Is There Any Difference?

You Decide

Is There Any Difference?

You Decide

Chaplain Gene

Unless otherwise noted, Scripture translations are from the New King James Version (NKJV)…

Other translations cited are the King James Version (KJV), the New World Translation (NWT), and the Joseph Smith Translation (JST).

Quotations of the Qur'an, unless otherwise specified, are from *The Holy Qur'an, Text, Translation and Commentary* by A. Yusuf Ali 1934 edition

Cover image from iStock Photo.

For information or additional copies contact:
New Creations Ministries, Inc.
2660 Horizon (Suite 205)
Grand Rapids, MI. 49546

Contents

Acknowledgments

This book has been a labor of love for God and for all who will read it with the goal of finding truth. I firmly believe it is the right of every person to believe what he or she wants to believe, but I also believe each person should hear the alternatives and is accountable for the decisions about what to believe.

In writing a book, thanks are due to those who have helped an author. I thank God for allowing me to be involved in New Creations Ministries, which carries on various ministries to inmates in the prisons of Michigan.

I also want to thank my family for their encouragement, especially my wife, Ruth, who never complained when I spent hours researching. Also, I am grateful for her quiet accompaniment while I was writing during the past several years. For almost two years now, Ruth has been in an assisted living center; she suffers from spinal stenosis and Alzheimer's disease. This has been an on-and-off, highly emotional trial, but through it all God has given grace. When I express how sorry I am for what she goes through, Ruth often says, "It could be worse." She is one remarkable example of trusting the Lord.

Thanks to Robert Bowman at the Institute for Religious Research for his review of and input into the chapters about Jehovah's Witnesses and Latter-Day Saints (LDS) doctrine.

I have a new appreciation for those who birth the many articles and books that are a source of help during the trials of this journey called life, but more than that I now sense personal growth in compassion for those who suffer daily. Maybe compassion will be the subject of the next book or booklet, the Lord willing, or as my Muslim friends would say, *Inshallah*.

I thank God for opportunities to share His Word. May He receive all the praise and glory. He truly is good.

Chaplain Gene

Preface

There are times in a person's life when he sees God's hand clearly involved in the fruit of his labor. Often this evidence is seen after the event takes place. Although you sense God's leading when you work on a book, your labor comes to fruition after publication and the benefit to those who have an opportunity to read the book's contents.

It is my desire to give this book to those incarcerated in jails and prisons. My involvement in prison ministry, and the exposure to the confusion associated with the various religions represented in prison, encouraged me to write this book. Are all those representative religions an acceptable approach to God? I trust and pray that you, the reader, will benefit from the research, the reading of many books, and the work that have gone into this book. I have made every effort to be intellectually honest in all cases.

Any proceeds from the sale of this book will go to a foundation that will continue to provide Bibles and other materials to those incarcerated, for they are so often forgotten, and for other worthwhile investment in eternal things.

God gave me the privilege to write two booklets, *Paths Worth Choosing* and *Straight Up*, that are also free to inmates. More than 200,000 copies have been distributed to inmates.

I never cease to be amazed that God uses a character like me, who has often strayed from His path. Each time I have been restored to that most important and intimate relationship with my heavenly Father, who delights in mercy and grace. His forgiveness is so reflective of His great love for His children.

Furthermore, I believe the hour is near for some serious developments in the world that you will read about in this book. Because of that, I would like to reach out to some who will miss the rapture and will go through those future developments believing world peace has finally become a reality. But do not be deceived, for real peace will not be achieved until the true Prince of Peace arrives on the scene, and He will not arrive until after the world goes through the worst tribulation ever to happen to it and its inhabitants.

Therefore it is imperative that I present to you the following scenario. If you have obtained a copy of this book during the reign of the Antichrist and have been told that you must receive the "mark" in order to buy and sell, please read this book carefully. What is presented in this book will relate the consequences for receiving that "mark of the beast."

What value is there in surviving for this short span of life on earth at the expense of being separated eternally from God and all the glory He has planned for those who accept His offer? That offer is presented within the pages of this book.

Chaplain Gene
Founder of New Creations Ministries

Chapter 1

Is There Any Difference?

One day I decided to fly an airplane, so I went out to the local airport, where I saw a beautiful Navajo airplane parked on an apron outside a hanger. I jumped into the left seat in the cockpit, looked over the instrument panel and some of the controls, and thought, *This looks like something I could handle on my own without the instruction manual or an instructor.* I got the engines started—it was a twin engine—and in no time I was taxiing toward the end of the runway. I was ready to take off! But I couldn't figure out why the tower was flashing a red light at me. Well, I took off, and I was flying through the skies, maneuvering in and out of the clouds, having a great time. I was flying! It was now time to land, and the tower was still flashing that red light, but I was able to land the plane and taxi back to the hanger. There I was met by a lot of cars with flashing lights. I wondered what they wanted. Probably to congratulate me on the success of my first flight.

By this time you are saying to yourself, *This guy is lying through his teeth.* You would be right.

I was a pilot, but I didn't learn to fly that way. It took hours of ground school to learn why an airplane flies, what all the controls do, fuel management, weather, dead reckoning, charts, instruments, flying in a simulator, and the many other functions associated with flying. Then came hours of flying with an instructor before I was allowed to solo.

Is there a difference? Of course. I needed to rely on the source documents for flying, the instruction manuals that gave me truthful information. Partial truth in flying is devastating. We need the truth, and nothing but the truth, so help us God. Doesn't that sound familiar? In a court of law, partial truth or untruths are not acceptable. In fact, the jury's job is to settle on that which is true.

After retiring from a business career, I became involved in prison ministry. I have been asked many times, "What's the difference between Christians and Muslims, or Baptists and Catholics, or Christians and Mormons, or Christians and Jehovah's Witnesses?" This question generally is followed by comments such as, "Don't we all acknowledge the same God?" "Is this true?" "Is there any difference?"

I must admit that in my first encounters with people who asked these questions, I didn't have a lot of researched information to share, but that experience did start me on a course of finding out what were the differences. I sincerely hope my quest over the years will be an honest approach to the most important issues of life that will result in benefit to your ultimate eternal destiny.

In my eighteen years in prison ministry, I have had many interviews and discussions with inmates who were followers of one of the many religions that are recognized by prison authorities. I have sensed the conflict and confrontation that go on in the cell blocks and day rooms of the incarcerated, all in the name of religion. The Russian communist Vladimir Lenin is credited with the statement, "Religion is the opiate of the people," and in a sense I agree with this. I don't believe in religion! Religion is people's attempt to please God through their own efforts of trying to keep certain rules and rituals that are imposed by their religious leaders. Failure to measure up to the expectations of those rules and regulation often leads to despair and hopelessness.

Religion has emotional highs and lows because it has such an impact on our feelings, but feelings do not determine truth. However, in today's culture it seems that if it feels good, do it, because if it feels good it must be okay. If that's what I believe, then that is truth to me and becomes my religion, whether it's true or not. Here's where we must be intellectually honest and seek a source that is truth. To dig down deep inside our inner being and to examine what we have held onto as truth is a difficult task, especially when it disturbs the spiritual equilibrium we have managed to develop over time.

Whatever conclusions we come to should be based on truth. To believe something that is not true puts us on a path of error and false hope. Often people will seek out and find "truth" that in fact is not truth, but it fits their philosophy and the lifestyle they want. Then that becomes truth to them, regardless of whether their source of truth is true or not. Of course, there are those who know something to be true but disregard it because it hampers their lifestyle.

Our lifestyle and mindset, therefore, are motivated by what we believe or don't want to believe; if I really believe I shouldn't live in a certain way, I wouldn't. But many times we ignore what is true, or we allow our emotions to override what we loosely believe, to dictate our attitudes and actions. As a result our attitudes and actions sometimes hurt others as well as ourselves, because we are not practicing truth with love.

Beliefs are at the core of our thought processes: "As a man thinks in his heart [inner being] so is he." What we hang onto as our core values does determine our attitudes and actions.

As I mentioned earlier, in the story about learning to fly, whatever we believe must be based on truth. Otherwise, our thinking is flawed. To rely on our internal compass for truth may point us in the wrong direction. Truth is important and must come from a source that is truth, a written document that is true. To base our belief in a source that rests on flawed thinking would lead to wrong conclusions. Therefore, to determine whether a religion is based on truth, we have to look at the source documents. Are the sources reliable? That is the crucial question each person must answer based on the information presented. Another crucial question is whether the teachings from the source documents are being presented truthfully.

We should be searching seriously for that source of truth that brings about a way of life that is one of freedom and inner peace. This freedom and inner peace come from the true Source of life and not a life of repetitious ritual and pious rules that places us in chains. These-self imposed religious disciplines can bring a sense of self-satisfaction, but they never are able to bring fulfillment and lasting joy. Sometimes an overwhelming sense of hopelessness and frustration sets in because people wonder if they have accomplished enough to satisfy the rules and rituals of their religion. Often this leads to rejecting any further search for that which is truth, and even throwing overboard what they once thought was truth. They close the mind, thus settling for a false foundation that can never bring true freedom and inner peace.

The difficulty of obtaining ultimate truth is that even though a source document is interspersed with elements of truth, it is the untruths that cause conflicts and confusion. Any religion developed by humans has some truths, and its followers will accept or ignore the untruths that are being taught along with the truths. If the source comes from a higher power of flawless intelligence, why would that higher power pass along untruths, or declare a truth and later alter or reverse that truth? That would mean the prior truth was not truth to begin with. Truth never has to be abrogated. Time does not erode truth, because truth is changeless and timeless. It has always been there, although it appears as new truth to someone to whom it hadn't been exposed before.

Truth must come from an infinite intellect that is from a higher power than the finite intellect of humans. Man's attempt at establishing truth always contains flawed thinking and often false sources. However, truth never has to be changed or modified to adapt to the culture or the trends of the day. Truth never has to be compromised, for when it is compromised, truth is twisted to fit the circumstances. This is happening today in societies and religions around the world. Human opinions, feelings, and emotions have replaced the source document of truth and have become the basis for people's beliefs and lifestyle.

If the source document of a religion is not absolutely true, then the teachings are in error. Any religion must stand the scrutiny of the doctrines taught to see if they are absolutely true. People will say, "There are no absolutes." That statement, however, is an absolute.

My sincere hope is that when you consider these writings you will be in a position to view the teachings of the various source documents and determine whether they have the ring of validity.

There have been and are today many prophets, people who supposedly have received a message of truth, who claim their message is from a higher source and thus divinely inspired. Sometimes these messages are recorded and reported to be holy writings. But are they? People accept the teachings of a prophet without investigating the source for the teaching because the message challenges them or makes them feel good. Emotions can trap people in such a way that they are willing to give their all to a religious movement that enslaves them to a life of repetitious ritual. Beliefs founded in emotions can be carried to extremes. Beliefs can be a powerful motivator resulting in good or evil.

Another word for "belief" is "faith." Everyone exercises faith, whether it is in truth or theory. How strong is that faith? Does that person buckle under when that faith is tested? Does the person back away from that faith when serious trials are encountered, often blaming others and God? In the arena of everyday life, those encounters separate the defeated from the victors.

Standing up for what I believe does not mean being obnoxious or threatening the existence of others. If what I believe is truth, I must present that truth in a loving manner using the source document of truth but not demanding that a person accept what I believe. I must, however, point out differences in the teachings of the source documents from which their prophet or prophets teach. Each person must then decide whether what is being presented is trustworthy or not.

I would like to challenge you to keep an open mind and look at the beliefs and teachings from the source documents of Mormons, Jehovah's Witnesses, Islam, and Christianity. Yes, there will be some contradictions that will be pointed out, but that's where you decide what is truth.

What are the main source documents and the prophets of these religious groups?

Mormonism: The King James Bible or Smith's Version, *Book of Mormon, Doctrines and Covenants, Pearl of Great Price*

Jehovah's Witnesses: New World Translation of the Bible, *The Watchtower, Awake* (publications)

Islam: Qur'an; the sunna, which relates the practice and example of the prophet Muhammad, is the second authority for Muslims and belief in the sunna is a requirement of the Islamic faith; the Hadith are the books of traditions connected with the life of Muhammad

Christianity: The Bible's sixty-six books are considered the final authority for all matters of faith and life

Who are the main characters, prophets, and founders of these religious groups?

Mormonism: Prophet Joseph Smith, founder; Brigham Young followed Smith, and after Young came many other presidents who are also regarded as prophets to the church. There are many other positions within the Church of Jesus Christ of Latter-Day Saints (LDS).

Jehovah's Witnesses: Dr. Charles Taze Russell, founder; followed by many leaders whose teachings are published through *The Watchtower* and *Awake* publications, which are the authoritative sources for what is taught in the Kingdom Hall assemblies

Islam: Muhammad, considered a prophet; many succeeding teaching leaders within the two main groups; the Sunnis and Shiites; there are other sects within and outside those two main groups

Christianity: Jesus of Nazareth is the central figure; his twelve apostles preached his message. Many denominations and religious groups place themselves under the Christian umbrella.

Regarding the founders and followers of these religious groups we must look at the background of their life and the integrity of their message. What brought them to the teachings that they came to? Were their goals and life consistent with their teachings? In this book I seek to answer those questions in a truthful way. But you are the one who either accepts or rejects the truthfulness of the teachings. You must decide!

It has been my experience that I can be "down on things I am not up on." It is easy to shove something aside if I don't want to take the time to "get up on it." So I better get up on it, because if I believe something that is untrue, I would like it to be replaced with the truth. My hopes and prayers are that you will examine these writings with an open mind and heart as you search for the truth. After all, we are spiritual beings having a human experience, not human beings having a spiritual experience.

There will be a temptation to go to the chapter that may challenge your particular religious leaning. However, I would urge you to read all the chapters, because you will benefit from knowing all the differences.

Let's take a look at them.

Chapter 2

Jehovah's Witnesses

It was a Saturday morning more than fifty years ago. The doorbell rang, and when I opened the front door, an older gentleman and a much younger man stood on the front steps. They greeted me and asked if they could share some things from the Bible. I told them yes, if they would tell me who they were with. They were somewhat reluctant to do this but did finally say they were from a certain Kingdom Hall. They were Jehovah's Witnesses (JW).

The older man piqued my interest when he told me he used to be a pastor of a Reformed church but had discovered he had been believing things that were not true. He said he found out that there is only one God, and His name is Jehovah. I asked him, "What about Jesus?" He said, "He was a god." I knew enough about JW doctrine to realize that the man would deny Jesus' deity, but I was interested in hearing his views.

Later, I shared some portions of Scripture with the men. They spent a little more time and said they had to go. I appreciated their zeal. At that time I wondered how the JW organization started, and I wanted to know more of what they taught and what their teaching was based on. I would have to look into that sometime. That "sometime" developed into research over the years and more recently by exposure to other Witnesses. This is what I found out.

A Brief History of the Jehovah's Witnesses

Charles Taze Russell was the founder of the Jehovah's Witnesses. He was born in the Pittsburgh, Pennsylvania, area on February 16, 1852, and grew up with Congregational and Presbyterian influences. He came to a point where he rejected all organized religion and the prior eighteen hundred years of the teachings of historic Christianity. Rebelling against those earlier religious influences, Russell became interested in the teaching of Adventism, which had started with William Miller, who predicted that the second advent (return) of Christ would take place in 1843. When that did not happen, Miller revised his prediction to say that Christ would return in 1844. That also did not happen.

Later, some of the followers of Adventism went on to form the Seventh-day Adventist denomination. Some of the teachings of Adventism were incorporated into Russell's preaching and writings. Those teachings included the belief that no personal soul exists after physical death; that there is no hell; that the wicked are annihilated; and some unusual views of divine judgment.

For a time, Russell felt he had lost his way, but with these new teachings he had a restored "faith." His newfound beliefs inspired him to start a Bible class during the 1870s in the Pittsburgh area. The study centered around the Scriptures about Jehovah's kingdom and the second coming of Christ, the advent. Although Russell was never a Seventh-day Adventist, he taught variations of Adventist beliefs. Russell had a strong leadership role in this study group, even though he was a teenager without any theological training. He was an impressive individual and a great orator who could sway his audiences.

During those days, the Seventh-day Adventists distanced themselves from Russell because of his changes to Adventist doctrines. In a similar way, many present-day Jehovah's Witnesses attempt to distance themselves from Russell while still holding to his teachings. I believe another reason for their distancing is due to a lawsuit initiated by the *Brooklyn Daily Eagle,* during which Russell perjured himself when he stated under oath that he knew the Greek alphabet. When he was asked to read and interpret Greek, he had to admit that he couldn't do so.

At the age of twenty-seven, Russell began a magazine that is generally known today as *The Watchtower*. This magazine is published in more than 180 languages, and each printing is well into tens of millions of copies.

Russell died in 1916, and Joseph F. Rutherford, who had been legal counsel for the Watchtower Society, took over leadership of the group. Rutherford practiced authoritarian leadership and introduced the program of literature distribution and door-to-door witnessing that is still used today. Many

Jehovah's Witnesses soon left to start other sects after Rutherford took the helm. Rutherford gave them an ultimatum: If they did not return, they would suffer destruction at Armageddon, which was to come soon.

Following Rutherford's death in 1942, Nathan H. Knorr became the organization's leader. Under his guidance, the Watchtower Society published large amounts of literature, along with their translation of the Bible, called the New World Translation of the Holy Scriptures (NWT).

In 1977, Frederick W. Franz replaced Knorr as president. After the death of Franz, Milton Henschel became president of the Watchtower Society, and he was succeeded by Don Adams.

A few years ago, the Jehovah's Witnesses underwent a significant organizational change that separated its governmental body (teaching leaders) from its corporate leaders and the society's assets. Some observers believe this change was accomplished to separate the liability associated with their teachings from the assets of their corporate structure. This sounds like a good business move, because there are possible lawsuits by advocates for children who have died as a result of having been denied blood transfusions (JW teaching forbids blood transfusions).

Source Documents of Jehovah's Witnesses

The New World Translation of the Holy Scriptures

The New World Translation of the Holy Scriptures (NWT) is the source document used by Jehovah's Witnesses to substantiate their teachings as revealed by the leaders of the Watchtower Society. The NWT was done by a translation committee, but the names of the committee members were withheld, so that it is difficult for any critic to challenge their credentials in the area of translation. In addition, the committee seemed to disregard in various places literal language from the Old Testament Hebrew, a few Old Testament chapters that were written in Aramaic, and especially the New Testament in Greek, which are the original languages of the Bible. Yet the title page states the NWT was rendered from the original languages. Is that statement true? Is the NWT a reliable translation? To answer these questions, we first need to understand something about the process of making a Bible translation.

Bible Translation

A great deal of preparation goes into producing a valid translation of the Bible. Translators, above all else, must follow as closely as possible the literal intent of the original texts. Translators are not to interject their biases or personal beliefs. This requires intellectual integrity, along with scholarly qualifications. In addition, translators should rely on the earliest manuscripts available and newer, updated translations that are based on scholarly work, again without interjecting personal biases or beliefs.

The texts of the Old Testament Scriptures were handwritten in Hebrew on scrolls and copied using painstaking procedures that produced accurate duplicates. Some copies, handwritten on papyrus and leather and dating back to about 150 BC, were discovered in the caves at Qumran, near the Dead Sea, in 1947. Other scrolls were found later in surrounding caves. These copies are called the Dead Sea Scrolls. This remarkable discovery validated the accuracy of the Hebrew Scriptures, because the text is the same as the copies that have been used to produce numerous modern English translations.

For several centuries, Greek was widely used as a universal language, including many Jewish communities. Therefore, Hebrew scholars translated the Hebrew Scriptures (what Christians call the Old Testament) into Greek. That translation, called the Septuagint, was started around 280 BC and completed around 150 BC.

At least some copies of the Septuagint kept a word called the Tetragrammaton that was in the Hebrew Scriptures. *Tetra* means "four," and *grammaton* means "letters." So, the Tetragrammaton is a word of four letters. In English this word is written YHWH, and it is the divine name. This name was considered so holy that when pious Jews read the Hebrew Scriptures, they would call God *Adonai*, a Hebrew word that means "Master" or "Lord," to show respect for the holiness of the name YHWH.

In the Septuagint, used in Greek-speaking Jewish communities, the Tetragrammaton, YHWH, was translated as *Kyrios*, which is the Greek word for "Lord," and less often by the word *Theos*, meaning "God." In English, it is generally accepted to use Jehovah as God's name, but the name Jehovah is derived from a combination of the Hebrew consonants YHWH and the vowels from *Adonai*. Therefore YHWH should be spelled Yahweh (pronounced Yah-way), rather than Jehovah

In English translations of the Old Testament, you sometimes will find the word *Lord* written in small capital letters (LORD). Be alert, because LORD translates instances where God is referred to as YHWH.

What about the New Testament? The New Testament was written in Greek, and today we have more than five thousand Greek manuscripts that date from the very early days of the Christian church. In all of these manuscripts, the divine name always appears as *Kyrios*. Why is this fact so important? Because the translators of the NWT properly translated the divine name in the Old Testament as Jehovah, but they disregarded the earliest Greek New Testament manuscripts, in which the divine name is always *Kyrios* ("Lord"). This is how the divine name appeared in the Septuagint, which was quoted by Jesus Himself and by the apostles. The apostles, throughout their original inspired writings, used the Greek word *Kyrios* as the divine name.

Many centuries later, the New Testament Scriptures were translated from Greek into Hebrew for the purpose of reaching Jewish communities with the message of Jesus the Messiah. The earliest of those translations came about in AD 1385. The New World Translation committee relied on this Hebrew translation from the original Greek, rather than the early Greek manuscripts, to produce their translation.

The committee seemed to disregard in various places the literal language from the Old Testament Hebrew, a few Old Testament chapters in Aramaic, and especially the New Testament in Greek, which are the original languages of the Bible. The purpose for translating the Bible into the other languages of the world is to reveal the truth of God's Word to specific language groups, not to change the meaning of the Scriptures to fit the doctrinal positions of a particular religious group.

Is the Divine Name Translated Properly?

In chapter 12 of *The Divine Name in the New World Translation*, the committee gives its reasons for translating the divine name as it does. This chapter is reproduced in Appendix A of my book, or it may be obtained from www.tetragrammaton.org. If you are interested, it is possible to request a download of the complete book.

In reading chapter 12 of *The Divine Name in the New World Translation*, it is helpful to remember that the divine name is translated 237 times as Jehovah in the New Testament of the NWT, whereas in the Greek New Testament the divine name is always *Kyrios* ("Lord"). If the Christian writers were divinely inspired by the Holy Spirit, which is what Christians believe that Scripture teaches, then the divine name *Kyrios* in the Greek New Testament must be translated "Lord."

If you examine the Scriptures carefully, you will discover that God has many names. *Adonai* is a divine title for God that is often used in the Old Testament. For instance, in Genesis 15:2, Abram speaks to the divine person as *Adonai*, as does Gideon in Judges 6:15. David, speaking to God, says in Psalm 38:15 (NKJV), "For in You, O LORD [*Yahweh*], I hope; You will hear, O Lord [*Adonai*] my God [*Elohim*]." I believe all the titles given for God in His Word are respectful of God, and it is appropriate to call on Him using those names. If you eliminate the teaching of the Tri-unity in Scripture, then you would have to recognize the person of Jesus as Yahweh at the exclusion of the Father and the Holy Spirit as God.

You can see that there will be some major differences between Jehovah's Witnesses' and Christians' beliefs. The translators of the NWT rely on the Hebrew translation of the Greek New Testament to deny that Jesus and the Holy Spirit are truly God. These teachings will be explained further in the section about the beliefs of Jehovah's Witnesses.

Additional Source Documents

In addition to the New World Translation, the greatest source for communicating the doctrines and teachings of the Watchtower Society is *The Watchtower* magazine, which effectively functions as the ultimate authority for Jehovah's Witnesses. The content of the magazine is written by members of the Watchtower Society, whose headquarters is in Brooklyn, New York. Their writings, which since 1942 have been anonymous, are considered the final word of truth. Individual Witnesses are taught that the true interpretation of Scripture must come from the Watchtower Society.

In fact, Russell stated of his "Scripture Studies" in the September 15, 1910, issue of *The Watchtower*:

> If the six volumes of "Scripture Studies" are practically the Bible, topically arranged with Bible proof texts given, we might not improperly name the volumes, "The Bible in an Arranged Form." That is to say, they are not mere comments on the Bible, but they are practically the Bible itself. Furthermore not only do we find that people cannot see the divine plan in studying the Bible by itself, but we see, also, that if anyone lays the "Scripture Studies" aside, even after he has used them, . . . and goes to the Bible alone, though he has understood his Bible for ten years, our experience shows that within two years, he goes into darkness. On the other hand, if he had merely read the "Scripture Studies" with their references and had not read a page of the Bible as such, he would be in the light at the end of two years, because he would have the light of the Scriptures.

This means that the "Scripture Studies" are more significant than the Bible, and Witnesses who return to relying only on the Bible will leave JW teaching.

Awake magazine expresses the views of the "Anointed Leaders" of the society concerning contemporary issues. Several other influential books that were the basis for early JW beliefs are *Reasoning from the Scriptures*, *You Can Live Forever on Earth*, *The Truth Shall Make You Free*, *Make Sure of All Things*, *Let God Be True*, and *New Heavens and New Earth*.

All of these source documents are or have been utilized in carrying out the Jehovah's Witnesses' mission as the only "true witnesses" of Jehovah God. Witnesses are required to go door to door in neighborhoods to get out their message, along with offering their publications to those who are interested.

Beliefs of Jehovah's Witnesses

Creation

The Witnesses believe that the only uncreated being is Jehovah, who has always been eternally existent and was before anything was ever created. Jehovah's first creation was the pre-human Jesus (50a).[1] However, Witnesses also teach that Jesus in his pre-human spirit form was previously Michael the archangel. However, if Michael was the pre-human Jesus, Michael, not Jesus, would had to have been the creator of the "other things." This in itself is contradictory, because the NWT in Colossians 1:15-16 says, speaking of Jesus, that He created the "other things." The word *other* is not in the original Greek, and Scripture teaches that God created everything: all things, not just some things.

Only God could create things out of nothing (Colossians 1:15-17 NWT):

> He is the image of the invisible God, the firstborn of all creation; because by means of him all [other] things were created in the heavens and upon the earth, the things visible and the things invisible, no matter whether they are thrones or lordships or governments or authorities. All [other] things have been created through him and for him. Also, he is before all [other] things and by means of him all [other] things were made to exist.

1 The parenthetical references reflect the sources used in each chapter of this book. See the Reference Materials.

In the early editions of the NWT, there was no bracketing in this text. Qualified scholars of Greek challenged the NWT translating committee on the addition of the word *other* to their translation. The committee was forced to bracket the word *other*, because it was not in the manuscripts they were using for their translation.

Now look at Colossians 1:15-16 in the New King James Version (NKJV):

> He is the image of the invisible God, the firstborn over all creation. For by Him all things were created that are in heaven and that are on earth, visible and invisible, whether thrones or dominions or principalities or powers. All things were created through Him and for Him. And He is before all things, and in Him all things consist.

Both translations begin with "He," which refers to Jesus the Christ. Notice also that the NWT claims "He" is the firstborn *of* all creation, which could imply that the pre-human Jesus was created. The NKJV states that Jesus is the firstborn *over* creation, which means that He is the rightful heir to everything, because He created all things. They are rightfully His.

Note the confirmation of God creating all things in a correct translation from the Greek manuscripts to English (John 1:1-3 NKJV): "In the beginning was the Word, and the Word was with God, and the Word was God. He was in the beginning with God. All things were made through Him, and without Him nothing was made that was made." Not just "other things" but "all" things were created by Him. That's a huge difference, wouldn't you agree?

God

Jehovah's Witnesses teach that there is only one God, and His name is Jehovah. They believe if you can't understand the Trinity from a physical and human perspective, then it can't be so.

I once had a discussion with a man, Stanley, who worked in a company where I was the general manager. Stanley was a sincere and devout Jehovah's Witness who frequently wanted to give me literature or enter into conversations regarding the Trinity. During a work break, Stanley called me over to his work bench, where he had arranged three identical brass cups, and asked, "Are these three one?" I replied, "No, but they are all of the same material." He turned away, exasperated with me. Stanley was reasoning strictly from a physical and human perspective that is often flawed. Remember, "With God all things are possible"—even for there to be one God in three persons, a Tri-unity.

One of the proof texts that Witnesses like to use is found in Deuteronomy 6:4 (NKJV), which states "Hear, O Israel: The LORD our God, the LORD is one!" The NWT translates this as, "Listen, O Israel: Jehovah our God is one Jehovah." The text is then often quoted to prove there is one God, Jehovah. Therefore, according to Witnesses, the Trinity of the Godhead is a manufactured teaching with no biblical basis. But is this true?

The Hebrew word for "one" used in Deuteronomy 6:4 is the same word used in Genesis 2:24 to describe the union within marriage: The two shall become one flesh. Both the word *God* (*Elohim*) and the word *one* allow for a plurality. God's Word in Genesis 1:26 states, "Then God said, 'Let Us make man in Our image.'" Only those who are the "Us" and "Our" of the Godhead (Tri-unity) would have the power to create through the spoken word and to make man from the dirt of the earth, which had been created earlier. Would anyone but God be capable of creating something out of nothing, and then use that something to make something else?

Something else to think about: How did the writer of the book of Genesis know that man was made from the dirt of the earth when the human science of that day would have no knowledge of the chemical structures of dirt that today we know are contained in the human body?

Christ Jesus

If I am asked what is the significant difference between what Jehovah's Witnesses believe and what I believe the Scriptures teach, it is that Witnesses teach that Jesus is a created being. As a created being, Jesus could not be God in human form.

In JW writings, Jesus was the first son that Jehovah brought into existence (50b), but they also declare that Michael the archangel is the only begotten Son of God, who became Jesus Christ (51a). This also is contrary to the teaching of Scripture. There are only fives references to Michael the archangel found in Scripture (Daniel 10:12-14, 21; 12:1; Jude 9; Revelation 12:7). On the basis of these references, it would be difficult to interpret Jesus to be Michael.

It's interesting that in Scripture, the seraphim are the highest-ranking angels. An archangel is just above the rank of an angel. Scripture states that Jesus Christ is the Lord of lords and King of kings; He has first place in all things (Colossians 1:18).What does this say about the Lord Jesus Christ to describe Him as an archangel, a created and lower-ranking being?

According to JW teaching, Jesus subjected Himself to God and humbled Himself to a disgraceful death on a torture stake (50c), after which God raised him as a mighty, immortal spirit Son (50d). Witnesses do not believe that Jesus was raised with a body of flesh, but a spiritual body (49a).

What does the Bible relate after Jesus' death on a cross, His resurrection, and His encounter with two of His disciples on the road to Emmaus (Luke 24:38-43)?

> And He said to them, "Why are you troubled? And why do doubts arise in your hearts? Behold My hands and My feet, that it is I Myself. Handle Me and see, <u>for a spirit</u> does not have flesh and bones as you see I have." When He had said this, He showed them His hands and His feet. But while they still did not believe for joy, and marveled, He said to them, "Have you any food here?" So they gave Him a piece of a broiled fish and some honeycomb. And He took it and ate in their presence.

Why would Jesus tell His disciples He was not a spirit if He was? He further proved He was still in His flesh and bones by eating something.

Witnesses say Jesus is a "lesser god" than the Father because Jesus said, "The Father is greater than I" (John 14:2) (46a). Also, Scripture says, "The head of Christ is God" (1 Corinthians 11:3) (46b). However, there is no contradiction with Jesus' deity in those proof texts because Jesus said in another portion of Scripture, "I and my Father are One" (John 10:30). Jesus says that the Father, who is God, is in Him; He (Jesus) is in the Father, which indicates that there is the one God in the Father and the Son. Jesus was speaking of His deity when He said, "I and My Father are One."

A distinction must be considered between Jesus' humanness and His divineness. I feel comfortable with the position that Jesus in His humanness was lesser than His Father, but in His divinity He and His Father were one.

The real nature and character of you and me is not our temporal mortal body but our eternal inner being: our soul, our spirit. Our problem is that our soul and spirit inherited a sinful nature from Adam so that we are impure and prone to sinning. Jesus, by contrast, had a pure, sinless nature, because He was the living Word with the fullness of God in a human vessel.
Philip, one of Jesus' followers, questions Jesus (John 14:7-11):

> "If you had known Me, you would have known My Father also; and from now on you know Him and have seen Him." Philip said to Him, "Lord, show us the Father, and it is sufficient for us." Jesus said to him, "Have I been with you so long and yet

> you have not known Me, Philip? He who has seen Me has seen the Father; so how can you say, 'Show us the Father'? Do you not believe that I am in the Father, and the Father in Me? The words that I speak to you I do not speak on My own authority; but the Father who dwells in Me does the works. Believe Me that I am in the Father and the Father in Me, or else believe Me for the sake of the works themselves."

The NWT has translated this part of Scripture to read that Jesus was in union with the Father and the Father was in union with Jesus:

> "If YOU men had known me, YOU would have known my Father also; from this moment on YOU know him and have seen him." Philip said to him: "Lord, show us the Father, and it is enough for us." Jesus said to him: "Have I been with YOU men so long a time, and yet, Philip, you have not come to know me? He that has seen me has seen the Father [also]. How is it you say, 'Show us the Father'? Do you not believe that I am in union with the Father and the Father is in union with me? The things I say to YOU men I do not speak of my own originality; but the Father who remains in union with me is doing his works. Believe me that I am in union with the Father and the Father is in union with me; otherwise, believe on account of the works themselves. Most truly I say to YOU, He that exercises faith in me."

The word *union* does not appear in the original Scriptures and again shows that the NWT translators incorporated words to accommodate their teaching that Jesus was not God in flesh. But a translation of Colossians 2:9 (NKJV) that accurately reflects the Greek text says, "In Him [Christ] dwells all the fullness of the Godhead bodily." Clearly this teaches that in Jesus there is all of God in a human body. Furthermore, "He [Christ] is the image of the invisible God" (Colossians 1:15 NKJV). The Bible does not teach there are three gods, but one God in three persons, a Tri-unity.

What other Scriptures confirm that Jesus the Christ is God in human form? Let's look at some. John's Gospel strongly represents Jesus as the Christ and God who dwelled among us. John 1:1-3 (NKJV) states, "In the beginning was the Word, and the Word was with God, and the Word was God. He was in the beginning with God. All things were made through Him, and without Him nothing was made that was made." The NWT mistranslates this by saying, "the word was *a* god," because the translators knew that John 1:14 says, "the Word became flesh and dwelt among us," which would lead a reader to conclude that the Word, who was God, took up His dwelling in a human body the body of Jesus. This is what an authentic translation of Scripture teaches.

Jehovah's Witnesses hold to the non-Trinity doctrine of Jehovah as the one God; however, by referring to the Word as *a god* (small "g") they are admitting to other gods. Their teaching is that Jesus is a god among many gods, but can there be other gods? If there are other gods, then God cannot be the truly sovereign God. Yet, does not Scripture say that we are to have no other gods but the one God? Therefore their teaching of many gods is polytheism. The difference is that true Christians do not worship three gods but one God manifested in a Tri-unity of the Father, the Son, and the Holy Spirit, which is the Godhead.

By translating YHWH in the Old Testament as Jehovah, the NWT translation committee verified the teaching of Scripture that Jesus is Jehovah. The NWT prophecy in Isaiah 40:3 reads, "Listen! Someone is calling out in the wilderness: 'Clear up the way of <u>Jehovah</u>, YOU people! MAKE the highway for our <u>God</u> through the desert plain straight.'" This is prophecy fulfilled in Matthew 3:3 (NWT) as "This, in fact, is the one spoken of through Isaiah the prophet in these words: 'Listen! Someone is crying out in the wilderness, "Prepare the way of <u>Jehovah</u>, YOU people! Make his roads straight."'"

Isn't it interesting that in both the NWT and the NKJV New Testament it is John the Baptist's voice crying out in the wilderness? If you read the context of this Scripture portion carefully, you will discover that John the Baptist is without a doubt referring to Jesus the Christ and therefore, according to the NWT, Jesus would have to be Jehovah.

I was having some sessions with a Jehovah's Witness regarding the deity of Jesus the Christ, and one time I asked him, "Is Jehovah God?" He answered emphatically, "Of course." I then shared Isaiah 40:3 and Matthew 3:3 (NWT) with him. When he saw that this was talking about Jesus as Jehovah, he threw up his arms and declared, "Now I see."

A similar example comes from Hebrews 1:8, which in the NWT says, "But with reference to the Son: God is your throne for ever and ever." However, in the NKJV Hebrews.1:8 it states, "But to the Son He says: <u>Your throne, O God</u>, is forever and ever." Obviously, there is a significant difference in the meaning.

Again, Colossians 1:15-16 (NKJV) states, "He [Christ] is the image of the invisible God, the firstborn over all creation. For by Him all things were created that are in heaven and that are on earth, visible and invisible, whether thrones or dominions or principalities or powers. All things were created through Him and for Him." Colossians 2:9 adds, "For in Him [Christ] dwells all the fullness of the Godhead bodily." These two portions of the Word of God commit to Jesus as the Creator of "all things" and that there is all of God in a human body.

Jesus also made this statement in John 8:58 (NKJV) when He said to the Pharisees, "Most assuredly, I say to you, before Abraham was, I AM." This was said in loving rebuttal to the religious traditionalists when they were putting down Jesus. They said they knew who their father was, claiming it was Abraham, and stating that Jesus possessed a demon and implying He didn't know who His father was.

Another interesting encounter Jesus had with the religious legalists of His day is found in John 10:33 (NKJV): "The Jews answered Him, saying, 'For a good work we do not stone You, but for blasphemy, and because You, being a Man, make Yourself God.'" Why would the Jews want to stone Him if He were just a god (small "g")? There is no blaspheming a god that is not God. The Jews knew that Jesus knew what He was implying.

It is apparent there is a vast difference between the JW position that Jesus is a created being and the biblical position of Jesus as all of God in a sinless human body. Only God could be and is sinless.

The Holy Spirit

Witnesses are vocal in denying the deity of Christ, so to be consistent they would have to deny the deity of the Holy Spirit. Also, Witnesses say the Holy Spirit is not a person (46c).

According to JW teaching, the Holy Spirit is an "active force" of God to accomplish God's will (46c, 50e). The Holy Spirit does not have a name, so Witnesses recognize the Holy Spirit as an "it" and not a person (46c, 46d). Their reasoning is that many people being filled with the Holy Spirit at the same time proves that the Holy Spirit is not a person (46c). That would be true that if the Holy Spirit cannot be in more than one place at a time; then He would not be God. He would not be an entity or a person and could not indwell every true believer, as Scripture teaches in 1 Corinthians 6:19 (NKJV): "Or do you not know that your body is the temple of the Holy Spirit who is in you, whom you have from God, and you are not your own?"

The Scriptures do teach that God is all-powerful (omnipotent), is able to be everywhere at the same time (omnipresent), and knows everything (omniscient). Why is it so difficult for the Holy Spirit to be a person of the Tri-unity? Just because our human wisdom is limited and we can be in only one place at a time, why must we confine God the Holy Spirit to these same restrictions? To further illustrate that the JW consider the Holy Spirit is an active force, turn to Genesis 1:2 in the NWT, and you will read that "God's active force was moving to and fro over the surface of the waters." The proper translation is "the Spirit of God" and not an active force.

The God of the Bible is awesome in all of His attributes. He is not limited to time, to space, in energy, or in power. If He were, He would not be the God of the Bible. Just because the human intellect finds it difficult to comprehend the Tri-unity of God, and the Holy Spirit as a person, it is no reason to change the Scriptures to accommodate limited human intellect and reasoning. To have to admit limitations to our intellect and reasoning power in understanding the awesomeness of God from a human perspective wounds our pride.

With the God of the Bible all things are possible, because the Word of God says so. If people find this difficult to believe that's their privilege, but that doesn't give them the right to change the Scriptures.

Regarding the Holy Spirit, read what the NWT states in Acts 5:1-4:

> However, a certain man, Ananias by name, together with Sapphira his wife, sold a possession and secretly held back some of the price, his wife also knowing about it, and he brought just a part and deposited it at the feet of the apostles. But Peter said: "Ananias, why has Satan emboldened you to play <u>false to the holy spirit</u> and to hold back secretly some of the price of the field? As long as it remained with you did it not remain yours, and after it was sold did it not continue in your control? Why was it that you purposed such a deed as this in your heart? You have played <u>false, not to men, but to God</u>."

Notice the underlining and then the corresponding portion in the NKJV:

> But a certain man named Ananias, with Sapphira his wife, sold a possession. And he kept back part of the proceeds, his wife also being aware of it, and brought a certain part and laid it at the apostles' feet. But Peter said, "Ananias, why has Satan filled your heart <u>to lie to the Holy Spirit</u> and keep back part of the price of the land for yourself? While it remained, was it not your own? And after it was sold, was it not in your own control? Why have you conceived this thing in your heart? <u>You have not lied to men but to God</u>."

It is apparent that the sin of lying is recorded as a sin against the Holy Spirit, who is confirmed as God. To draw any other conclusion is to deny the Holy Spirit His rightful title as God. To say the Holy Spirit does not have a name, or call the Holy Spirit an "it" or an "active force," as JW teaching does, is to deny the Holy Spirit's deity (46c, 50e).

Many other biblical accounts make it evident the Holy Spirit is God. For instance, in John14:26 (NKJV), Jesus is speaking to His apostles: "But the Helper, the Holy Spirit, whom the Father will send in My name, He will teach you all things, and bring to your remembrance all things that I said to you." The Holy Spirit would indwell and inspire the apostles.

The apostle Paul in Galatians 2:20 (NKJV) says, "I have been crucified with Christ; it is no longer I who live, but Christ lives in me; and the life which I now live in the flesh I live by faith in the Son of God, who loved me and gave Himself for me." How does Christ live in us? By the Holy Spirit living in us. You ask, "Isn't this double talk?" It would be if God were not one.

Look at John 14:16-17 (NKJV):

> "And I will pray the Father, and He will give you another Helper, that He may abide with you forever—the Spirit of truth, whom the world cannot receive, because it neither sees Him nor knows Him; but you know Him, for He dwells with you and will be in you."

Note the emphasis on the Holy Spirit as a person. The Holy Spirit's indwelling is also revealed in Acts 1–2.

Further, in John 16:12-15 (NKJV) Jesus says:

> "I still have many things to say to you, but you cannot bear them now. However, when He, the Spirit of truth, has come, He will guide you into all truth; for He will not speak on His own authority, but whatever He hears He will speak; and He will tell you things to come. He will glorify Me, for He will take of what is Mine and declare it to you. All things that the Father has are Mine. Therefore I said that He will take of Mine and declare it to you."

This clearly teaches the Holy Spirit will dwell in believers. The Holy Spirit's ministry is to reveal the truth of the glorified one, Jesus the Christ. Once again, we see the uniqueness of the Godhood. In all that They do there is complete unity, harmony, and a oneness.

Sin

The JW teaching about sin has some similarities to orthodox Christianity, as well as some differences. Witnesses proclaim that Adam and Eve plainly disobeyed God's law; that sin is falling short of God's standard of perfection and transgressing His righteous law; all humankind inherits sin from the first man, Adam; and all are born in sin (49b). Witnesses also claim that Adam at death returned to dust but then depart from biblical teaching by adding that Adam also returned to nonexistence (51b). More about nonexistence will be said regarding "soul-sleep" under the heading "Eternal Destiny."

Witnesses say sin caused perfect human life to lose its perfection with all its rights and earthly prospects (50f).

Salvation

JW teaching on salvation mixes believing in the Jesus of the Watchtower Society, which describes Jesus as a spirit being who is void of His human body. Witnesses say Jesus never was God in flesh, which is different from what John 1:14 states, that the Word (God) became flesh and dwelled here on earth.

In addition to belief in the Jesus as described by the Watchtower Society, Witnesses must carefully follow all the teachings of the society, which is considered God's authoritative organization speaking for God on earth. If Witnesses break from the teachings of the "anointed" of the society as set forth in Watchtower publications, they are considered heretics and are in jeopardy of annihilation.

In essence, JW teaching is that salvation is dependent on accepting the Watchtower Society's teachings and faithfully following them. This sets them apart from the biblical position that clearly reveals that salvation and being righteous in God's sight depend only on faith in Jesus Christ, who by His accomplishment on the cross has given us pardon and everlasting life. Faith, and nothing else, is required.

Witnesses teach that there are two classes of saved people. First, there are the 144,000 who are the "anointed" class. They will share in the heavenly glory and will not be on the earth (59g).

The second class, the "other sheep," will enjoy life here on earth during the millennium (a thousand years), which occurs after the battle of Armageddon. If Witnesses are faithful during this thousand years, then they will continue to live here on earth; otherwise they will be annihilated after the judgment (59g).

The ranks of the 144,000 have been filled in the past with first-century Christians only, plus any JW converts since the 1800s. After the first century and up to the 1800s, all of Christendom was apostate, according to Charles Taze Russell. He appeared on the scene to rescue Christendom from the "false teaching" of the past seventeen hundred years. The Watchtower Society has determined that the ranks of the 144,000 have been filled, and so any future JW followers, or those given a second chance, are now the "other sheep."

There are fewer than 10,000 of the 144,000 "anointed" remaining alive today. This is after years of decline, and then the number went up. Today this number is not reported by the organization. Don't you wonder why? Those who are members of the "organization," the "governing body" of the Watchtower Society, are part of the 144,000. Each person of the "great crowd" must prove his or her faithfulness by faith in "Jehovah's baptism, that they abide in him, keeping a good conscience, through faith and loyal service" (50h).

Said in another way, all who have faith in Jehovah God and in Christ Jesus and dedicate themselves in doing the will of God by carrying out that dedication "will be rewarded" with eternal life (50g). Notice "will be rewarded," that is, a person earns his or her salvation. If salvation is obtained that way, how does one know that he or she has followed that dedication to the will of God in a way that is acceptable to God?

When a religion departs from the Scripture's teaching of salvation obtained by grace through faith alone, then the only alternative is to follow a works-based salvation imposed by the teachings of its leaders, who hold their followers through an underlying motivation of fear. This is not freedom but slavery.

It is truthful and fair to say there is a vast difference between JW teachings and those of the unchangeable Word of God regarding salvation.

Eternal Destiny

As mentioned earlier, this section will explain the JW position regarding "soul-sleep." The teaching that a person is no longer conscious at physical death is regarded as "soul-sleep." Again, Witnesses point to proof texts that seemingly prove their position. Witnesses do not believe that the body, soul, and spirit of a person are separate entities; they do believe that all are as one in a state of nonexistence at death.

Let's look at some Scripture. Immediately my mind reflects on Dives (this Latin word means "rich man") and Lazarus, who had different lives prior to their deaths and different destinies after death.

Look at what was taught in Luke 16:19-31 (NKJV):

> "There was a certain rich man who was clothed in purple and fine linen and fared sumptuously every day. But there was a certain beggar named Lazarus, full of sores, who was laid at his gate, desiring to be fed with the crumbs which fell from the rich man's table. Moreover the dogs came and licked his sores. So it was that the beggar died, and was carried by the angels to Abraham's bosom. The rich man also died and was buried. And being in torments in Hades, he lifted up his eyes and saw Abraham afar off, and Lazarus in his bosom.
>
> "Then he cried and said, 'Father Abraham, have mercy on me, and send Lazarus that he may dip the tip of his finger in water and cool my tongue; for I am tormented in this flame.' But Abraham said, 'Son, remember that in your lifetime you received your good things, and likewise Lazarus evil things; but now he is comforted and you are tormented. And besides all this, between us and you there is a great gulf fixed, so that those who want to pass from here to you cannot, nor can those from there pass to us.'
>
> "Then he said, 'I beg you therefore, father, that you would send him to my father's house, for I have five brothers, that he may testify to them, lest they also come to this place of torment.' Abraham said to him, 'They have Moses and the prophets; let them hear them.' And he said, 'No, father Abraham; but if one goes to them from the dead, they will repent.' But he said to him, 'If they do not hear Moses and the prophets, neither will they be persuaded though one rise from the dead.'"

While he lived, the rich man had great luxury and no compassion. He shunned Lazarus, who existed with great poverty, sores, and pain. His "care givers" were dogs who licked his sores.

Notice the *consciousness* after death. This life/death experience was told by the Lord Jesus Himself, who explains that the rich man, whose body was evidently put in a grave, finds his conscious self in a place of torment. He feels, sees, and senses severe agony. He was separated from comfort, he thirsted, and he could consciously communicate. He spoke to those in Abraham's place who consciously existed in comfort. Abraham was not experiencing agony. He was separated by a great distance from the place of the rich man. There was no possibility of transport from one place to the other.

Isn't it interesting to see the role reversal between the rich man and Lazarus? The rich man becomes the beggar, and Lazarus lives in comfort. The rich man finds no comfort and doesn't want his brothers to come to him. No one in Hades wants anyone to come there. I've often heard people say, "If I die and go to hell, I'll have lots of friends there." They won't enjoy friendship but will experience awful torment. Hell is a place of remorse, agony, and crying out for relief.

There was another Lazarus in Scripture, who was the brother of Mary and Martha. Lazarus was sick and dying, and his sisters called for Jesus to come and heal him. Read what Jesus says in John 11:11-13 (NKJV): "These things He said, and after that He said to them, 'Our friend Lazarus sleeps, but I go that I may wake him up.' Then His disciples said, 'Lord, if he sleeps he will get well.' However, Jesus spoke of his death, but they thought that He was speaking about taking rest in sleep."

After Lazarus had died and had been in the tomb for four days, Jesus arrives and says, "Lazarus, come forth," and Lazarus in his grave wrappings comes forth from the tomb.

These biblical events indicate awareness and a consciousness after death, and that death is referred to as the body sleeping. Even when people are sleeping, their mind is still active. A lot of people don't like to face the reality of God's Word when they have their own philosophies and way of living, so they ignore and reject the Scriptures. I'm sure that's what the rich man did while alive. After death it was different.

The apostle Paul, inspired by the Holy Spirit, wrote some specific Scripture about Christians' body and soul after death. Keep in mind that Paul refers to the body as a house, a tent, or a building in 2 Corinthians 5:1-8 (NKJV):

> For we know that if our earthly house, this tent, is destroyed, we have a building from God, a house not made with hands, eternal in the heavens. For in this we groan, earnestly desiring to be clothed with our habitation which is from heaven, if indeed, having been clothed, we shall not be found naked. For we who are in this tent groan, being burdened, not because we want to be unclothed, but further clothed, that mortality may be swallowed up by life. Now He who has prepared us for this very thing is God, who also has given us the Spirit as a guarantee.

> So we are always confident, knowing that while we are at home in the body we are absent from the Lord. For we walk by faith, not by sight. We are confident, yes, well pleased rather to be absent from the body and to be present with the Lord."

Paul gives additional insight to consciousness after death in his epistle to the Philippians (1:21-23 NKJV): "For to me, to live is Christ, and to die is gain. But if I live on in the flesh, this will mean fruit from my labor; yet what I shall choose I cannot tell. For I am hard-pressed between the two, having a desire to depart and be with Christ, which is far better."

These Scriptures indicate that as a Christian, the real me leaves my earth-suit at death and is translated into the presence of the Lord, which is consistent with the promises of Jesus the Christ, who said in John 14:3 (NKJV), "And if I go away I will come again and receive you unto myself; that where I am, there you may be also."

In 1 Corinthians 15:17-19 we read, "And if Christ is not risen, your faith is futile; you are still in your sins! Then also those who have fallen asleep in Christ have perished. If in this life only we have hope in Christ, we are of all men the most pitiable." The underlined words indicate that a person can be absent from the body. This is very clear in the text and context that the real person, the soul, is to be differentiated from the mortal body. Often in Scripture the body is referred to as a tent or a tabernacle, and as such it is temporal—that is, a temporary housing unit until an eternal body is available. This portion of Scripture is talking about the Christian being in the physical presence of the risen Lord Jesus. While here on earth the believer has Christ's indwelling presence through the Holy Spirit:

> Now this I say, brethren, that flesh and blood cannot inherit the kingdom of God; nor does corruption inherit incorruption. Behold, I tell you a mystery: We shall not all sleep, but we shall all be changed—in a moment, in the twinkling of an eye, at the last trumpet. For the trumpet will sound, and the dead will be raised incorruptible, and we shall be changed. For this corruptible must put on incorruption, and this mortal must put on immortality. (1 Corinthians 15:50-53 NKJV)

Again, this portion of Scripture is written to Christians. Our mortal bodies, because of their corruptness, cannot dwell in the heavenly presence of the holy God. This corrupt body must be changed to an incorruptible body, one that is like the eternal body of the Lord Jesus. We will need to exchange a mortal body for an immortal body, one that will last for all eternity.

The great hope of the Christian is the coming of Jesus Christ for His church, which is His mystical body comprised of all Christians. Listen to what the Scripture says concerning His coming in 1 Thessalonians 4:13-18 (NKJV):

> But I do not want you to be ignorant, brethren, concerning those who have fallen asleep, lest you sorrow as others who have no hope. For if we believe that Jesus died and rose again, even so God will bring with Him those who sleep in Jesus. For this we say to you by the word of the Lord, that we who are alive and remain until the coming of the Lord will by no means precede those who are asleep. For the Lord Himself will descend from heaven with a shout, with the voice of an archangel, and with the trumpet of God. And the dead in Christ will rise first. Then we who are alive and remain shall be caught up together with them in the clouds to meet the Lord in the air. And thus we shall always be with the Lord. Therefore comfort one another with these words.

Those Christians who are "asleep in Christ," meaning that their bodies are inanimate in the grave, will be resurrected and given a changed body like the resurrected body of Jesus. How can those who have predeceased the living Christians come with the Lord, who is coming from the heavenly throne room, if they were not with Him? The teaching here is that the "sleeping body" will be changed and united with the conscious soul and spirit that had been with the Lord Jesus in heaven.

Although there are other views held by Christians, I believe the Scriptures teach that all those Christians who are alive at Christ's coming, will be changed by receiving a new body to go along with their redeemed soul. This event is known as the rapture, the calling away of the Christians who are alive at Christ's coming in the clouds. Those Christians who are "asleep" at this time will have their bodies resurrected and changed to be new, incorruptible bodies. Both those who were alive and those whose bodies were asleep will meet the Lord in the air, not on the earth, and will go on to the heavenly realm in new eternal bodies.

After this rapture the world will go through the "great tribulation," a period of seven years that ends with the second coming of Christ. He returns to earth at the Mount of Olives, across from the eastern gate to Jerusalem. This event will take place at the end of the great tribulation, when the horrendous battle of Armageddon involving all the nations of the world is shaping up. This battle takes place at Megiddo, north of Jerusalem.

Another JW doctrine is that of annihilation, the complete destruction of all those who are not in one of the two groups of Witnesses. There is a third group (not JWs or failed JWs, but souls that are to receive another chance) who Witnesses say were resurrected after the battle of Armageddon and had not achieved everlasting life. They were given a second chance by living a resurrected life during the millennial reign of Christ and failed. Therefore, they were annihilated. But nowhere in the Word of God do we read of a second chance after death; in fact, Scripture says in Hebrews 9:27, "And as it is appointed for men to die once, but after this the judgment . . ." To believe in a second chance indicates that humankind will merit salvation by behaving well, which is contrary to what the Word of God teaches about salvation by grace through faith. "How shall we escape if we neglect so great a salvation?" (Hebrews 2:3).

According to JW teachings, "everlasting" punishment means those involved will be dismissed from the presence of God forever and will not be involved in "eternal" torment but will be annihilated immediately. Witnesses state there is a difference between the words *eternal* and *everlasting*, but both words are translated from Greek root words having the same meaning in the original New Testament Scriptures. "Eternal" and "everlasting" can only mean the same thing.

For example, look at the state of the evil trinity, who are Satan, the Antichrist (beast), and the false prophet, during the thousand-year reign of Christ. (The beast and the false prophet are evil personages in human bodies, who are respectively the Antichrist and the messenger for the beast.) Where are they? Satan is bound and thrown into the bottomless pit, and the Antichrist and the false prophet are in hell, the place of torment.

Satan is unbound for a short season at the end of the thousand years to carry out his last mission. It is evident the Antichrist and the false prophet still exist at the end of a thousand years. They were not annihilated. During his last mission, Satan gathers together all those who had resisted Christ during His thousand-year reign. Satan's goal was to dethrone Jesus the King of kings, but his mission fails. Satan is sent to hell, where the beast and false prophet are still imprisoned. If there was annihilation, why weren't they destroyed?

Read the Scriptures to see if these things are as stated (Revelation 19:19–20:15 NKJV):

> And I saw the beast, the kings of the earth, and their armies, gathered together to make war against Him who sat on the horse and against His army. Then the beast was captured, and

with him the false prophet who worked signs in his presence, by which he deceived those who received the mark of the beast and those who worshiped his image. These two were cast alive into the lake of fire burning with brimstone. And the rest were killed with the sword which proceeded from the mouth of Him who sat on the horse. And all the birds were filled with their flesh.

Then I saw an angel coming down from heaven, having the key to the bottomless pit and a great chain in his hand. He laid hold of the dragon, that serpent of old, who is the Devil and Satan, and bound him for a thousand years; and he cast him into the bottomless pit, and shut him up, and set a seal on him, so that he should deceive the nations no more till the thousand years were finished. But after these things he must be released for a little while. And I saw thrones, and they sat on them, and judgment was committed to them. Then I saw the souls of those who had been beheaded for their witness to Jesus and for the word of God, who had not worshiped the beast or his image, and had not received his mark on their foreheads or on their hands. And they lived and reigned with Christ for a thousand years. But the rest of the dead did not live again until the thousand years were finished. This is the first resurrection. Blessed and holy is he who has part in the first resurrection. Over such the second death has no power, but they shall be priests of God and of Christ, and shall reign with Him a thousand years.

Now when the thousand years have expired, Satan will be released from his prison and will go out to deceive the nations which are in the four corners of the earth, Gog and Magog, to gather them together to battle, whose number is as the sand of the sea. They went up on the breadth of the earth and surrounded the camp of the saints and the beloved city. And fire came down from God out of heaven and devoured them. The devil, who deceived them, was cast into the lake of fire and brimstone where the beast and the false prophet are. And they will be tormented day and night forever and ever.

Then I saw a great white throne and Him who sat on it, from whose face the earth and the heaven fled away. And there was found no place for them. And I saw the dead, small

> and great, standing before God, and books were opened. And another book was opened, which is the Book of Life. And the dead were judged according to their works, by the things which were written in the books. The sea gave up the dead who were in it, and Death and Hades delivered up the dead who were in them. And they were judged, each one according to his works. Then Death and Hades were cast into the lake of fire. This is the second death. And <u>anyone</u> not found written in the Book of Life was cast into the lake of fire.

Notice how the New World Translation translates Revelation 20:10: "And the Devil who was misleading them was hurled into the lake of fire and sulphur, where both the wild beast and the false prophet [already were]; and they will be tormented day and night forever and ever."

By dropping the word *are* and by replacing it with the bracketed words *already were* accommodates their teaching about annihilation. This translation is an example of changing the text of Scripture to suit one's beliefs.

There is one more powerful incident in Scripture that gives evidence of people being conscious after death. This is during the time between Jesus' crucifixion and His resurrection. Matthew 27:50-54 says:

> And Jesus cried out again with a loud voice, and yielded up His spirit. Then, behold, the veil of the temple was torn in two from top to bottom; and the earth quaked, and the rocks were split, and the graves were opened; <u>and many bodies of the saints who had fallen asleep were raised; and coming out of the graves after His resurrection, they went into the holy city and appeared to many.</u> So when the centurion and those with him, who were guarding Jesus, saw the earthquake and the things that had happened, they feared greatly, saying, "Truly this was the Son of God!"

The bodies of the saints who were raised were joined with their souls and spirits from paradise, and is it possible they were to be a witness to those in Jerusalem that a resurrection of the dead can happen and surely would be the case for Jesus. The Scripture gives every evidence that physical death is not the ceasing of life but rather an afterlife experience of either paradise or hades.

Prophecies of the Jehovah's Witnesses

This is an area that requires careful consideration and depth of thinking that doesn't merely dismiss the results as human error. It is not just human error when the declared prophecies are said to be divine revelations communicated through God's only spokespersons, the Watchtower Society, and are published in *The Watchtower*.

The Watchtower Society says about its role, "We belong to NO earthly organization. We adhere only to that heavenly organization. All the saints now living or that ever lived during this age, belong to OUR CHURCH ORGANIZATION: such are all ONE CHURCH, and there is NO OTHER recognized by the Lord" (69a).

Jehovah's Witnesses believe the Watchtower Society is God's only channel through which truth is dispersed, and belonging to that organization is the only means of salvation. Now I am sure there are individual Witnesses who may deny this, but that is the official statement of the organization, and to disagree with the society is to be an apostate with annihilation as one's end.

Here's what a former JW wrote:

> We were taught that we must adhere absolutely to the decisions and scriptural understanding of the Society, because God had given *it* this authority over His People (69b). To gain eternal life, I was told certain things were necessary (1) I should study the Bible diligently, and only through Watchtower publications (70a).

If the society declares that it is the only channel for God, then its channeled messages from God must be 100 percent correct (see Deuteronomy 18:20-22). Would God channel through the Watchtower organization a prophetic event that didn't take place at the time it says God said it would? This has happened several times, with such events calling for later adjustments in attempts to clarify the failed prophecies.

There are hundreds of the prophecies in holy Scripture that have been fulfilled with perfect accuracy, so there is no reason to believe that those that remain won't be fulfilled exactly as prophesied. However, when humans make predictions that are declared to be divinely inspired but do not come to fulfillment, then you must question their truth in other areas. Remember that a prophet has to be 100 percent correct in the prophetic messages, or the prophet is not a prophet of God.

Its "anointed leaders" and the Watchtower organization, who say they are Jehovah's voice to humankind and make His messages available in their official publications, have made various predictions that have not come to pass as prophesied.

A prophecy of Armageddon coming in 1914 first appeared in *Zion's Watch Tower* (July 15, 1894), which declared, "We see no reason for changing the figures nor could we change them if we would. They are, we believe, God's dates, not ours. But bear in mind that the end of 1914 is not the date for the *beginning,* but for the end of the time of trouble" (68a). Did this happen?

Another prophecy: "In view of the strong Bible evidence . . . we consider it an established truth that the final end of the kingdoms of this world, and the full establishment of the Kingdom of God, will be accomplished by the end of AD.1914 . . . and that the 'battle of the great day of God Almighty' (Rev.16:14), which will end in A.D. 1915 with the complete overthrow of the earth's present rulers, is already commenced" (67a). Did this happen?

It is apparent the rulers of the kingdoms of this world are still ruling and the Kingdom of God Almighty on earth has not yet been established. If God's Kingdom has been established on earth either physically or spiritually, as Witnesses say, then why is there such chaos, increasing sinfulness, hatred, terrorism, people rejecting Christ, and wars in the world today? The Scriptures teach that when Christ has established His millennial kingdom, their will be no wars. Peace will reign. The lion will lay down with the lamb.

The same resurrected Lord Jesus, who was the rejected King, went back to heaven and has not yet physically returned to earth in "power and great glory" as He said He would. In the Acts 1:9-11 we read,

> Now when He had spoken these things, while they watched, He was taken up, and a cloud received Him out of their sight. And while they looked steadfastly toward heaven as He went up, behold, two men stood by them in white apparel, who also said, "Men of Galilee, why do you stand gazing up into heaven? This same Jesus, who was taken up from you into heaven, will so come in like manner as you saw Him go into heaven."

When will He come in "power and great glory"? In Matthew 24:29-30, Jesus says:

> "<u>Immediately</u> <u>after the tribulation of those days</u> the sun will be darkened, and the moon will not give its light; the stars will

> fall from heaven, and the powers of the heavens will be shaken. Then the sign of the Son of Man will appear in heaven, and then all the tribes of the earth will mourn, and they will see the Son of Man coming on the clouds of heaven with power and great glory."

This time of great tribulation occurs during the last three and a half years of the seven-year peace treaty that the Antichrist negotiates with Israel and the nations. At the end of that tribulation, Jesus rescues Israel and sets up His earthly kingdom and thousand-year reign. He will rule with a rod of iron. Sin and unrighteous deeds will be dealt with immediately. Righteous justice will be administered..

The Bible says in Mark 13:32 and Acts 1:6-7 that no man can predict the exact time of Christ's second coming to rescue His people at the end of the tribulation. The rapture of the true church, who are the members of the body of Christ, will take place before the tribulation.

Some other failed prophecies are these:

> 1918, the downfall of "Christianity": "Also in the year 1918, when God destroys the churches wholesale and the church members by millions, it shall be that any that escape shall come to the works of Pastor Russell to learn the meaning of the downfall of "Christianity." (*The Finished Mystery*, 1918, 404, 485)

> 1925, it is "definitely settled": "1925 is definitely settled by the Scriptures, marking the end of the typical jubilees." (*The Watchtower*, April 1, 1923, 106)

> 1925, the date is "definitely and clearly marked": "the year 1925 is a date definitely and clearly marked in the Scriptures, even more clearly than that of 1914." (*The Watchtower*, July 15, 1924, 211)

> 1925, the "faithful prophets will return": "That period of time beginning 1575 before A.D. 1 of necessity would end in the fall of the year 1925, at which time the type ends and the great antitype must begin. . . . Therefore we may confidently expect that 1925 will mark the return of Abraham, Isaac, Jacob and

> the faithful prophets of old." (*Millions Now Living Will Never Die*, 1920, 88-90)
>
> 1925, "it may or may not be": "The year 1925 is here. With great expectation Christians have looked forward to this year. Many have confidently expected that all of the body of Christ will be changed to heavenly glory during the year. This may be accomplished. It may not be." (The Watchtower, January 1, 1925, 3)

Similar statements were made for 1930, 1931, 1933, 1939, 1940, 1941, 1942, 1943, 1944, 1946, 1950, 1953, 1955, 1958, 1973, 1974, 1975, 1992, 2005, and 2006. With so many failures in dates determined for Armageddon, you might think that the Watchtower Society would refrain from any more date setting. However, in 2006 no specific year is given, as it was in the past: "Soon it [this world] will come to its end . . . and Armgeddon is but a short time off" (40a).

What a trail of failed prophetic declarations. Jesus said that neither men nor the angels know the day or the hour of future prophetic events, so why do people still attempt to predict the date for Armageddon? I would suggest that it's to obtain a following and build a group of adherents through the sensationalism associated with supposedly knowing something no one else does. This will always draw a crowd. Could there be human glory and pride involved?

Interpretation of Scripture

There is another area that needs to be looked at, and that is the many times Scripture has been interpreted one way only to be totally changed later. Now anyone can change their minds on certain positions, but not when those changing their minds are the only earthly spokepersons for God.

In 1985, the Kingdom Interlinear Translation, which is the official Greek New Testament of Witnesses, applies the Greek *ho theos*, which in English is "the God" to Jesus (John 20:28, p. 513); however, *The Watchtower* of July 1, 1986 (31) states that *ho theos* does not apply to Jesus.

Or, *Man's Salvation Out of World Distress at Hand* (1975, 208) says of Matthew 13 that the Sower is Satan; however, *The Watchtower* (October 1, 1975,.600) says Jesus is the Sower.

Awake (August 22, 1978, 28) declares the "Alpha and Omega" is Jehovah, but *The Watchtower* (October 1, 1978) says the "Alpha and Omega" is Jesus.

One day I was asked by an inmate who had been reading the book of Revelation what the "Alfalfa and Omega" meant. I had the opportunity to share with him that this talks about the Lord Jesus Christ and that it says He is the Beginning and the End, thus indicating His eternal existence.

Let's look at some flip-flops in JW interpretation:

"Resurrection" of the men of Sodom (Genesis 18:16-19):
They will be resurrected. (*Zion's Watch Tower* reprint, July 1879, 7)
They will not be resurrected. (*The Watchtower*, June 1, 1952, 338)
They will be resurrected. (*The Watchtower*, August 1, 1965, 479)
They will not be resurrected. (*The Watchtower*, June 1, 1988, 30-31)

The "Lord" in Romans 10:12:
Lord refers to Jesus. (*Zion's Watch Tower* reprint December 1, 1903, 3282)
Lord refers to Jehovah. (*The Watchtower*, July 1, 1940, 200)
Lord refers to Jesus. (*The Watchtower*, May 1, 1978, 12)
Lord refers to Jehovah. (*The Watchtower*, February 1, 1980, 16)

How can these inconsistencies be justified coming from the Watchtower organization, which claims to be God's spokesmen on earth?

Once the NWT translators started changing the Scripture to comply with their teachings there were bound to be some portions of Scripture they would have difficulty translating and consequently would conflict with their teachings.

When Scripture is silent, I must remain silent. When I look at Genesis 1:26 and the Word of God says, "Let Us make man in Our image, according to Our likeness," some things are irrefutable. There are other things for which I could have an opinion; for example, man has God's image, and therefore man must look like God. But I must not build a dogmatic doctrine on an opinion that is not clearly stated in Scripture. This is what I believe happens when people try to reason out some of the things of God from a human perspective. Often human reasoning conflicts with the teachings of God's Word and results in a departure from the truth of Scripture.

Then, to substantiate their doctrines, people declare themselves to be an apostle or a prophet of God and have to come up with supposedly divine revelations. These conflicting revelations are meant to replace the true teachings of Scripture, or they twist teaching of Scripture in a way to fit the person's or the group's doctrines. This leads to extra scriptures and/or translations that disregard scholarly translations from the original Scriptures.

Once a position is taken that is not consistent with the teachings of Scripture, additional claimed divine inspiration or revelation must be found to combat those who make justifiable criticism of their teachings and scriptures.

It is tragic when intellectual honesty is lost. The mind then becomes open to teaching that is found on the pathway of vain deception and human philosophy. Supposedly sophisticated intellectualism that disregards the truth of God's Word misses what God intended for us.

Summary

It appears that the doctrines of Jehovah Witnesses are guided from a human perspective that attempts to supplant the holy Scriptures when the human mind has trouble reasoning from God's perspective. God says in His Word, "For My thoughts are not your thoughts, nor are your ways My ways" (Isaiah 55:8), In essence, the worldly mind does not discern the things of God. Discernment requires illumination from the Holy Spirit, who never reveals any teaching contrary to the Word of God.

Although Witnesses claim their final authority is the Bible, partial authority rests on the NWT, which mistranslates some texts to fit JW doctrinal positions. There is strong language in the Word of God condemning those who would add to or subtract from the Scriptures.

My heart goes out to the followers who must accept the Watchtower Society's word as the final authority. The society states that there is no infallible human authority, but their teachings say otherwise. Jehovah Witnesses must follow the authoritarian system and studies established by the "anointed leaders" of the Watchtower organization.

True Christians have a love relationship with Christ, the Father, and the Holy Spirit that produces a loving concern for those who are following a system of manmade doctrines, rules, rituals, and traditions. True Christians have a genuine concern for those who trust in their works rather than accepting God's grace and placing their faith in the person of Jesus the Christ and His once-for-all sacrifice for the sins of the world. Faith is taking God at His Word, and that faith comes by hearing, and hearing by the Word of God (Romans 10:17). Without that faith it is impossible to please God (Hebrews 11:6).

Faith alone in Christ alone, excluding manmade religion with all its traditions, rules, and regulations, determines whether a person is a Christian. The Scripture is clear in Galatians 2:16 ("for by the works of the law no flesh will be justified") and in Titus 3:5 ("not by works of righteousness which we have done, but according to His mercy He has saved us").

All we are and have comes through God's overwhelming generosity, including gifts of His grace, such as everlasting life, forgiveness, mercy, and unconditional love. All are made possible by taking God at His Word, believing that He will deliver what He has promised. This requires faith, which God honors. That's what trusting Him is about: "Faith comes by hearing and hearing by the Word of God" (Romans 10:17).

One would have to admit there are important major differences between JW source documents and their beliefs, compared with the Christian claim that the Word of God alone is the final authority. You alone must consider and come to a conclusion, because both cannot be true. If you are in a state of uncertainty, please look over the section on Christianity.

You must decide. Neutral you cannot be. Remember, no decision is a decision.

Chapter 3

Mormonism

We were a young family on a vacation in the western United States. We took in all the sights at Yellowstone National Park: Old Faithful and the other geysers, the animals, the hot springs, the paint pots, the nearby lakes that reflected the majestic Teton Mountains. With those beautiful scenes of God's creation impressed on our minds, we left that area for Utah. We wanted to see and possibly swim in the Great Salt Lake in Utah. While we were there we had an opportunity to visit the Mormon Museum and the Mormon Tabernacle with its impressive pipe organ. From the tabernacle the Mormon Tabernacle Choir airs its inspiring annual Christmas musical program.

During our walk around the area we headed towards the magnificent temple only to find out that we were not permitted inside that impressive structure. Entry to it is available only to faithful Mormons. We moved on to the museum, which took us on a trip through the history and growth of the Mormon church. The growth was brought about by its founder, Joseph Smith, and his successor, Brigham Young, who blazed the wilderness trail to the Salt Lake area. Today, you will find the headquarters of the Mormon church there.

I learned a lot and was impressed with the presentation about the Mormon religion. I tried to incorporate this into the traditional Christianity I knew, but there seemed to be some differences. I would have to dig into this.

I have always been impressed by the close-knit Mormon families, their personal cleanliness, good business sense and endeavors, and the zeal of their missionary program.

The History of the Church of Jesus Christ of Latter-Day Saints (LDS)

Mormonism began with Joseph Smith Jr., who was born in 1805 and died in 1844. He started the Church of Christ in Palmyra, New York, in 1830. Today this church is known as The Church of Jesus Christ of Latter-Day Saints (LDS Church), or more commonly, the Mormons.

Joseph Smith claimed his "first vision" took place in 1820, in which God the Father and Jesus Christ told him that all the churches were false. Later, an angel told him where he would find some gold plates from which he would be able to translate the *Book of Mormon*. That book was officially published in 1830, when Smith was twenty-four. He considered himself responsible for restoring the one true church.

In another of his books, Smith relates his first vision. In it he encountered two personages with whom he had a dialogue: "I asked the Personages who stood above me in the light, which of all the sects was right (for at this time it had never entered my heart that all were wrong) and which I should join. I was answered that I must join none of them, for they were all wrong; and the Personage who addressed me said that all creeds were an abomination in his sight" (54a). In this vision, he was also told by God the Father, "this [the second personage] is my beloved Son, hear Him."

Joseph Smith Sr., the father of Joseph, spent a lot of time digging for hidden treasure around Sharon, Vermont, searching for Captain Kidd's treasure. He got into trouble with authorities when he decided to mint his own money. Joseph's father took him along on digging trips on which he used divining rods and peek stones to find hidden treasure. Perhaps this background influenced the younger Smith.

It would appear that Joseph was having difficulty finding his way and became involved in the religious community.

According to Orsamus Turner, an apprentice printer until 1822, he and young Smith were members of a juvenile debating club in their teens. Turner recalled that Joseph, "after catching a spark of Methodism . . . became a very passable exhorter in the evening meetings" (71a). He was welcomed and allowed to exhort during the Methodists' evening preaching.

In 1823, at the age of eighteen, Joseph says he experienced the appearance of the angel Moroni, son of Mormon, who told him where to locate gold plates that would contain data about the ancient Americas. The plates would be written in "reformed Egyptian Hieroglyphics" and declare the fullness of the everlasting gospel, which had been sent to the ancient peoples of the Americas. He would also find a pair of transparent stones set in silver to use as glasses in translating the plates.

When the plates were found, Smith was told not to take them then. He would have to wait. After several more visits by the angel Moroni, Smith was allowed to take the plates. He recovered the plates in 1827, in the hill Cumorah near Palmyra.

On recovering the plates, Smith translated the text on them. He was aided by scribes who were separated from him by a curtain. Smith would translate and tell the scribes what he was translating. The plates were said to have been inscribed with "reformed Egyptian Hieroglyphics," which Smith translated over a two-year period and had published in 1830 as the *Book of Mormon*.

It was during the first month of translation that Smith and one of his scribes, Cowdry, received a visit from John the Baptist that restored them into the Aaronic priesthood. Later, we are told, the Lord's apostles, James, Peter, and John, appeared and ordained them into the Melchizedek priesthood. Every worthy adult male Mormon is considered to be in one of those two priesthoods.

On the basis of those visits and revelations, Smith and five of his followers officially started a church that would become The Church of Jesus Christ of Latter-Day Saints. The year 1831 brought Smith another revelation that told him to move his followers to Ohio and Missouri. It was just prior to this that the group adopted the name The Church of Jesus Christ of Latter-Day Saints.

Within a short time Smith and his followers pulled stakes and moved to Kirtland, Ohio, and in the presence of the twelve apostles of the newly formed church they elected Smith as leader. When Smith was in this area, he joined the Masons. The Masonic Lodge rituals that Smith was exposed to influenced the rituals that are practiced in the LDS temple ceremonies.

Some of Smith's followers had settled in Zion, Missouri. However, in 1839, the governor of Missouri ordered the Mormons to leave that state because some of Smith's followers had been implicated in serious crimes. Smith then led a group to Illinois and settled in a city later called Nauvoo. It was here that Smith introduced his teachings of polygamy, which allowed a man to have more than one wife.

Smith apparently got into trouble with the authorities for trying to destroy a local newspaper office because it took a stand against the Mormons' illegal practices. Both Smith and his brother were arrested and jailed in Carthage, Illinois. An angry mob stormed the jail and shot Smith and his brother on June 27, 1844. Both were considered martyrs for the cause of Mormonism.

During this time of tragedy, many of Smith's followers rallied around Brigham Young, who emerged as the "first President," and as such was considered the new leader and prophet of the Mormons. His teachings became the dogma of their church. Due to adverse publicity, a vast number of Mormons left the Midwest and followed Young to settle in the Salt Lake Valley of Utah. Young was a man of vision and established the headquarters of the church in what today is called Salt Lake City. Young ruled the church as its president/prophet and determined its theology.

In 1857, a large group of non-Mormon immigrants arrived. These people were headed for California, but orders were given to Bishop John D. Lee to get rid of them. In what came to be called the Mountain Meadows Massacre, 150 non-Mormons were destroyed.

This is a very brief overview of the early years of The Church of Jesus Christ of Latter-Day Saints. Another group, based in Missouri, called the Reorganized Church of Jesus Christ of Latter-Day Saints, does not accept some of the teachings of the LDS. This group took a new name, Community of Christ, in 2001.

Since the death of Brigham Young there have been several succeeding presidents/prophets who have guided the LDS church with what they declare are divine revelations. Their recitations or messages are considered the same as holy Scripture. If the LDS considers each president/prophet and his counselors as "the Presidency," and if their words are scripture, then how does one reconcile when previous scripture is declared incorrect by a later presidency? This is difficult to understand, since the LDS says it accepts the King James Version Bible as Scripture, and the King James Version says in Deuteronomy18:20-22:

> "But the prophet who presumes to speak a word in My name, which I have not commanded him to speak, or who speaks in the name of other gods, that prophet shall die. And if you say in your heart, 'How shall we know the word which the LORD has not spoken?'—when a prophet speaks in the name of the LORD, if the thing does not happen or come to pass, that is the thing which the LORD has not spoken; the prophet has spoken it presumptuously; you shall not be afraid of him."

Consequently, a prophet of the Lord's message had to be 100 percent correct. To be other than that is to be a false prophet.

Also, the Bible states in Revelation 22:18-19:

> For I testify to everyone who hears the words of the prophecy of this book: If anyone adds to these things, God will add to him the plagues that are written in this book; and if anyone takes away from the words of the book of this prophecy, God shall take away his part from the Book of Life, from the holy city, and from the things which are written in this book.

Since the prophecies in Revelation are consistent with and confirm prophecies from the Old Testament and the New Testament, then this warning would apply to those books as well. When leaders of other religions change the words of the Bible or make predictions that don't come to pass or that contradict or change the words, then this warning in Revelation would apply. It's unwise to tamper with God's Word. There are eternal consequences.

Source Documents of the LDS Church

The Book of Mormon

The King James Bible is referred to for some LDS teaching; however, Joseph Smith's translation of the Bible is considered to have corrected and clarified parts of the Bible and thus has greater authority. Other books that have precedence over the Bible include *Doctrine and Covenants*, *Book of Mormon*, and *The Pearl of Great Price*. *The Pearl of Great Price* also contains the Book of Abraham, the Book of Moses, and others. All of these books serve as the basis for LDS teachings.

The original *Book of Mormon*, written on the golden plates, is claimed to have been written by several people over a period of time from 600 years before the birth of Christ to 421 years after His birth and tells that there were migrations of people to the Americas. One migration supposedly took place at the time of the Tower of Babel, which was built before 2000 BC. Those migrant peoples, called Jaredites, all perished because of their apostasy. Around 600 years before the birth of Christ there was another migration of a group of Jews who were told by God to leave Jerusalem before the Babylonian captivity occurred. This group of Jews was led by a man named Lehi and his son Nephi, who the LDS believe to have crossed the Indian and Pacific oceans before landing in the Americas. This group of Jews split into two opposing nations, the Nephites and the Lamanites.

Due to their wickedness, the Lamanites were cursed with dark skin and are considered to be the ancestors of Native Americans. This is difficult to accept, since Native Americans were originally from the continent of Asia and not of Jewish ancestry.

The *Book of Mormon* proclaims that the Nephites recorded prophecies concerning the coming of Christ and that He visited the Nephites after His resurrection, at which time He instituted communion, baptism, and the priesthood of the Nephites. Later, the Nephites were all killed in a battle with the Lamanites (about AD 421). Before being killed in this battle, Mormon and his son Moroni buried the golden plates on which were engraved the revelations of the *Book of Mormon*. These were the plates recovered by Joseph Smith fourteen hundred years later.

The Authority of the Book of Mormon and the Bible

The Mormon church says the *Book of Mormon* is divinely inspired and equal to the Bible when the Bible is translated correctly. This allows the *Book of Mormon* to take precedence over the Bible when it differs. It was Joseph Smith's opinion that the transcriptions from the original writings of the Bible were so corrupted that a great deal of the original word was lost. Therefore he was called on to correct those gross errors with his translation. In the process of correcting these errors, Smith changed the text of the book of Revelation.

For an example of Smith's changes, let's look how he translated John 1:1: "In the beginning was the gospel preached through the Son. And the gospel was the word, and the word was with the Son, and the Son was with God, and the Son was of God" (Joseph Smith Translation [JST]). In the New King James Version (NKJV), the same portion says, "In the beginning was the Word, and the Word was with God, and the Word was God."

The JST does satisfy the doctrinal position of Mormonism which is that Jesus was the son of a god, but not the Son of God but certainly differs from Christian teaching. Mormons justify these differences by saying that the original writings of the apostles were not copied correctly; even though hundreds of copies of the earliest Greek manuscripts of the Gospel of John have survived and do not allow for Joseph Smith's translation of John 1:1.

Even though the Bible is respected as a holy book by the Mormon church, the *Book of Mormon*, *The Pearl of Great Price*, and *The Doctrine and Covenants* are considered of greater significance. In fact, people who believe that the Bible is God's final revelation and not to be changed, added to, or replaced are ridiculed in the *Book of Mormon*: "Thou fool, that shall say: A Bible, we have got a Bible, and we need no more Bible. . . . Wherefore, because that ye have a Bible ye need not suppose that it contains all my words; neither need ye suppose that I have not caused more to be written" (*Book of Mormon*, 2 Nephi 29:6, 10). This is a necessary statement to justify adding to or changing the Word of God. But why would God reveal something later that was so contradictory to what He had revealed earlier? Is God a God of duplicity and confusion?

Smith claimed the plates from which he translated the *Book of Mormon* were buried in 421 and recovered in 1827, but more than five hundred verses of the plates came directly from the King James translation of the Bible. The King James Version was translated 1611 into the common English language of that day. How is it that the words of Christ to His apostles were on plates that were buried in 421 contain text and words from the King James Version of 1611? That's about twelve hundred years before the King James Version was published.

More than two thousand corrections have been made to the *Book of Mormon* since it was first published in 1830. Wording has been changed over the years, in spite of the claim that Joseph Smith's original translation was divinely inspired. Those who question the *Book of Mormon* find it difficult to accept the validity of a source document as divinely inspired given that the writings in that book were based on a language called "reformed Egyptian Hieroglyphics." There were no known authoritative translators of that language, if it ever existed, in the world.

Mormons expect sincere questioners of the authenticity of the *Book of Mormon* to accept the Mormon church's teaching that the Bible is not reliable because it supposedly contains many translation errors. This is especially the case when the Bible conflicts with teachings from Mormon source documents.

But how can a person be expected to accept the *Book of Mormon* as divinely inspired when its writings contains accounts of the history, geography, culture, and foods of Native Americans (who are claimed to be dispersed Jews) that are totally inaccurate? Also, DNA testing indicates that the Native Americans are from the Asian bloodline, and not the Israelite, as proposed by Mormon source documents. Isn't it difficult to accept such historical and ethnic inconsistencies as divine revelation?

The Book of Abraham

Within *The Pearl of Great Price* is a portion identified as The Book of Abraham. This book was translated from an Egyptian papyrus that Smith and some of his followers had purchased from a man who was traveling from city to city displaying those papyri along with some Egyptian mummies. The traveling man was Michael H. Chandler, who was convinced that Smith was capable of translating the "Egyptian hieroglyphics" of the papyri.

According to Smith, The Book of Abraham was written by Abraham's own hand in "Egyptian hieroglyphics" that supposedly had been lost since the time of Abraham (the same Abraham spoken about in the book of Genesis in the Bible). It is that book, The Book of Abraham, from which Mormon doctrine is derived. One of those teachings is that black people were under a curse and could not serve in the priesthood of the church. This teaching, however, was rescinded in 1978. How can this be?

Joseph Fielding Smith, in *Doctrines of Salvation* (vol. 1, p. 186, 1954) is quoted as follows:

> **What is Scripture?** When one of the brethren stands before a congregation of the people today, and the inspiration of the Lord is upon him, he speaks that which the Lord would have him speak. It is just as much scripture as anything you will find written in any of these records, and yet we call these the standard works of the Church. We depend, of course, upon the guidance of the brethren who are entitled to inspiration.

This being the case, why should the writings of Joseph Smith and Brigham Young be changed or rescinded later if they were divinely inspired scripture when originally spoken or written?

Although Smith's translations of the papyrus have been discovered to be completely erroneous, there was much joy among Mormons when the papyrus was first purchased and the great discoveries of truth from the writings of Abraham were translated into English from the "Egyptian hieroglyphics." This was considered a monumental confirmation to LDS followers that the *Book of Mormon* taken from the golden plates written in "reformed Egyptian Hieroglyphics" and translated by the prophet Smith was truly divinely inspired scripture.

There was no challenge to the authenticity of Smith's translation of the papyrus at the time, because there were no Egyptologists in the United States who could decipher those hieroglyphic writings. Several years earlier, the code for Egyptian hieroglyphics was broken, although that fact was not then known in the United States. Egyptology was in its infancy, the Rosetta Stone had been deciphered, but scholars had not yet reached the point of translating other Egyptian hieroglyphic texts with any confidence. Today, however, authoritative sources in Egyptian studies conclude that the papyrus Smith translated, rediscovered many years later in the archives of the New York Museum, contained nothing more than a portion of an Egyptian Book of Breathing. The papyrus had nothing to do with Abraham. It contained funerary rites, a document describing a prominent Egyptian priest's burial, and the dead man's travel to the other world.

Today, there is much confusion in the Mormon church and among its followers as they try to explain away this wrong translation that Smith had of the so-called Egyptian hieroglyphics after he claimed the document to be divinely inspired. Smith was using an untranslatable language, which he evidently didn't know either, to perpetuate teachings that in many areas contradicted the Bible.

For an in-depth study regarding this lost book, I recommend *By His Own Hand Upon Papyrus*, written by Charles M. Larson and published by the Institute of Religious Research (IRR) in Grand Rapids, Michigan.

President/Prophet

It is this office of the LDS church that is considered the authority and final word for beliefs and practices. The president/prophet is considered the voice of God to the LDS members.

In a devotional assembly with LDS students at Brigham Young University, President Ezra Taft Benson lectured on "Fourteen Fundamentals in Following the Prophets" (February 26, 1980). He confirmed the president/prophet must be the final authority for the church. Here's his summary of that speech:

> In conclusion, let us summarize this grand key, these "Fourteen Fundamentals in Following the Prophet," for our salvation hangs on them.
>
> **First:** The prophet is the only man who speaks for the Lord in everything.
>
> **Second:** The living prophet is more vital to us than the standard works.
>
> **Third:** The living prophet is more important to us than a dead prophet.
>
> **Fourth:** The prophet will never lead the Church astray.
>
> **Fifth:** The prophet is not required to have any particular

earthly training or credentials to speak on any subject or act on any matter at any time.

Sixth: The prophet does not have to say "Thus saith the Lord" to give us scripture.

Seventh: The prophet tells us what we need to know, not always what we want to know.

Eighth: The prophet is not limited by men's reasoning.

Ninth: The prophet can receive revelation on any matter, temporal or spiritual.

Tenth: The prophet may be involved in civic matters.

Eleventh: The two groups who have the greatest difficulty in following the prophet are the proud who are learned and the proud who are rich.

Twelfth: The prophet will not necessarily be popular with the world or the worldly.

Thirteenth: The prophet and his counselors make up the First Presidency—the highest quorum in the Church.

Fourteenth: The prophet and the presidency—the living prophet and the First Presidency—follow them and be blessed; reject them and suffer.

I testify that these fourteen fundamentals in following the living prophet are true. If we want to know how well we stand with the Lord, then let us ask ourselves how well we stand with His mortal captain how closely do our lives harmonize with the words of the Lord's anointed—the living prophet—the President of the Church, and with the Quorum of the First Presidency?

May God bless us all to look to the Prophet and the Presidency

> in the critical and crucial days ahead, is my prayer. In the name of Jesus Christ. Amen.

The problem with this doctrinal position is when an authoritative pronouncement from one of their prophets, living or dead, was later changed or contradicted by another living prophet. Is God so changeable regarding His revelations to these leaders of the LDS church?

All of the doctrines and teachings of the Mormon church that are based on their source documents should be questioned as to their divine origin, along with the teachings of their current prophets.

There is a great difference between the teachings of the Bible and those from the sources upheld by LDS authorities. Much of the above writings come from materials that were researched by IRR. Let's look into some of what Mormons teach.

Teachings from Mormon Sources

God

When Brigham Young, the president/prophet of the church, was in office, he taught that the Adam of Genesis was none other than the heavenly Father:

> Now hear it, O inhabitants of the earth, Jew and Gentile, Saint and sinner! When our father Adam came into the garden of Eden, he came into it with a *celestial* body, and brought *Eve, one of his wives,* with him. He helped to make and organize this world. He is MICHAEL, *the Archangel,* the Ancient of Days! About whom holy men have written and spoken He *is* our Father *and our* God, *and the only God with whom we have to do.* Every man upon the earth, professing Christians or non-professing, must hear it, and *will know it sooner or later.* (from the *Journal of Discourse*, vol. 1, p. 50, April 9, 1852)

Today, this teaching is officially denied by Mormon leaders. Spencer W. Kimball is quoted as follows:

> We warn you against the dissemination of doctrines *which are not according to scriptures* and which are *alleged* to have been taught by some of the General Authorities of past generations.

> Such for instance is the Adam-god theory. We *denounce* that **theory** and hope that everyone will be cautioned *against this and other kinds of* ***false doctrine.*** (*Church News*, October 9, 1976)

Isn't it interesting that what was once called divine revelation is now called theory and false doctrine? Mr. Kimball traces his priestly line of authority directly back to Brigham Young, and if Brigham Young taught false doctrine, he should be considered a false prophet according to Deuteronomy 18:21-22:

> "And if you say in your heart, 'How shall we know the word which the LORD has not spoken?'— when a prophet speaks in the name of the LORD, if the thing does not happen or come to pass, that is the thing which the LORD has not spoken; the prophet has spoken it presumptuously; you shall not be afraid of him."

Mr. Kimball had the difficult problem of explaining how he obtained his own authority from a false prophet.

The Mormon scriptures state that the God the Father has flesh and bones, just as humans do. In fact, Joseph Smith believed that God "was once as we are now, and is an exalted man" (72a). God once dwelled on a planet as a man and through self-effort became God.

On the basis of these assumptions Smith taught that all good Mormons can become gods. Mormons teach that all humans existed in eternity past as spirit beings before they became flesh and blood on earth. According to Mormon source documents, the heavenly Father with a heavenly Mother birthed as spirit beings all who were to become human beings.

Let's reiterate the LDS views of God:

1. He is the Father of all spirit beings.
2. He is the Father of Jesus Christ in the flesh.
3. He was once a man as we are now.
4. He is the only God with whom we have to do, although there are other gods of other worlds in the universe;
5. And as such, He is our heavenly Father.

Also, God by nature is a physical being and is not omnipresent, and thus He can only be in one place at a time. The Bible, however, teaches that God is Spirit and can be everywhere at the same time, knows all, and is all-powerful.

Christ

Jesus the Christ, according to the Mormon *Doctrine and Covenants*, said, "I was in the beginning with the Father, and am the Firstborn . . . ye were also in the beginning with the Father" (53a).

Jesus was created in the same way that we were created, but as a spirit being. Lucifer (Satan) was a created spirit being as a son of god, and Jesus, a created being, is Satan's spirit brother. Mormons teach that at one time Jesus was the physical son of the god who lives with his many wives near the star Kolob, where he procreates spirit children through natural means. This god came down to earth in the flesh to be the physical father of Jesus through Mary. This means that Mormons would have to conclude that the birth of Jesus was not a literal virgin birth.

Mormons also have taught that Jesus, a polygamist, was the husband of Mary and Martha, the sisters of Lazarus; Jesus was also the husband of Mary Magdalene.

According to Mormon doctrine, if Jesus had not been married during his earthly life, after his resurrection and return to heaven he could rise only to the level of an angel. This is based on the Mormon doctrine that unmarried people and couples whose marriages are not sealed by the temple endowments can become only angels in heaven and not a god. Only marriages that take place in the temple are sealed, and only then in the spirit world can the couple become gods.

Was there a Mormon temple in Jesus' day? If not, the so-called marriage of Jesus would not be valid, and He would not be permitted entrance into the highest heaven, the celestial realm.

Can the Jesus of Mormon teaching possibly be the Jesus of the Bible?

The Holy Spirit

The "Holy Spirit" has been recognized as an impersonal presence and a spiritual force, energy, or an electricity-like emanation from God that influences individuals in varying degrees. Mormon teaching says the Father and the Son have physical bodies, but Mormons do not ascribe a physical presence to the holy spirit. The holy spirit sometimes is called the light of Christ. It is the holy spirit that can be an influence throughout all of space, thus enabling the Trinity to know all that is going on.

In Mormonism there is apparently a difference between the "holy spirit" and the Holy Ghost.

The Holy Ghost is considered the third God of the Mormon Godhead. The Holy Ghost supposedly looks like a man in form but has a spirit body. In this bodily form the Holy Ghost can be in only one place at a time, which is what the LDS church believes about all gods. Today, however, there is some thought that the Holy Ghost can be present with people in different places at the same time.

Salvation

The Mormon Articles of Faith 3 state that the atonement that Christ perfected on the cross is the means by which all humankind can and will be resurrected. After the resurrection of all humankind, each person can attain to one of the three eternal kingdoms. The only exception is for those who were so vile and heretical that they go into perdition, or the blackness of outer darkness.

To reach the celestial kingdom, which is the highest attainment, a person must be a Mormon in good standing having declared faith in Jesus Christ; experienced repentance; baptism by immersion for the remission of sins; eternal marriage; and the laying on of hands for the gift of the Holy Ghost. This person must live in obedience to many Mormon regulations.

Some of these rites and rituals must be administered in a temple of the Mormon church and all must be administered by a member of the Mormon priesthood. This implies that rituals extended through human efforts are necessary to meet the requirements for justification and acceptance by God.

This in essence teaches that people attain salvation on their own merits, earned by adhering to Mormon teachings and observance of the Mormon temple rituals. Is this not salvation by achieving?

This is entirely different from the biblical doctrine of salvation by grace through faith alone in the person of Christ alone and His sacrificial work on the cross.

Eternal Destiny

In *Doctrine and Covenants* section 76 it is taught that there are three places of eternal abode for humankind after their death on earth. They are the celestial, the terrestrial, and the telestial. These are three separate, distinct heavenly kingdoms, and a person's qualification for entrance is dependent on his or her level of attainment or the lack thereof in the Mormon church.

The highest kingdom, the celestial, has three levels or degrees, the highest of which is reserved for those who have been faithful to the teachings and rituals in the temple, including water baptism, and the commandments of the Mormon church. Only those Mormons who have had their marriages sealed by the temple endowments will earn this highest level and achieve godhood.

The terrestrial kingdom is for those who have lived good lives but did not accept the Mormon gospel, or for Mormons who were unfaithful to the temple rituals. This will also be for those who did not receive the gospel on earth but did accept the testimony of Jesus in the spirit world. This is saying there is a second chance after death. Sounds good, but is it true?

The telestial kingdom is reserved for those who have led unclean lives on earth. After they have spent some time being punished for their sins, they will be part of the telestial realm.

The Mormon church believes that very few people will receive eternal punishment, since the three kingdoms are reachable because of the atoning work of Christ. They believe the atonement makes provision for just about everyone with the exception of the "sons of perdition," those who accepted Mormonism but fell away and became apostate. If a Mormon turns away from and denounces the Mormon church and its teachings, he or she is considered apostate and is destined to the place of "outer darkness."

One can readily see that the only way to obtain eternal status in any of the three kingdoms depends on the efforts of the individual. In other words, one earns one's way into one of the heavenly kingdoms.

There is a great emphasis placed on the need for water baptism, administered by a priest, as an absolute requirement for salvation. This is further evidenced by the practice of being baptized for those who have died but who were not Mormons. Being baptized for someone who has passed on makes it possible for that person in the afterlife to become a Mormon and attain godhood. That is to become a god.

A great deal of time is spent reviewing family trees to determine those deceased relatives who were not Mormons and the need of being baptized for them.

Thus, to the Mormon, baptism is essential for entrance into the kingdom of heaven and an indispensable step to salvation and eternal exaltation as a god.

Finally, the eternal outcome and a place within the three kingdoms are dependent on how closely a person follows the teachings and ordinances of the Mormon church. No where in the Bible will you find any teaching for an opportunity after death to obtain a second chance for a place in one of "3 heavenly kingdoms," or in fact any teaching of three separate kingdoms within heaven.

Did LDS Prophecies Come to Pass?

Prophet Joseph Smith, in the *History of the Church of Jesus Christ of the Latter-Day Saints* (5:394), prophesied that the United States government would be overthrown in the 1800s. This was a failed prediction.

Smith also prophesied that a temple would be built in Missouri in his "generation" (53b). This never came to pass.

Brigham Young prophesied in the *Journal of Discourses* (10:250) that the Civil War would fail to end black slavery.

Journal of Discourses 13:271 indicates that both the sun and moon were inhabited. There is no evidence that this has happened or could happen.

Furthermore, Brigham Young (*Journal of Discourses*, 13:95) states, "I have never yet preached a sermon and sent it out to the children of men, that they may not call Scripture." He is saying that his sermons are of divine revelation and are Scripture; thus they are equivalent to the Bible.

This is perplexing if the prophecies are not true. How then can the messages be from God? How could the prophecies be divinely inspired? How can they be called Scripture?

Summary

Many teachings of the LDS have been changed later, and revelations of dated prophecies have failed. The LDS scriptures have been rescinded as indicated in some areas. When the foundation of a religious movement has been laid and found to be unstable, then the whole structure is unsound, even if the structure was built with good intentions. Source documents must be beyond reproach and reliable. Is God so fickle and capricious to say this is what will happen, this is the truth, and then change what will happen? The original revealed truth of the past wasn't true after all. It required changing. Would that be a God you could depend on?

Now that I have researched and discovered the basis for Mormon teaching, I know why I was having difficulty with the information presented while touring the Mormon museum.

In the chapter about Christianity, the vast differences between Christianity and Mormon doctrines will become even more apparent.

Chapter 4
Islam

It was in the mid-1980s. I was sitting in one of the small lobbies in the old historic section of the Taj Intercontinental Hotel in Bombay, India, along with two of my traveling companions as we waited for a fourth person in our party. Seated in a corner of the lobby, not far away from where we were seated, was a man dressed in Arab garments. I noticed he was observing us somewhat, so I waved to him, and he acknowledged my gesture. I invited him to come and join us. He did.

We introduced ourselves, and he told us his name was Mohamed. He seemed to need a friend. He was probably wondering what we were doing in India, and he asked, in English, "Are you from America?" He then asked what we were doing in India. I told him we were from America and that we raised funds in the United States to pay for Bibles and lessons to be printed and distributed in India. He seemed to be impressed by that.

I then asked him why he was in India. He said he was from Bahrain and that he came to India to get away for a little while. He had a son who had attended Oxford University in England and then went to New York University, where he got involved in the drug culture. When he came back to Bahrain during midterm, he was found dead early one morning in his car by the side of the highway. He had overdosed.

My heart went out to this father who was grieving the loss of his son. I told Mohamed I would remember him in my prayers. He seemed to be comforted by that. I told him I had something for him, but it was in my room, and if he had a few moments I would get it for him. I assumed he could read English and found out later he did. I left and returned with a tract written by Billy Graham, "Steps to Peace with God." He said he had never heard about Billy Graham.

Mohamed asked to be excused, because he wanted to go to his room to get something for us. He returned with four small metal bars in plastic cases and gave one to me and one to each of my traveling friends. Later we found they were solid gold, worth at that time about $125 each. He then invited us to be his guests for dinner that evening in the five-star restaurant on the top floor of the hotel. I told him we were flying back to the United States that evening and at 8:30 p.m. I had to get our seat assignments. He said, "We will be finished in time." I said, "Not in India." He laughed, because he knew what I was talking about, but he assured me we would be through in time. We agreed to meet him in the main lobby at 6:00 p.m. When we met him, he had an entourage with him, and as I recall it was about ten men. I wondered what was going on!

We went to a luxurious dining room on the seventeenth floor of the hotel, where there was a long table beautifully set up just for our group. Mohamed was seated at the head of the table, and I was seated at his right hand. Seated to my right was an interpreter. Although Mohamed understood and could converse in English, he was more comfortable with Arabic, his mother tongue.

Through dinner, we had some interesting conversation, and during our discourse Mohamed told the interpreter to tell me that he would like me to visit his country soon. When the interpreter said His Highness wanted me to visit his country, I began to wonder who this person was. It was getting late and we had to leave, but I assured him I would make a visit to his country on one of my return trips from India. This was my first time to have such close exposure to and dialogue with a Muslim.

When I got home, I did some investigation regarding Bahrain and found out that Mohamed was Sheikh Mohamed, a member of the royal family. His oldest brother, Sheikh Isa, according to tradition, was the emir, or the ruler, of Bahrain. Mohamed and his two brothers were also related to the royal family of Saudi Arabia.

Why did our paths cross? This meeting wasn't planned by me, and I don't believe it was coincidental. I must say that our meetings and conversations were always amiable and gave us opportunity to relate our positions in a civil atmosphere. That's the way it should be, but not always the way it is.

A Brief History of Islam

Development and Growth During Muhammad's Lifetime

Although Muslims are taught that Islam has been around from time immemorial, it was developed over twenty-three years by its prophet, Muhammad. He says he had many sessions with the angel Gabriel, who revealed writings from a Mother Book in heaven. The revelations to Muhammad were gathered and published as the Qur'an, which is highly respected by Muslims as the Word of Allah. Allah is the name used for God in Arabic.

Muhammad was born in the area of Makkah (Mecca), Saudi Arabia, as a member of the Quraysh tribe in AD 570. At the age of forty (in 610) Muhammad received his first revelation from an angel. His second revelation came three years later and was followed by many more revelations until he died in 632.

Muhammad was considered unlettered (unable to read or write), so his followers wrote his recited revelations on pieces of bone, leather, and other items. Some revelations were memorized by others but were not written down, but later, after Muhammad's death, these were eventually written in what is known as the holy Qur'an.

The Qur'an is considered to be eternal (always having been existent), as God is. If the Qur'an is eternally existent and God is eternally existent, then that would indicate two separate, eternally existent causes. That would essentially mean two gods, or one God who is a duo-unity. Two gods would be inconsistent with the teaching of Islam that there is only one God. A one-God duo-unity would be consistent with one eternal cause.

Muhammad had some sorrowful events occur in his early childhood. His father, Abdullah (or Abd Allah), died about six months before Muhammad's birth. The Quraysh tribe, and thus Muhammad, was reported to have descended from Ishmael, who was the son of Abraham and Hagar. Hagar was an Egyptian maidservant to Abraham's wife, Sarah. Because she could not have children, Sarah offered Hagar to Abraham so he could father a son with her. Genesis 16:8-12 relates what happened:

> And He [God] said, "Hagar, Sarai's maid, where have you come from, and where are you going?"
>
> She said, "I am fleeing from the presence of my mistress Sarai."
>
> The Angel of the LORD said to her, "Return to your mistress, and submit yourself under her hand." Then the Angel

> of the LORD said to her, "I will multiply your descendants exceedingly, so that they shall not be counted for multitude."
> And the Angel of the LORD said to her:
>
> "Behold, you are with child,
> And you shall bear a son.
> You shall call his name Ishmael,
> Because the LORD has heard your affliction.
> He shall be a wild man;
> His hand shall be against every man,
> And every man's hand against him.
> And he shall dwell in the presence of all his brethren."

Muhammad's mother died when he was six years old. At that time his grandfather stepped into the picture, but shortly after, when Muhammad was eight, his grandfather passed away. Then Muhammad went to stay with one of his uncles, Abu Talib, who lived in Mecca, which was the commercial and religious center of the Arabian Peninsula. Muhammad traveled the trade routes by leading his uncle's camel caravans north to Syria and as far south as Egypt. Along those trade routes, Muhammad undoubtedly encountered both Christian and Jewish communities.

Muhammad likely obtained some of his views of Christianity and Judaism during those travels. He learned of the teaching of Judaism about one God and the erroneous teaching of a Christian sect that taught the Father, Mary the mother of God and the Son were to be worshiped as deity. History would indicate that Muhammad was a very reflective and mystical person who was looking for something more than the idolatrous religions of the Arabian area.

In the course of their caravan trade, Muhammad and his uncle established a business connection with a wealthy widowed merchant woman named Khadijah. Eventually, Muhammad was put in charge of all her camel caravans. This business arrangement led to a fondness for one another, and Khadijah at the age of forty proposed to and married Muhammad, who was twenty-five.

Muhammad began to enjoy a more leisurely lifestyle that gave him the opportunity to spend time pursuing answers to spiritual matters that perplexed his mind and soul. He often retreated to a cave on Mount Hira, outside of Mecca, for spiritual reflection. At the age of forty, during one of his retreats in the month of Ramadan, he had his first vision, which caused him great mental distress in regard to its source. His wife and her cousin Waraqah convinced him he was being called as a prophet to his people. Waraqah declared himself to be a Christian who read the Scriptures and learned from those who followed the Torah and the Injil, which are the Old Testament and the New Testament. Warraqah told Khadijah, "He is the prophet of this people" (24a).

Muhammad's next vision was not until three years later, and during that interim period he was concerned as to whether or not Allah was pleased with his life. Thereafter Muhammad's visions became more frequent, with the angel Gabriel giving him revelations that confirmed to him the one God, Allah. Muhammad became very disturbed by the pagan practices of his own Quraysh tribe and the other tribes who worshiped the 360 idol gods in the shrine of the Ka'aba ("Cube"; a building).

The Ka'aba, located in Mecca, housed not only the idols but also the Black Stone. This stone, revered as a religious shrine, is reported by Muslims to have been founded by Abraham and his son Ishmael. For a considerable time, the Ka'aba and Mecca were the religious center of the Arabian Peninsula. To it worshipers made pilgrimages to do homage to their particular idol or idols.

Muhammad was displeased by paganism and became a warner with a clear message confronting those who worshiped false gods and idols. Muhammad's messages not only condemned economic oppression and idolatry but also disturbed the people of Mecca, including his own Quraysh tribe. These messages of the one God, Allah, and the warning of judgment because of their pagan practices became a threat to the economic welfare of those who made their living from the religious pilgrims.

When Muhammad's message was vigorously rejected, especially by those of his own tribe, he became angry with his people and the Meccans. At this time, as the warner to the people, Muhammad became very upset with his uncle Abu Lahab for rejecting his message and pronounced a curse on him and his wife: "May the hands of Abu Lahab perish! May he himself perish! Nothing shall his wealth and gains avail him. He shall be burnt in a flaming fire, and his wife, laden with faggots, shall have a rope of fiber around her neck!" (sura 111:1-5, from the Qur'an).

In 622, which became year 1 of the Muslim calendar, the situation in Mecca deteriorated to such a degree that an assassination attempt caused Muhammad, along with a few followers, to hide in caves to save their lives. Eventually he and his followers fled to Madinah (Medina), a city about 260 miles north of Mecca.

In Medina, Muhammad found refuge and supporters of his message, and over time many residents became followers of Islam. Using Medina as their home base, Muhammad and his growing army of Muslims raided the camel caravans to sustain themselves. These raids led to many battles. Most battles involved residents of Mecca, who opposed his message and his raids.

It is my opinion, after reading some of the resource material on the traditions and the early writings of the Qur'an, that Muhammad was trying to persuade Jews and Christians to acknowledge that he was a prophet of God. He encouraged Muslims to learn from the people of the book and their Hebrew and Christian Scriptures. Also, he accepted Abraham and Jesus as prophets.

As time passed, however, Muhammad's ongoing revelations differed greatly from Jewish and Christian teachings, and this caused tension. As a result, Muhammad had skirmishes with the populous Jewish tribes in Medina, who would not accept him as a prophet. In the last battle against the Jews of Medina, more than six hundred Jewish men were killed and their wives and children taken as booty.

Eventually Muhammad took political control of Medina and with his growing army increased the raids on the caravans coming out of Mecca. This situation worsened to the extent that the Meccan leaders in 624 commanded an army three times the size of Muhammad's and attempted to defeat him in Medina, but to no avail. They were soundly defeated in what was called the Battle of Badr.

What to do with the spoils of war became a problem solved through a revelation to Muhammad, which is quoted in the Qur'an: "Know that whatever ye take as spoils of war, lo! a fifth thereof is for Allah, and for the messenger and for the kinsman (who hath need) and orphans, and the needy, and the wayfarer, if ye believe in Allah and that which We revealed unto Our slave on the Day of Discrimination, the day when the two armies met" (sura 8:41). This would mean Muhammad received 20 percent of the bounties of war and then distributed that booty for care of mosques, orphans, and other causes.

Muhammad, during his time in Medina, surrounded himself with Muslims who were willing to carry out his orders to eliminate those who did not want to accept him as a prophet or his message (8c).

In 630, with an army of 10,000, Muhammad returned to Mecca and took the city without much resistance or bloodshed. Most Meccans could not and would not resist this powerful military leader and submitted to becoming Muslims. Many Jews and Christians, who did not submit to Islam, were placed under Muslim control and required to pay tribute.

After his military victory in Mecca, Muhammad had all the stone idols in the shrine of Ka'bah destroyed, and he commanded that the religious practices of Islam must be followed. Muhammad's military occupation of Mecca allowed him to rule from Medina but exercise political, religious, and military control over the tribes of the Arabian territory.

It was a short time after Muhammad's return to Medina that he died in 632. Muhammad is buried in Medina. It became known as "the city of the Prophet" and today is considered a holy city of Islam along with Mecca. The religious shrines and mosques of both cities are off limits to unbelievers, that is, non-Muslims.

From Muhammad's Death to the Present Day

After Muhammad's death there was a struggle over who was to become the next religious, political, and military leader of Islam. The person who came forth with the blessing of some of Muslim leaders was Abu Bakr, Muhammad's father-in-law. However, there was much disagreement among some of the Arabian tribes, and for two years these factions were suppressed by Abu Bakr, who eventually extended his control over the entire Arabian Peninsula. As a result, a standing army of thousands emerged, which during and after Abu Bakr's rule went on conquering through succeeding leaders, known as caliphs, from India and China, to the northern countries of Africa, and to Spain.

The third caliph, Uthman, failed to bring the factions together, and that resulted in a division that remains today between the two groups called Sunnis and Shiites. The Sunnis represent about 80 to 90 percent of Muslims and Shiites about 10 percent. Iran and the southern part of Iraq are predominately Shiite; Shiites want "Israel and its Satanic ally the U.S." to be destroyed.

There are other sects within Islam, among them the Sunni Wahhabis. This sect was founded in the eighteenth century by Muhammad ibn' Abd-al-Wahhab in an attempt to return Islam to a more literal observance of the Qur'an and its Muslim roots. This sect has many followers in Saudi Arabia and has influenced Osama bin Laden and the Taliban in Afghanistan, who believe they have literal authority and a mandate from the Qur'an to fight a holy war (*Jihad*). They believe they are told by Allah to follow those portions of the Qur'an that calls for the extermination of "unbelievers." They believe the world must be purged from unbelievers and infidels before their messiah, the *Mahdi*, returns (8b).

Muslims in Nations of the World

Today, there are more than a billion Muslims in the world. Islam, though heavily concentrated in Middle Eastern countries, extends from the Philippines to Indonesia, throughout Africa, Turkey, Europe, England, India, Afghanistan, Pakistan, and North and South America. The largest population in any one country is in Indonesia.

It is because of the financial backing from the oil-rich Islamic nation of Saudi Arabia that Islam has been and is increasing its outreach with literature, with Muslim religious missionaries, and with the building of mosques throughout the world. All of this has led to significant numbers of conversions to Islam taking place in the last fifty years.

During the last fifty years also, millions of innocent people have been killed as a result of genocide, terrorism, suicide bombings, and persecution; however, the horror of September 11, 2001, and merciless terrorist killings applauded in the streets by Muslims have caused some to rethink their Islamic beliefs in light of this violence in the name of Allah.

It seems that when terrorism is condemned, Muslims bring up the horror of the Crusades. The Crusades were wrong. There is a difference, however, behind the motive. Let me reiterate, the Crusades had no foundation in the Bible, the Word of God. Christian doctrine does not sanction those wars. The medieval church, corrupt and politically motivated, had fallen away from biblical truth, had entrenched human traditions and rituals, and controlled governments and peoples. The religious leaders were fearful of seeing their world collapsing and opposed those who were a threat.

However, from the Muslim perspective the conquest of nations and terrorism do have their foundation in the Qur'an. In the minds of radical Muslims, this can be justified by more than one hundred *ayahs* (verses) mentioned in the Qur'an that encourage Jihad. (For more background about Jihad, including its religious and political aspects, see Appendix C.)

There is evidence that terrorists and the horror of their actions are driving many moderate Muslims away from Islam. Joel C. Rosenberg, an authority on Middle Eastern politics and world views (75), reports:

> After crisscrossing the Islamic world over the last several years and interviewing more than 150 pastors and ministry leaders operating deep inside the most difficult countries for "Inside the Revolution" [a book written by Rosenberg], I can report that in Iran, more than 1 million Shia [Shiite] Muslims have turned to Christ since 1979. In Pakistan, there are now more than 2.5 million followers of Jesus Christ. In Sudan, there are now more than 5 million followers of Christ. Not every country has seen millions leave Islam to become adherents of the New Testament teachings of Jesus. In Syria, there are between 4,000 and 5,000 believers, but this is up from almost none in 1967. In Saudi Arabia, there are about 100,000 followers of Jesus now, up from almost none in 1967. But overall, the trend has been dramatic and largely unreported.

> For many Muslims, despair and despondency at what they see as the utter failure of Islamic governments and societies to improve their lives and give them peace, security, and a sense of purpose and meaning in life are causing them to leave Islam in search of truth. Some have lost their way entirely and become agnostics and atheists. Others, as we have seen, have sadly turned to alcohol and drug abuse. But millions are finding that only Jesus Christ heals the ache in their hearts and the deep wounds in their souls.

As long as the rulers of Islamic nations continue to follow their stated goal to eradicate the so-called enemies of Allah, peace will be impossible in the Middle East and throughout the world. Jihad will continue as long as radicals are a prominent force within Islam.

Source Documents of Islam

The Origin of the Source Documents

The Qur'an is the most revered book of Muslims. It, along with the Hadith (traditions) is the foundation for faith and practice. The Hadith, which were published many years later than the Qur'an, are books containing handed-down traditions and are considered a compilation of Muhammad's sayings, actions, and lifestyle. From these two sources comes the *sunna*, or the Muslim way of life as Muhammad is said to have lived it. If they are to have any hope of paradise, Muslims are to copy his actions. Some even follow his manner of dress. In addition, the Bible is used as a source document when it supposedly favors Islam, even though Muslims state the Bible has been altered and corrupted.

The Muslim promotional booklet "Understanding Islam and the Muslims" states, "What is the Quran? The Quran is the exact words revealed by God through the angel Gabriel to the Prophet Muhammad. It was memorized by Muhammad and then dictated to his Companions, and then written down by the scribes, who cross-checked it during his lifetime. Not one word of its 114 chapters, *suras*, has been changed over the centuries, so that the Quran is in every detail the unique and miraculous text which was revealed to Muhammad fourteen centuries ago." According to Muslim teaching from the Qur'an, Allah will not allow His Word to be altered or changed.

Collecting the Qur'an

Since Muhammad did not literally write the Qur'an, who was responsible for gathering the various suras, settling on the 114 chapters, and compiling them into the Qur'an?

Sometime after Muhammad's death, many of his followers who had memorized the Qur'an were being killed in battles. Thus, portions of Muhammad's recitations were lost. Umar, who later became the second caliph of Islam, ordered the collection of the Qur'an because he feared that the knowledge of it would soon fade away. Zayd ibn Thabit, one of Muhammad's most trusted secretaries, was appointed to this task. According to Zayd's testimony, "during the lifetime of the prophet the Qur'an had been written down, but it was not yet united in one place nor arranged in successive order." Umar and Abu Bakr confronted Zayd with this problem, and Zayd's statement about this is preserved in the *Sahih* of Al-Bukari:

> Fearing that more battles would claim more lives of those who had memorized the Qur'an and thus may lose a large part of the Qur'an a conversation took place that was recorded as follows; Umar speaking, "Therefore I suggest you (Abu Bakr) order that the Qur'an be collected." I said to Umar, "How can you do something which Allah's Apostle did not do?" Umar said, "By Allah, that is a good project." Umar kept on urging me to accept his proposal till Allah opened my chest for it and I began to realize the good idea which Umar had realized.
>
> Then Abu Bakr said (to me) "You are a wise young man and we do not have any suspicion about you, and you used to write the Divine Inspiration for Allah's Apostle. So you should search for (the fragmentary scripts of) the Qur'an and collect it (in one book)." By Allah! If they had ordered me to shift one of the mountains, it would not have been heavier for me than this ordering me to collect the Qur'an. . . . So I started looking for the Qur'an and collecting it from (what was written on) palm-leaf stalks, thin white stones and also from the men who knew it from heart.

Contrary to this account from Al-Bukari, Muslim theory holds that the Qur'an was arranged in the same form we have today, under the direct supervision of Muhammad and the angel Gabriel. Later, however, it was reported to Uthman, the third caliph, that several Muslim communities were using different versions of the Qur'an, and he feared great confusion would be the outcome. Word from General Hadhaifa in the campaign of Armenia brought word to Uthman that such debates were going on even among his troops.

Uthman had all the variant versions of the Qur'an collected, and once again with oversight by Zayd bin Thabit, had them compiled into one version, which is recognized as the Qur'an of today. All the other variant versions of the Qur'an were recalled and destroyed, and the new, authoritative copies were sent to the major centers of the Islamic empire. But were all of the variant copies destroyed (24b, 18a)?

Different Versions Available?

Archaeologist Arthur Jeffery, in *Materials for the History of the Text of the Qur'an*, states, "Contrary to popular belief, not all Muslims today accept one and the same version of the Qur'an. The Sunnite Muslims accept the *Sahih* tradition of Masud, one of the few people authorized by Muhammad to teach the Qur'an, as authoritative. Yet the *Ibn Masud* book of the Qur'an by them has multitudinous variations from the Uthman recension. In the second sura alone there are nearly150 variations" (24c).

Isn't the Qur'an supposed to be the exact copy of the Mother Book in heaven that was given to Muhammad by the angel Gabriel? Weren't all the collected copies originally recited to Muhammad's followers? Why would a collection have to take place after all of the critical review that went into compiling an accepted copy? Why destroy the copies? Weren't they some of Muhammad's recitations? The only reason to get rid of any of the copies would be due to variations between the copies, yet according to Muslims the Quran can neither be altered nor changed. Historical records, however, indicate the Qur'an was altered and changed.

One can only draw the conclusion that there were several variant versions of the writings of Muhammad's recitations that were rejected as the Qur'an, which is contrary to the Muslim teaching that the Qur'an is the exact copy of the Mother Book in heaven, and thus considered the greatest of miracles.

Seven Different Readings Allowed by the Prophet

Furthermore, an incident involving two followers during the time of the Prophet (Muhammad) is related from the *New England Review* website, "Which Koran?"

> Narrated 'Umar b. al-Khattäb: I heard Hishäm bin Hakïm bin Hizäm reciting *Surat-al-Furqän* in a way different to that of mine. Allah's Messenger had taught it to me (in a different

> way). So, I was about to quarrel with him (during the prayer) but I waited till he finished, then I tied his garment round his neck and seized him by it and brought him to Allah's Messenger and said, "I have heard him reciting *Surat-al-Furqän* in a way different to the way you taught it to me." The Prophet ordered me to release him and asked Hishäm to recite it. When he recited it, Allah's Messenger said, "It was revealed in this way." He then asked me to recite it. When I recited it, he said, "It was revealed in this way. The Qur'än has been revealed in seven different ways, so recite it in the way that is easier for you."

Doesn't it cause one to wonder about the position held by Muslim theologians that the Qur'an is the exact copy of the Mother Book in heaven?

Various Hadiths record how the Qur'an was revealed to the Prophet in seven different ways, in Arabic *Sab'atu ahruf.* The word *ahruf* is often translated as "seven sets of readings" or sometimes "dialects," though strictly speaking *ahruf* is the plural of *harf* ("letter"; more than forty interpretations have been offered for this puzzling word). By changing the inflections and accents of words, it is claimed, the Qur'anic text may be read in the seven dialects of the Quraysh, Ta'i, Hawäzin, Yaman, Saqïf, Hudhayl, and Tamïm (74a).

Followers of Islam are compelled to uphold the position that the Bible has been altered and corrupted because the Bible and the Qur'an differ in many areas, and Muslims had to establish a reason for the differences.

However, Muhammad did state in the Qur'an that the Old Testament and the New Testament are Scriptures to be followed by Muslims, Jews, and Christians. Why would Muhammad want Muslims to follow the Old Testament and New Testament Scriptures if they were corrupted? The Bible that Christians relied on at the time of Muhammad is the same Scripture we have today; the Apocrypha and "extra" gospels were not included. The teachers in Muhammad's day expounded views based on the Apocrypha and the "extra" gospels, but these views conflicted with the teachings from canonical Scripture.

Many differences between the Qur'an and the Bible will be shown later (see below, and Appendix B), but we must bear in mind that contradiction means that only one of the sources, either the Qur'an or the Bible, can be true—not both.

The Teachings of Islam

The Goal of Islam

Islam in Arabic means "submission," but some Muslims like to indicate it means "peace." However, in its purest form Islam means that all humans must submit to Allah as God and Muhammad as his last messenger or prophet. One who submits is called a Muslim.

Traditional Islam believes there are only two areas in the world. The first is *Dar al-Islam*, the "house of peace," whose territories in the world are under the control of Islamic rulers. The second area, all the other territories in the world not under the control of Islam, is known as *Dar al-Harb*, or "house of war." The latter territories are yet to be conquered through holy war [Jihad] and to be brought under the domination of Islam, resulting in *Shari'a* law being imposed on the conquered. This is what Muhammad taught and tried to accomplish and what some of his successors almost succeeded in doing.

It is an explicit part of Islamic doctrine that when all peoples of the world are submissive to Allah and under control of Muslims, a universal theocratic government and society will be ruled by Shari'a law. This means a mandatory death sentence for disrespect for the Prophet and a life sentence for desecration of the Qur'an (15b).

Muslims believe once this world order under Islam comes about, then the return of the Muslim messiah, Mahdi, will come to pass, and everyone will acknowledge Allah as supreme.

Because of this worldview, any nation that is considered Christian, and all Jews, are unbelievers. Therefore, according to Islam, the United States and Israel are evil nations whose ruler is Satan. Many Arab nations in the Mideast continually promote this doctrine through Islamic leaders and teachers who have for years taught their children to hate the United States and Israel. They are taught that it is their privilege to carry out acts of terrorism for the cause of Allah and Islam.

What is confusing is that Muslims are told in the Qur'an to accept the teachings of the Old Testament, the Psalms, and the gospel of Jesus. Jesus in the Gospels says to "turn the other cheek" and "to love your enemies." One incident recorded in the Gospels is that of a woman caught in adultery being brought before Jesus. According to Mosaic law, the woman should be stoned to death. The religious leaders who brought the woman to Jesus were trying to put Him on the spot. But Jesus told them that whoever was without sin should cast the first stone. I wonder how this would have been be handled under Shari'a law.

In what is called the Sermon on the Mount, Jesus tells the multitudes, "You have heard that it was said, 'You shall love your neighbor and hate your enemies.' But I say to you, love your enemies, bless those who curse you, do good to those who hate you, and pray for those who spitefully use you and persecute you, that you may be sons of your Father in heaven" (Matthew 5:43-45). This is disregarded under Islam, because many radical Muslim religious leaders, supposedly basing their teachings on the Qur'an, encourage Muslims to continue to terrorize and kill Christians, Jews, and even other Muslims (see Appendices C and D).

In the Iran-Iraq war, more than a million Muslims were killed, and in recent years fighting between Muslims and Christians has destroyed the lives of hundreds of thousands of Sudanese. Yet the claim is made that Islam means peace. One cannot deny that all of those Muslim militant actions can be interpreted as sanctioned from the Qur'an, and to say it is a matter of defending oneself is being disingenuous.

History would prove that Muhammad and his small group of followers in the early days were pursued with the intent to get rid of them. They needed to defend themselves, but later military ventures went to the extent of going out to conquer and bringing the conquered under submission to Allah and his messenger. It seems when Muslims have political and military power, Islam means "submission" for those under their rule, and when Muslims are a minority, then Islam means "peace."

Sura 9:29 tells how Christians should be treated in a Muslim country: "Fight those who believe not in Allah nor the Last Day, nor hold that forbidden which hath been forbidden by Allah and His Messenger, nor acknowledge the religion of Truth, (even if they are) of the People of the Book, until they pay the Jizya with willing submission, and feel themselves subdued."

How were Christians subdued in Muhammad's day? Under Muslim control, Christians were, not allowed to witness to Muslims to convert them to Christianity; a Muslim's conversion to Christianity was punishable by death. Crosses were not allowed on top of a church. Jews or Christians had to wear some outward means of identifying themselves as such; they were to pay the *jizya,* which was like a poll tax, which generated vast income for Muslim rulers. Some of this attitude still exists, and it is becoming apparent that Christians and Jews are second-class citizens in Muslim-controlled countries.

There is a great deal of sentiment among Muslims that they are being persecuted in the United States. In fact, a new film, just released, deals with this issue and is being shown in American theaters. The title of the film is *Mooz-Lum* (I believe indicating a slur on how the word *Muslim* is pronounced). It is not right for non-Muslims to make slurs. But the persecution of Christians in Muslim-controlled countries is far more serious and increasing in frequency. For instance, Joel Rosenberg reports:

> It is not receiving nearly enough attention in the mainstream media, but a disturbing development is underway in the Middle East: followers of Jesus Christ in the epicenter have endured a dramatic surge of violence and persecution at the hands of religious and political extremists in recent weeks and months.
>
> In Iraq, Christians have been attacked and killed in their homes and in public, forcing nearly a thousand families to flee from Baghdad and Mosul to the safer Kurdistan region in the north. A separate siege on a Baghdad church on October 31 killed 58 followers of the Lord Jesus and wounded 67others. (83)

In *Christian Heroes* (published by Tyndale) an incident that took place in Pakistan is reported in detail. A Christian girl shared the Good News with a Muslim friend, and that girl became a Christian. The Christian girl, her family, and their pastor were arrested and tortured. The Muslim girl was killed by her brother (73a).

In Israel, extremists firebombed an Arab Christian church in Jerusalem in November 2010. In December 2010, Kristine Luken, an American evangelical Christian, was stabbed to death not far from Jerusalem in what many believe to have been an act of terror. Her friend Kay Wilson, an Israeli believer in Jesus, was also severely wounded in the attack.

In Iran, Ayatollah Ali Khamenei, the so-called supreme leader, publicly warned against the "network of house churches" that "threaten Islamic faith and deceive young Muslims." Then, during Christmas, at least seventy Iranian Christians were arrested in their homes and separated from their families.

Coptic Christians in Egypt have also suffered severe persecution since 2011 began. As a result of two recent violent attacks, nearly thirty people have died and dozens more have been wounded.

Jesus Christ warned His followers that in the last days "they will deliver you to tribulation and will kill you" (Matthew 24:8). The Lord also warned His followers that "an hour is coming for everyone who kills you to think that he is offering service to God" (John 16:2). The good news is that the Lord Jesus also promised, "I will build My Church and the gates of Hell shall not prevail against it" (Matthew 16:18) Overall, the church is growing. More people in the epicenter are coming to faith in Jesus Christ than at any other time in history, and this is a cause for great rejoicing. History indicates when the members of the body of Christ are martyred, the church grows.

There is an abundance of speeches from Muslim leaders and of articles in Middle Eastern Islamic media reflecting hatred for the decadent United States. These sources also condemn Israel for taking territory that they believe belongs to the Arabs. In the Old Testament, which Muslims are told in the Qur'an to accept, are unilateral covenants of God and prophecies that gave the land to Israel. These prophecies include more territory than Israel occupies today. Although it doesn't seem that these prophecies, in light of today's events, will be fulfilled, ultimately they will. The fulfilled biblical prophecies have come to pass exactly as foretold. In the Mideast today it appears that the Arab Muslim role is center stage and winning political control. Israel is being forced to make concessions for peace. But God has His own plans laid out in the Scriptures. It's best to bet on God!

Most Muslims and Muslim converts in the United States will deny that the goal of one world under Islam is part of Islamic teaching, but the Qur'an and the speeches and publications of many Muslims leaders say otherwise. I know many Muslims are saddened by the violence that is going on today. Yet they must be careful how they condemn militant Muslims because the militants can quote the Qur'an to support their position, and some militants can suppress those who speak against them. Many non-militants are very religious, sincere in their beliefs, kind, and have decent families. However, even if they gained control over the militants, their religion, rituals, and traditions would leave them without the assurance of salvation and eternal life.

I too am saddened and concerned, and that is why I bring these issues out in the open for observation and reflection. It doesn't do any good to suppress the issues. Conflicting views must be exposed and analyzed so the reader can without bias properly reason, evaluate, and decide what is true. As Alexander Solzhenitsyn said, "Violence can only be concealed by a lie, and the lie can only be maintained by violence. Any man who has once proclaimed violence as his method is inevitably forced to take the lie as his principle."

The Five Foundations for the Beliefs of Islam

It would appear that these five beliefs are what the five pillars of Islam rest on. Each Muslim is to practice the five pillars daily and annually.

Underlying the teachings of Islam is the doctrine that Allah (God) is one and there can be no partners with Him. To do so is to commit the sin of *shirk*, for which there is no forgiveness (sura 4:48).

Muslims believe in angels, who are the means through whom Allah reaches people, for God is transcendent and unreachable in the highest heaven. Gabriel is the top-ranking angel; he is generally considered the revealer of the Qur'an to Muhammad. Gabriel is followed by other rankings of angels; the lowest being in this hierarchy is the *jinn,* who Muslims believe were created from fire. Jinn are generally bad creatures who are able to possess people that Allah ordains. Muslims are taught that two angels are assigned to each human. One angel records the person's good deeds and the other bad deeds. From this record a person's eternal destiny is determined.

Allah sent prophets to the various nations to preach the message of the one God, and there have been 124,000 prophets sent since the beginning of time, from Adam to Jesus, with many prophets in between. However, Muhammad is the prophet for all time and the "seal of the prophets," which means there are no further revelations and messages from God.

Muslims consider several books to be holy. Moses was given the *Tawrat* (Torah). David was given the *Zabur* (Psalms). Jesus was given the *Injil* (Gospels). Muhammad was given the Qur'an. Muslims believe only the Qur'an has been kept in an uncorrupted state.

On judgment day, each person will stand before Allah, and all of his or her deeds will be weighed on a balance scale. If a person's good deeds outweigh the bad deeds, that person will enter paradise; those who fall short will be cast into hell. Only Allah knows whether a person passes or fails. If He deems you worthy, you enter paradise; otherwise, you are destined to hell. There can be no assurance of paradise while here on earth, except for those Muslims who give their lives in Jihad.

The Five Pillars of Islam

In addition to the five foundational beliefs, there are the five pillars of faith, carried out as religious rituals and practices.

The *Shahada,* which means "to bear witness," is recited frequently. This is the declaration of a Muslim's faith. In Arabic it is *la ilaha illa 'Llah, Muhammadun rasula 'Llah* (There is no god except Allah; Muhammad is the messenger of Allah).

Prayers (*Salat)* are an obligation of a Muslim and are performed five times daily while facing Mecca. Prayers are said at dawn, noon, midafternoon, sunset, and nightfall. Muslims usually use a prayer carpet and utilize various postures when they pray (for example, kneeling). These prayers contain verses from the Qur'an and are said in Arabic, the language of the revelations; however, prayers of supplication can be said in one's own language.

Zakat is considered a redistribution of wealth that purifies the possessions of the giver and prunes the possessions to bring growth. Generally 2.5 percent of one's capital is given annually. This money is distributed to the needy.

Fasting is practiced by all faithful Muslims. Every year during the month of Ramadan, a fast is observed from the first light of dawn until sundown, which requires abstaining from food, drink, and sexual relations. The purpose of the fast is to be cut off from worldly comforts and to remind oneself of those who are poor and hungry. Principally the fast is considered a method of self-purification.

The *Hajj* (pilgrimage) is an obligation of those who are financially and physically able to perform this trip to Mecca, where specific rites are followed. More than two million people make this trip annually during the month of Ramadan. Special clothes, simple in design, are worn by each pilgrim, thus erasing any distinctions of class or wealth. Pilgrims in this attire circle the Kaa'ba seven times; the rites that are said to be from Abraham in origin. Prayers ask for Allah's forgiveness, as pilgrims stand on the wide plains of the Arafa. This is considered a preview of the last judgment. The Hajj ends with a festival celebrated with prayers and the exchange of gifts.

The Bible, Jews, and Christians

The following are key points of Islamic teaching that differ vastly from the teachings of the Bible.

Muslims are emphatic that the holy Scriptures, both the Jewish Old Testament (*Torah*, or law) and the Christian New Testament (*Injil*) have been corrupted by human changes to the original revelations of the Word that was given to the prophets. However, Muslims do accept some parts of the Bible as true, when they perceive it to help their position.

Muslims teach that any portion of the Bible that contradicts the Qur'an is corrupted or altered. But how can this be? The Old Testament Hebrew and the New Testament Greek Scriptures we have today are the same as Muhammad had in his day. Also, in the Qur'an Muhammad states that Muslims of his day could verify the teachings of Islam by the Scriptures available from the Jews and Christians, so when were the Scriptures corrupted or changed? There should still be some copies of the uncorrupted and corrupted Scriptures of that day. They couldn't have all been lost or destroyed.

If the Jews had corrupted the Scriptures, Christians would have justifiably exposed their tampering, and vice versa. Historians would have recorded those events. We must also understand that neither the Old Testament nor the New Testament was translated into Arabic until AD 900 to 1200. So, how would those who could read only Arabic, and Muhammad, who was illiterate, know which Scriptures were corrupted? Muhammad's understanding of the Hebrew and Greek Scriptures was conveyed to him from others who had exposure to later, "extra" gospels.

We know the "extra" gospels were written long after the early Gospels and contained doctrines that were inconsistent with the Bible that was accepted by the early church. By the way, you couldn't go to a Bible bookstore in Muhammad's day and obtain a complete Bible, because each book was transcribed by a scribe. It would be difficult to believe that Muhammad had all sixty-six books, and if he didn't, how would he know what Scriptures were corrupted? Also, to maintain the position that the Bible was corrupted is to say that God didn't continue to protect the Scriptures. Didn't Muhammad say in the Qur'an that Allah would protect and preserve His Word?

Muslims say that Jesus was not crucified. Someone else died on the cross in His place, probably Judas (see the section below about Jesus Christ). The consistent record in the four Gospels of the life, death, burial, and resurrection of Jesus is considered completely false. But, contrary to the Muslim position, historical evidence is totally on the side of the Bible.

Muslims say the Trinity is a manufactured false teaching, because it is not possible for God to have a partner (see the section below about God).

Are these true evaluations, or are they unfounded arguments in an attempt to validate Muslim teachings?

Muslims deny or completely change the crucifixion events pertaining to Jesus the Messiah in the New Testament that were prophesied hundreds of years earlier in the Old Testament and perfectly fulfilled later in the New Testament. Notice how the apostle Paul wrote about the Old Testament prophets foretelling the new covenant of grace and righteousness to come through Christ: "But now a righteousness from God, apart from law, has been made known, to which the Law and the Prophets testify. This righteousness from God comes through faith in Jesus Christ to all who believe. There is no difference, for all have sinned and fall short of the glory of God" (Romans 3:21-23).

The apostle Peter also refers to the Old Testament prophets, who had the Spirit of Christ within them declaring the prophecies of Christ's suffering and His future glories (1 Peter 1:10-12):

> Concerning this salvation, the prophets, who spoke of the grace that was to come to you, searched intently and with the greatest care, trying to find out the time and circumstances to which the Spirit of Christ in them was pointing when he predicted

> the sufferings of Christ and the glories that would follow. It was revealed to them that they were not serving themselves but you, when they spoke of the things that have now been told you by those who have preached the gospel to you by the Holy Spirit sent from heaven. Even angels long to look into these things,

Romans 3:21-23 and 1 Peter 1:10-12 refer to the prophecies of the Old Testament prophet Isaiah.

In the New Testament, Acts 8:26-40 tells about an Ethiopian eunuch who was reading from Isaiah 53:

> Now an angel of the Lord spoke to Philip, saying, "Arise and …………go toward the south along the road which goes down from Jerusalem to Gaza." This is desert. So he arose and went. And behold, a man of Ethiopia, a eunuch of great authority under Candace the queen of the Ethiopians, who had charge of all her treasury, and had come to Jerusalem to worship, was returning. And sitting in his chariot, he was reading Isaiah the prophet. Then the Spirit said to Philip, "Go near and overtake this chariot." So Philip ran to him, and heard him reading the prophet Isaiah, and said, "Do you understand what you are reading?" And he said, "How can I, unless someone guides me?" And he asked Philip to come up and sit with him. The place in the Scripture which he read was this:
>
> > "He was led as a sheep to the slaughter;
> > And as a lamb before its shearer is silent,
> > So He opened not His mouth.
> > In His humiliation His justice was taken away,
> > And who will declare His generation?
> > For His life is taken from the earth."
>
> So the eunuch answered Philip and said, "I ask you, of whom does the prophet say this, of himself or of some other man?" Then Philip opened his mouth, <u>and beginning at this Scripture, preached Jesus to him</u>. Now as they went down the road, they came to some water. And the eunuch said, "See, here is water. What hinders me from being baptized?" Then Philip said, "If you believe with all your heart, you may." And

> he answered and said, "I believe that Jesus Christ is the Son of God." So he commanded the chariot to stand still. And both Philip and the eunuch went down into the water, and he baptized him. Now when they came up out of the water, the Spirit of the Lord caught Philip away, so that the eunuch saw him no more; and he went on his way rejoicing. But Philip was found at Azotus. And passing through, he preached in all the cities till he came to Caesarea.

This event focusing on Isaiah 53 specifically refers to the sacrificial death of Jesus the Christ. The Ethiopian eunuch had that revealed to him. Philip undoubtedly told the Ethiopian of other prophesied events surrounding the crucifixion of Jesus that had recently taken place in Jerusalem. The Ethiopian put his faith in Jesus as the Son of God. He went on his way rejoicing in his newfound relationship with God through Christ.

Muslims point to the Old Testament Scriptures that say not a bone of Jesus would be broken in death; yet, they say, the soldiers who nailed Jesus' feet to the cross could not have done so without breaking His bones. Do Muslims not believe that with the Almighty "all things are possible" and He certainly could guide the nails through Jesus' feet?

Muslims who oppose Jesus as the Son of God and the God/Man will either ignore the Scriptures or misinterpret them according to flawed human perspectives. They find later revelations to promote their positions that are contradictory to the prior revealed Scriptures. They accept the Scriptures that are supposedly favorable to their teachings, usually taking texts out of context, but ignore other Scriptures that contradict the Qur'an by saying those Scriptures were altered or corrupted.

Interestingly, Jesus and the apostles frequently quoted from the Old Testament. Why would Jesus quote corrupted Scriptures? The evidence is overwhelming that the Scriptures we have today contain the same books and writings they had in Jesus' day.

If Jesus is God, why wouldn't He say that? This is one of the arguments presented by Muslims. He did, however, display the attributes that only God could have: performing miracles, healing, forgiving sins, His virgin birth, His sinless life, His death, resurrection, and ascension back to His Father. All of these aspects of His earthly life were observed by His apostles and many of His followers. Were the apostles wrong about their firsthand observations, but people who weren't there are right?

If the writings of the apostle Paul were untrue, numerous critics and contemporary historians would have jumped on the opportunity to deny his writings, especially 1 Corinthians 15:1-11:

> Moreover, brethren, I declare to you the gospel which I preached to you, which also you received and in which you stand, by which also you are saved, if you hold fast that word which I preached to you—unless you believed in vain. For I delivered to you first of all that which I also received: that Christ died for our sins according to the Scriptures, and that He was buried, and that He rose again the third day according to the Scriptures, and that He was seen by Cephas, then by the twelve. After that He was seen by over five hundred brethren at once, of whom the greater part remain to the present, but some have fallen asleep. After that He was seen by James, then by all the apostles. Then last of all He was seen by me also, as by one born out of due time. For I am the least of the apostles, who am not worthy to be called an apostle, because I persecuted the church of God. But by the grace of God I am what I am, and His grace toward me was not in vain; but I labored more abundantly than they all, yet not I, but the grace of God which was with me. Therefore, whether it was I or they, so we preach and so you believed.

When Paul refers to the Scriptures, he is referring to the Old Testament prophecies.

One of the many incidents in Scripture that graphically portrays Jesus' deity is His encounter with unbelieving Jews (John 10:22-39):

> Now it was the Feast of Dedication in Jerusalem, and it was winter. And Jesus walked in the temple, in Solomon's porch. Then the Jews surrounded Him and said to Him, "How long do You keep us in doubt? If You are the Christ, tell us plainly." Jesus answered them, "I told you, and you do not believe. The works that I do in My Father's name, they bear witness of Me. But you do not believe, because you are not of My sheep, as I said to you. My sheep hear My voice, and I know them, and they follow Me. And I give them eternal life, and they shall never perish; neither shall anyone snatch them out of My hand.

> My Father, who has given them to Me, is greater than all; and no one is able to snatch them out of My Father's hand. I and My Father are one.
>
> Then the Jews took up stones again to stone Him. Jesus answered them, "Many good works I have shown you from My Father. For which of those works do you stone Me?" The Jews answered Him, saying, "For a good work we do not stone You, but for blasphemy, and because You, being a Man, make Yourself God." Jesus answered them, "Is it not written in your law, 'I said, "You are gods"'? If He called them gods, to whom the word of God came (and the Scripture cannot be broken), do you say of Him whom the Father sanctified and sent into the world, 'You are blaspheming,' because I said, 'I am the Son of God'? If I do not do the works of My Father, do not believe Me; but if I do, though you do not believe Me, believe the works, that you may know and believe that the Father is in Me, and I in Him." Therefore they sought again to seize Him, but He escaped out of their hand.

Jesus refers to Psalm 86, where the context is about the mighty ones (gods) who acted as judges and are referred to as fulfilling among people a role on behalf of God, who is the supreme Judge. But more importantly, those opposed to Jesus considered Him to be a blasphemer because He was equating Himself with God. Had He not purposely escaped from them they would have stoned Him to death.

Muslims say that Jesus was not born in Bethlehem, but in Nazareth, where Mary gave birth to Jesus under a palm tree. According to history, however, Joseph and Mary had to leave Nazareth late in her pregnancy and go to Bethlehem for the census. Historical evidence confirms it was an edict by Caesar Augustus demanding that everyone had to return to the place of their ancestors to be enrolled so they could be taxed. It would have been more convenient and easier on Mary to remain in Nazareth when she was so far along in her pregnancy, but that was not an option. It was a requirement of the emperor. They had to go!

This is another attempt on the part of Muslim teachers to deny the teachings surrounding the birth of the Christ found in the four Gospels and foretold in the Old Testament prophecies that declared the Messiah's birth would be in Bethlehem. All of the historical events surrounding Jesus' birth as related in the New Testament accurately fulfilled the foretold events from the Old Testament, written centuries earlier. Only one of the records can be historically correct, either the Qur'an or the Bible. Which one is it?

Creation

What do Muslims teach about creation?

Yusuf Ali, one of the accepted Muslim translators of the Arabic Qur'an into English, is critical of the biblical creation sequence. In his footnotes on sura 41:9-12, where the creation span is eight days, Yusuf Ali describes the Qur'an's events of creation as follows:

> Our scheme is wholly different. (1) God did not rest, and never rests. "His throne doth extend over the heavens and the earth, And He feeleth no fatigue in guarding and preserving them."; (2) God's work has not ended; His activity still goes on: sura 32:5; 7:54; (3) Man in our scheme does not come in with land animals; (4) Our stages are not sharply divided from each other, as in the above ["above" refers to the biblical creation sequence] scheme where the stars and planets having been created on the fourth day, it is not intelligible how the first three days were counted, nor how vegetation grew on the third day. Our stages for earth and heaven are not in sequence of time for the heavens and the earth. Our six stages are broadly speaking, (1) the throwing off of our planet from cosmic matter; (2) its cooling down and condensing; (3) and (4) the growth of vegetable and animal life; (5) and (6) the parallel growth of the starry realm and our solar system.

Sura 57:4 refers to six days of creation, thus contradicting sura 41:9-12. In one part of the Qur'an, Muslims teach that God created man from a blood clot, and in another part, from clay. Also, Adam was created in paradise and not on the earth. Later, God placed him and Eve in the garden on earth.

This account differs completely from the explanation of creation in Genesis. Genesis is confirmed by the writings of Moses in Deuteronomy 4:32: "For ask now concerning the days that are past, which were before you, since the day that God created man on the earth, and ask from one end of heaven to the other, whether any great thing like this has happened, or anything like it has been heard." This is another proof of the internal consistency of the Bible and of the Qur'an differing with the Bible.

Furthermore, it seems that Yusuf Ali opts for six stages of creation that are totally different from the six days of a specific order of creation outlined in the Bible. Many scientists say is the sequence described in the Bible is the only one that would permit and sustain life on earth.

The following traditions are taken entirely from *The History of al-Tabari*, volume 1, *General Introduction and from the Creation to the Flood* (76a):

> We have stated before that time is but hours of night and day and that the hours are but traversal by the sun and the moon of the degrees of the sphere. Now then, this being so, there is (also) a sound tradition from the Messenger of God told us by Hannad b. al-Sari, who also said that he read all of the hadith (to Abu Bakr)- Abu Bakr b. 'Ayyash- Abu Sa'd al-Baqqal- 'Ikrimah- **Ibn Abbas**: The Jews came to the Prophet and asked him about the creation of the heavens and the earth. He said: **God created the earth on Sunday and Monday**. He created the mountains and the uses they possess on Tuesday. On Wednesday, He created trees, water, cities and the cultivated barren land. These are four (days). He continued (citing the Qur'an): "Say: Do you really not believe in the One Who created the earth in two days, and set up others like Him? That is the Lord of the worlds. He made it firmly anchored (mountains) above it and blessed it and decreed that it contain the amount of food it provides, (all) in four days, equally for those asking" for those who ask. **On Thursday, He created heaven. On Friday, He created the stars, the sun, the moon, and the angels, until three hours remained**. In the first of these three hours He created the terms (of human life), who would live and who would die. In the second, He cast harm upon everything that is useful for mankind. And in the third, (He created) Adam and had him dwell in Paradise. He commanded Iblis (Satan) to prostrate himself before Adam, and He drove Adam out of Paradise at the end of the hour. When the Jews asked: What then, Muhammad? He said: "Then He sat straight upon the Throne." The Jews said: You are right, if you had finished, they said, with: Then He rested. Whereupon the Prophet got very angry, and it was revealed: "We have created the heavens and the earth and what is

> between them in six days, and fatigue did not touch Us. Thus be patient with what you say."

According to this tradition from Ibn Abbas, Muhammad believed the earth and everything within it was created on the first four days, whereas the heavens and the constellations were created on Thursday and Friday. Hence, Muhammad believed that vegetation was created even before the heavens and the sun, a gross scientific error!

When the Bible says God rested from His creation, it means He ceased creating at this point, and then it says, "He saw it was good." In fact, "He saw it was very good." All of the processes of creation were completed in six days, with nothing to be added, all in a different sequence and time span from Muhammad's. Again, there are great differences between what the Qur'an teaches and the Bible's account. Can they both be correct?

God

Muslims believe that the essence and uniqueness of God is the transcendent undivided person of Allah. The attributes of Allah are summed up in the ninety-nine names that Muslims reflect on in their meditation and their prayers. Some Muslims believe when the Mahdi returns, he will reveal the one hundredth name for Allah.

Muslims believe that all humankind is to worship Allah, and anyone who refuses to do so and does not accept Muhammad as the last prophet is an unbeliever and an infidel. Only Allah is to be worshiped.

Muslims must submit to and practice Allah's will in the religion and rituals of Islam, but no Muslim can have a personal relationship with the creator and sustainer of creation, because Allah is unknowable in that sense. Allah has no partners. It is believed He has no need for anyone to carry out His will because Allah determines and destines everything. That is why humans cannot know their eternal destiny before judgment day.

For Muslims to even remotely consider that Allah has partners is considered blasphemy. God has no Son, because in Muslim thinking this lowers Allah to the realm of humankind. Allah is transcendent, beyond reach, residing in the highest place above all and everything. Allah would not lower Himself into the world of humans. Regarding an argument against the Trinity, Muslims use the mathematical logic that 1 + 1 + 1 = 3, so three cannot be one. But what about the logic of 1 x 1 x 1 = 1? Mathematics doesn't prove or disprove the Tri-unity of the Godhood. That proof depends on whether the source document is true that reveals the Creator/God.

The Qur'an says very little about a God of love. The emphasis is on Allah, who does not love unbelievers and sinners:

> As to those who believe and work righteousness, Allah will pay them (in full) their reward; but Allah loveth not those who do wrong. (sura 3:57)
>
> Say: "Obey Allah and His Messenger.: But if they turn back, Allah loveth not those who reject Faith." (sura 3:32)
>
> Serve Allah, and join not any partners with Him; and do good to parents, kinsfolk, orphans, those in need, neighbours who are near, neighbours who are strangers, the companion by your side, the wayfarer (ye meet), and what your right hands possess: For Allah loveth not the arrogant, the vainglorious. (sura 4:36)
>
> Fight in the cause of Allah those who fight you, but do not transgress limits; for Allah loveth not transgressors. (sura 2:190)
>
> Allah will deprive usury of all blessing, but will give increase for deeds of charity: For He loveth not creatures ungrateful and wicked. (sura 2:276)

All of the above suras, along with many others in the Qur'an, convey this image of Allah not loving the sinner or the unbeliever.

The Bible, however, says, "God is love" and loves sinners but hates their sin. The chapter about Christianity will present more on the one true God and His love for His creatures. Scripture emphatically declares that God loves sinners, but people refuse to accept God's provision for salvation that determines their eternal destiny.

Christ Jesus

In my encounters with Muslims they are quick to point out that they recognize Jesus as one of the prophets of Allah, or more exactly, the messenger of Allah to the Jews. Muslims want you to know that the Qur'an says Jesus spoke from the cradle. They also teach that Jesus as a lad brought life to clay birds. By this they want you to infer that the Qur'an is more complete because it fills in details about Jesus' infancy and childhood, whereas the Bible says little about His childhood.

What do Muslims generally teach regarding Jesus?

Jesus is one of 124,000 prophets who were sent to specific cultures over the past millennia; notable others were Noah, Abraham, and Moses, with Muhammad being the last and the seal of the prophets.

Jesus was born of a virgin as the Word from God but was not the Son of God. Muslims will agree that the Word of or the Word from God is eternal but that Christ Jesus prior to His human birth, who is the Word of God and thus eternal, was not. But is this being consistent? Look up John 1:1-14.

Jesus was sinless.

Jesus was not God in human flesh.

Jesus was not crucified and without dying ascended into heaven, where He is seated next to God. There are conflicting positions among Muslims regarding the crucifixion. Some say Judas the betrayer took Jesus' place on the cross. Others say Jesus did not die while on the cross but was rescued and later raised up to Allah without dying. Other Muslims say that Jesus did hang on the cross but was taken down before He died and later went to find the ten lost tribes of Israel. They say the search for those tribes took Jesus to Afghanistan and to Srinagar, Kashmir, where He died at the age of 120, and where His tomb is today. This is contrary to what the Qur'an says: that Jesus did not die but was raised up to the throne of God.

Jesus is referred to as the messiah and a sign from God.

Jesus will come in the future only to live and die and be buried next to Muhammad until the resurrection of all humankind on judgment day. Muslims deny that Jesus was placed in a tomb and arose on the third day.

These teachings raise some important questions to ponder. Is it possible for Jesus to be more than a prophet? Since Jesus is sinless and the Word from God, and the Word is eternal, wouldn't He be eternal? Why would Jesus' birth have to be a virgin birth if He was going to be only a human messenger? Why wouldn't he, like all the other prophets, have a human father? Please do not even consider that God had physical contact with the virgin Mary to bring forth the Christ child. Christians do not in any way believe there is the remotest possibility of this occurring. Instead, the Seed in Mary's womb was fertilized by the power of the Holy Spirit.

How could Jesus, according to the Qur'an, be the eternal Word of God who was sinless and who was returned to Allah without dying, not be divine? According to the Scriptures, Jesus was fully human and fully God. As a human Jesus could have sinned, but as God He would not sin. From a helpless fully human babe in the manger to a mature adult He needed to grow in wisdom and stature, but as God He was pure in thought and knew everything. He had to go through this human growth process without any shortcuts to be a fully human being.

Many of the unique attributes of Jesus need to be looked into to uncover their significance. It is not enough just to deny them because they are difficult to accept from a human perspective. There are serious differences between what Muslims believe and what the Bible teaches about Jesus that will be covered more fully in the chapter about Christianity.

I met Solomon Mattar, a Jordanian who was the keeper of the Garden Tomb outside old Jerusalem, near the Place of the Skull, where according to the Scriptures Jesus was crucified. He was visiting an assembly of believers in my city in the late 1950s to share with us the significance and authenticity of the Garden Tomb. My wife and I were asked by the elders of our assembly if we would house and care for him. We were honored to do so.

At his meetings in our assembly, Solomon related the history and the location of the tomb. His explanation, that this was the tomb of Joseph of Arimathea, where Jesus was buried, was convincing. Thousands of tourists make the tomb one of their stops while visiting Israel.

Solomon Mattar was responsible to oversee all that pertained to the care of this tomb and the surrounding gardens. He was a kind, humble, and gracious family man. During the six-day war in Israel (1967), it was risky for civilians to move about Jerusalem. Solomon's family was out of water, and as he ventured out to a well he was killed by a sniper's bullet.

A few years later, in the early 1970s, my wife and I went on a tour of the Holy Land. We saw the Garden Tomb, which was on the tour itinerary. It held a special meaning for us.

On one of our free days during the tour, we hired a cab and asked the Jordanian driver to take us to areas where tourists don't normally visit. As we went into some of the outskirts of Jerusalem, he said we had to be careful, for there was still political tension in those areas. Most of the taxi drivers in Jerusalem drove Mercedes cabs, and I noticed in the open-styled glove compartment of our cab what I thought was a miniature Bible. I asked if it was a Bible. He said, "Yes," and handed it back to me. The very small back cover had a Scripture verse printed on it, something that Jesus said: "Most assuredly, I say to you, he who hears My word and believes in Him who sent Me has everlasting life, and shall not come into judgment, but has passed from death into life" (John 5:24).

I asked the driver if he believed this, and he said, "Yes." I asked him how he became a Christian. He said, "My wife became a Christian first, and then I became a Christian." I asked how his wife had come to faith in Christ. He said, "There was a man in our neighborhood who held a Bible study in his home, and while attending those meetings she came to accept Jesus as her Lord and Savior." I asked if the teacher was a fellow Jordanian. He said, "Yes, his name was Solomon Mattar." Overwhelmed, I asked, "The keeper of the Garden Tomb?" He said, "Yes." What a small world. Of course we had to relate how we came to know Solomon Mattar and that I had heard that he had been shot and killed. Our driver was awestruck and surprised that we knew about Solomon and his death. Of all the cab drivers in Jerusalem, we were lined up with him!

This experience wasn't just a coincidence. It's God's way of confirming His hand at work in the lives of those in the Christian community who reach out to those in their world. Those who freely, not by force, put their faith in God's Word and accept Jesus the risen Lord as their Savior will know for certain that they are forgiven. They also receive God's free gift of eternal life. Jesus did arise! He is alive! The stone is still rolled away, and the tomb is still empty. My wife and I saw it firsthand.

The Holy Spirit

Muslims find it difficult to relate to and understand the attributes of the Holy Spirit. This will be best handled by expressing what the Bible teaches and what Muslims don't believe about the Holy Spirit.

The Bible teaches that the Holy Spirit is

> unlimited in power, knows everything, and can be everywhere at the same time;
>
> referred to as the Helper or Comforter to all true Christians, and the One who inspired the prophets of ages past to write the holy Scriptures;
>
> indwelling and ministering to the true believer the things of Christ from the Word of God;
>
> included with the Father and the Son in the benedictions of Scripture;

> referred to as a He, and one who has all the attributes of a person and all the attributes of God;
>
> the one person of the Godhood as fully God who caused Mary's Seed to be fertilized by His divine power that brought forth the holy child Jesus.

The biblical references for these truths will be covered in the chapter about Christianity.

The Qur'an, however, does refer to the Holy Spirit coming to Jesus. In sura 16:102, the Spirit is said to bring revelations to Muhammad: "Say, the Holy Spirit has brought the revelation from thy Lord in Truth, in order to strengthen those who believe, and as a Guide and Glad Tidings to Muslims." Also, sura 26:192-94 says, "Verily this is a Revelation from the Lord of the Worlds: With it came down the spirit of Faith and Truth to thy heart and mind, that thou mayest admonish."

To Christians, the Holy Spirit has all the attributes of a person and, according to Scripture, is to be respected as God, never despised or rejected.

Sin

Muslims believe that a child enters this world sinless. From the early chapters of Genesis we learn that death is the curse of sin, so a child born sinless would have no possibility of death until the child committed a sin. But babies do die. If they were without a sinful nature and sinless, why would infants die? Biblical teaching is that each person at birth has a sinful nature that is inherited from Adam. "Therefore, just as through one man (Adam) sin entered the world, and death through sin, and thus death spread to all men, because all sinned" (Romans 5:12). The reason we sin is because we have a sinful nature. We don't become sinners; we are sinners.

Another view of this is found in Psalm 51:5: "Behold, I was brought forth in iniquity, and in sin my mother conceived me." Here David is declaring he came from the womb a guilty sinner, and that his mother and father were sinners; therefore he inherited a sin nature.

One might use the argument that it would be impossible for Jesus to die because He was the Holy One from the womb and lived a sinless life. That would be true if He hadn't become sin for us. It was on the cross, when Jesus was forsaken of God, that He took all of our sins in His own body and became sin for us while making amends for our sins through the shedding of His blood and dying in our place. Second Corinthians 5:21 says, "For He made Him who knew no sin to be sin for us, that we might become the righteousness of God in Him."

Forgiveness of sins is not knowable to Muslims in this life. They will know if Allah has forgiven their sins only when they stand before Him at the final judgment. The Bible, however, teaches we can know forgiveness. Christians are told their sins are forgiven when they accept the person of Jesus the Christ and put their trust in His sacrificial death on the cross. God's Word says there can be no remission (forgiveness) of sins without the shedding of blood. In fact, Jesus confirms this in Matthew 26:28: "For this is My blood of the new covenant, which is shed for many for the remission of sins."

Some Muslims, however, do not believe Jesus died on the cross, so they do not and therefore cannot claim the redemptive work of Jesus. Muslims in essence hope their good deeds will be sufficient to outweigh their bad deeds. The Qur'an teaches that Allah will use a balance (scale) to decide whether a Muslim will enter paradise.

The position that only Allah knows if one is forgiven is contradicted by an illustration in "Understanding Islam," a booklet sponsored by the government of Saudi Arabia. This booklet relates from the Hadith a saying of Muhammad:

> "A man walking along a path felt very thirsty. Reaching a well he descended into it, drank his fill and came up. Then he saw a dog with its tongue hanging out, trying to lick up the mud to quench its thirst. The man saw that the dog was feeling the same thirst as he had felt so he went down into the well again and filled his shoe with water and gave the dog a drink. God forgave his sins for this action." The Prophet was asked: "Messenger of God, are we rewarded for kindness towards animals?" He said, "There is a reward for kindness to every living thing."

How did Muhammad know the man's sins were forgiven? Doesn't the Qur'an teach only God knows whose sins will be forgiven?

Islamic nations, under Shari'a law, have strong convictions against and severe punishment for the sins of adultery, pornography, homosexuality, and other actions within their communities. They consider the promiscuity promoted in Western society and movies as an affront to Allah. Christians believe the Bible calls those sinful actions as well, but they would still extend Christ's love and forgiveness to those who are practicing those lifestyles, trusting that the goodness of God can lead them to repentance. The difference between Islam and true Christianity is the way sin is handled. Islam would take vengeance on offenders to the extent of death or maiming of the body, such as like cutting off a hand and a foot from opposite sides of the body. True Christians would look for repentance from the transgressor and allow for forgiveness because they know judgment belongs to the Lord, who is long-suffering but will one day render righteous justice for unbelieving sinners (Revelation 20:11-15):

> Then I saw a great white throne and Him who sat on it, from whose face the earth and the heaven fled away. And there was found no place for them. And I saw the dead, small and great, standing before God, and books were opened. And another book was opened, which is the Book of Life. And the dead were judged according to their works, by the things which were written in the books. The sea gave up the dead who were in it, and Death and Hades delivered up the dead who were in them. And they were judged, each one according to his works. Then Death and Hades were cast into the lake of fire. This is the second death. And anyone not found written in the Book of Life was cast into the lake of fire.

The God of the Bible loves sinners but hates their sin. Islam says Allah hates sinners, as stated in the Qur'an. If God would render immediate justice every time people offended His laws, no one would be left alive. But don't be deceived. There will be a day of judgment for those who have not accepted God's provision for salvation and forgiveness that is offered in His Word, the Bible.

Salvation

In Muslim teaching regarding salvation, there is little certainty of anyone knowing he or she has forgiveness or is in good standing with Allah. This is due to the Qur'an's teaching that no one knows his or her eternal destiny until the final judgment day. Only Allah knows; He will determine on the day of judgment who will be saved and who will go to destruction. People have no part in determining their destiny, for Allah makes some stray and guides some: "We sent not an apostle except (to teach) in the language of his (own) people, in order to make (things) clear to them. Now Allah leaves straying those whom He pleases and guides whom He pleases: and He is Exalted in power, full of Wisdom" (sura 14:4). Muslims hope they are being guided by Allah. They must faithfully follow the five pillars: repetition of the creed, daily prayers, giving of alms, fasting at Ramadan, and the pilgrimage to Mecca, to have any possibility of being accepted by Allah.

In the finality of things Allah will send to paradise or hell whomever He wills. This is a fatalistic view that leads a person to be fearfully in doubt of his or her eternal destiny. There is no assurance of salvation for the Muslim, except for death associated in carrying out Jihad.

"And those who, having done something to be ashamed of, or wronged their own souls, earnestly bring Allah to mind, and ask for forgiveness for their sins and who can forgive sins except Allah and are never obstinate in persisting knowingly in (the wrong) they have done" (sura 3:135). This sura leaves people wondering whether they have been forgiven.

"And if ye are slain, or die, in the way of Allah, forgiveness and mercy from Allah are far better than all they could amass" (sura 3:157). If a person does not die in a Jihad, then paradise is attainable only by their righteous achievements, which Allah may or may not accept:

"If any do deeds of righteousness be they male or female and have faith, they will enter Heaven, and not the least injustice will be done to them" (sura 4:124). "Those who believe, and suffer exile and strive with might and main, in Allah's cause, with their goods and their persons, have the highest rank in the sight of Allah. They are the people who will achieve (salvation). Their Lord doth give them glad tidings of a Mercy from Himself, of His good pleasure, and of gardens for them, wherein are delights that endure" (sura 9:20-21). These two suras must be in compliance with sura 23:102-3: "Then those whose balance (of good deeds) is heavy,- they will attain salvation: But those whose balance is light, will be those who have lost their souls, in Hell will they abide."

Since the reward of paradise is based on one's good deeds outweighing one's bad deeds, a Muslim cannot know what Allah has recorded. Muslims live in constant wonder if they have done enough. Even Muhammad was not sure of going to paradise. Hadith 5:266 says, "Though I am the Apostle of Allah, yet I do not know what Allah will do to me."

All, whether good or evil, has been determined by Allah. This can be described as kismet, an attitude of "whatever will be will be," and that is fatalism.

How different this is from the Christian way of salvation, as we look at the apostle Peter's message to unbelieving Jews about the healing of a helpless man (Acts 4:8-10):

> Then Peter, filled with the Holy Spirit, said to them, "Rulers of the people and elders of Israel: If we this day are judged for a good deed done to a helpless man, by what means he has been made well, let it be known to you all, and to all the people of Israel, that by the name of Jesus Christ of Nazareth, whom you crucified, whom God raised from the dead, by Him this man stands here before you whole."

We must remember Peter was an eyewitness to the crucifixion and the resurrection. He visited with the resurrected Messiah, he saw the nail-scarred hands, and he saw the ascension of Jesus into the clouds of heaven. Peter was there when it happened. So were the other apostles eyewitnesses, as were hundreds of others. Why would the apostles of Christ want to perpetuate a lie, especially when the message would cost them their lives at the hands of others? Paul the apostle knew what it meant to be persecuted (2 Timothy 3:11-13): "persecutions, afflictions, which happened to me at Antioch, at Iconium, at Lystra—what persecutions I endured. And out of them all the Lord delivered me. Yes, and all who desire to live godly in Christ Jesus will suffer persecution. But evil men and impostors will grow worse and worse, deceiving and being deceived." He endured the persecutions and was kept from death until after his divinely appointed witness to those in Rome.

In Galatians Paul tells us that there were those who wanted to hold onto the Old Covenant Jewish practice of circumcision and to impose it on non-Jewish (Gentile) Christians. This was not necessary in the New Covenant, as Paul indicates (Galatians 3:12-13): "As many as desire to make a good showing in the flesh, these would compel you to be circumcised, only that they may not suffer persecution for the cross of Christ. For not even those who are circumcised keep the law, but they desire to have you circumcised that they may boast in your flesh." Paul goes on to say that being circumcised or not being circumcised isn't the important issue, but rather the keeping of God's commandments (1 Corinthians 7:17-19): "But as God has distributed to each one, as the Lord has called each one, so let him walk. And so I ordain in all the churches. Was anyone called while circumcised? Let him not become uncircumcised. Was anyone called while uncircumcised? Let him not be circumcised. Circumcision is nothing and uncircumcision is nothing, but keeping the commandments of God is what matters."

God's commandment for the New Covenant was heard at the time of the transfiguration of Jesus, who was accompanied by the apostles Peter, James, and John:

> behold, a bright cloud overshadowed them; and suddenly a voice came out of the cloud, saying, "This is My beloved Son, in whom I am well pleased. Hear Him!" And when the disciples heard it, they fell on their faces and were greatly afraid. But Jesus came and touched them and said, "Arise, and do not be afraid." When they had lifted up their eyes, they saw no one but Jesus only. Now as they came down from the mountain, Jesus commanded them, saying, "Tell the vision to no one until the Son of Man is risen from the dead." (Matthew 17:5-9)

Underlined above is the important command from God the Father that the apostles, and subsequently all, are to listen to and believe what His beloved Son Jesus had to say. The entire New Testament is record of the birth, life, death, resurrection, and teachings of Jesus as recorded by His apostles.

The New Covenant tells us that as the Son of Man Christ fulfilled all of the commandments of God on our behalf and thus brings release and freedom from the law's condemnation. In its place true Christians have Christ and His love living in them. This is the miracle of the engrafted Word of God in the hearts of those who have a relationship with the living Word of God, the very person of Christ.

Christians are still being persecuted and many are being killed for someone they believe was and is the promised Messiah Jesus, the one who fulfilled with precise accuracy more than one hundred prophecies written about Him concerning His first coming to earth. Is this coincidental, or is the Bible the inspired Word of God? That the Bible is the Word of God is confirmed in 2 Timothy 3:12-17:

> Yes, and all who desire to live godly in Christ Jesus will suffer persecution. But evil men and impostors will grow worse and worse, deceiving and being deceived. But you must continue in the things which you have learned and been assured of, knowing from whom you have learned them, and that from childhood you have known the Holy Scriptures, which are able to make you wise for salvation through faith which is in Christ Jesus. All Scripture is given by inspiration of God, and is profitable for doctrine, for reproof, for correction, for instruction in righteousness, that the man of God may be complete, thoroughly equipped for every good work.

From the teaching of the Scriptures we accept that Jesus is the means to our salvation (Acts 4:12): "Nor is there salvation in any other, for there is no other name under heaven given among men by which we must be saved."
Only in the name of Jesus can we, who were spiritually dead due to our sinful nature inherited from Adam, be made alive through a spiritual birth that gives us a new nature and makes us acceptable to a righteous and holy God. Jesus as fully God and fully man is the mediator between God and humankind (1 Timothy 2:3-7): "For this is good and acceptable in the sight of God our Savior, who desires all men to be saved and to come to the knowledge of the truth. For there is one God and one Mediator between God and men, the Man Christ Jesus, who gave Himself a ransom for all, to be testified in due time, for which I was appointed a preacher and an apostle—I am speaking the truth in Christ and not lying—a teacher of the Gentiles in faith and truth."

The Bible teaches that the one God is Spirit, not *a* spirit. Because He is Spirit and invisible to the human eye, He can be everywhere at the same time, knows everything that goes on, and is all-powerful. The fullness of the one God indwells and is manifested fully in the Father, Son, and Holy Spirit (John 4:24): "God is Spirit, and those who worship Him must worship in spirit and truth." In Colossians 1:15 we read, "He is the image of the invisible God, the firstborn over all creation." This tells us that Christ the Messiah, the Word of God in His human body, is the visible expression of the invisible God and the rightful heir to all creation, for it was by, through, and for Him, who is the Word of God, that everything was created.

Scripture, Muhammad, and Jesus

Muslims have identified Scriptures that they say tell the coming of the prophet Muhammad. Evidently those Scriptures were not among those that were corrupted or altered. This means we can rely on the text and context of those portions of Scripture that Muslims use to obtain the full meaning from the Word of God.

The following references came from an Islamic book published by Al-Shirkatul Islamiyyah, The London Mosque (1953) titled *Why Islam?*

Muhammad or the Holy Spirit (John 16:7-13)?

In sura 61:6 it says Jesus is foretelling a messenger who will come that is Muhammad: "And remember, Jesus, the son of Mary, said: 'O Children of Israel! I am the apostle of Allah (sent) to you, confirming the Law (which came) before me, and giving Glad Tidings of an Messenger to come after me, whose name shall be Ahmad.' But when he came to them with Clear Signs, they said, 'this is evident sorcery!'"

Muslims tie this sura to John 16:7-13, where Jesus says:

> "Nevertheless I tell you the truth. It is to your advantage that I go away; for if I do not go away, the Helper will not come to you; but if I depart, I will send Him to you. And when He has come, He will convict the world of sin, and of righteousness, and of judgment: of sin, because they do not believe in Me; of righteousness, because I go to My Father and you see Me no more; of judgment, because the ruler of this world is judged. "I still have many things to say to you, but you cannot bear them now. However, when He, the Spirit of truth, has come, He will guide you into all truth; for He will not speak on His own authority, but whatever He hears He will speak; and He will tell you things to come."

Islam claims that in these verses Jesus says the Helper (Comforter) refers to Muhammad, in that the Greek word *paraklutos* in Arabic means "Ahmad," thus Muhammad. The only problem is the Greek word used in the original Scriptures is not *paraklutos*, but *paraklitos*, which can only mean "Helper" or "Comforter" and is not to be translated Ahmad.

In this Scripture, Jesus is talking to His apostles about the promised coming of the Holy Spirit, who would later indwell the apostles and bring to their remembrance the things they saw Jesus do and the things He taught, some of which they recorded in their Gospels. The apostles were promised that they would be indwelled and inspired by the Holy Spirit and that would be the reason for the accuracy of the Scriptures they wrote. Thus their writings as the Word of God cannot be altered or changed, according to the Qur'an and Muslim teaching. In John 6, the apostle John relates the miraculous feeding of the five thousand. After the people were fed, Jesus told his disciples, "'Gather up the fragments that remain, so that nothing is lost.' Therefore they gathered them up, and filled twelve baskets with the fragments of the five barley loaves which were left over by those who had eaten. Then those men, when they had seen the sign that Jesus did, said, 'This is truly the Prophet who is to come into the world'" (John 6:12-14).

Notice the declaration that Jesus is the promised prophet who is to come into the world. This is a reference to Deuteronomy 18:15 and other portions of the Old Testament. *The* prophet, not just *a* prophet, the prophet Jesus.

Another reference to the Helper is found in John 14:15-18: "If you love Me, keep My commandments. And I will pray the Father, and He will give you another Helper, that He may abide with you forever—the Spirit of truth, whom the world cannot receive, because it neither sees Him nor knows Him; but you know Him, <u>for He dwells with you and will be in you</u>. I will not leave you orphans; I will come to you."

Notice Jesus says the Helper is the Holy Spirit. Notice the Holy Spirit is a person who is dwelling with them (the present) and will be in them (near future, during their lifetime). This future indwelling of the apostles and other believers took place at Pentecost, as recorded in the Acts1:4-5 and Acts 2:1-4. Another biblical prophecy fulfilled the way Jesus said it would! If this Scripture is talking about Muhammad, he would have had to be dwelling with the apostles of Jesus in the first century, not six hundred years later. Also, Muhammad did not indwell Christian believers as the Holy Spirit did at Pentecost and continues to do so to this day. Can you see that pulling texts out of context can lead to misinterpretation and error?

A Text Considered a Proof Text by Muslims (John 1:20-21)

Muslims consider John 1:20-21 as a proof text; the answer to the question, "Are you the prophet?" can only be Muhammad. John 1:20-21 says, "He confessed, and did not deny, but confessed, 'I am not the Christ.' And they asked him, 'What then? Are you Elijah?' He said, 'I am not.' 'Are you the Prophet?' And he answered, 'No.'"

These questions were being asked of John the Baptist, and if you read the <u>context</u> of this portion of Scripture, you will see the prophet being spoken about is Jesus the Messiah, not Muhammad. In John 1:22-23, we read John the Baptist's reply: "Then they said to him, 'Who are you, that we may give an answer to those who sent us? What do you say about yourself?' He said: 'I am "The voice of one crying in the wilderness: Make straight the way of the LORD,"' as the prophet Isaiah said." One can readily see that John the Baptist is not referring to Muhammad but to Jesus, just as it was prophesied in Isaiah 40:3.

Muslims claim many other Scriptures refer to Muhammad. However, by carefully examining the text and the context, and by comparing other Scripture, there is no possible way to render that Muhammad is ever found prophesied in the Bible. This is reading something into Scripture that isn't there, which is a serious offense to the God of the Bible.

You probably have detected that I have utilized a lot of material from both Muslim and Christian source documents and defenders of their faith. I have found that many times the material presented by Muslims about the teachings of Christians is not what Scripture says and not what Christians teach.

For instance, Ahmed Deedat is considered an authority among Muslims regarding error in Christian teaching. Deedat made a statement that Jesus never commented about His death and resurrection in the New Testament:

> Throughout the length and breadth of the 27 books of the new Testament, there is not a single statement made by Jesus Christ that "I was dead, and I have come back from the dead." The Christian has [wrongly] been belaboring the word resurrection. Again and again, by repetition, it is conveyed that it[the resurrection] is proving a fact. . . . [But] Jesus Christ never uttered the word that "I have come back from the dead," in the 27 books of the New Testament, not once. (77a)

This is not true, and Ahmed Deedat undoubtedly did not read the Scriptures, because Jesus did foretell of His death and resurrection. In the New Testament, Jesus told His disciples, "The Son of Man must suffer many things and be rejected by the elders, chief priests and the teachers of the law and <u>must be killed, and on the third day be raised to life</u>" (Luke 9:22). He also told His disciples a<u>fter His resurrection</u> that this was to fulfill the Old Testament prophecies written about Him:

> Then He said to them, "These are the words which I spoke to you while I was still with you, that all things must be fulfilled which were written in the Law of Moses and the Prophets and the Psalms concerning Me." Then He said to them, "Thus it is written, and thus it was necessary for the Christ to suffer and to rise from the dead the third day, and that repentance and remission of sins should be preached in His name to all nations, beginning at Jerusalem." (Luke 24:44, 46-47)

In Revelation 1:18, speaking of Jesus, it says, "I am the Living One; I was dead, and behold I am alive for ever and ever!" Furthermore, in Matthew 26:2, Jesus tells His disciples, "You know that after two days is the Passover, and the Son of Man will be delivered up to be crucified."

Jesus left no doubt in the minds of the high priest, scribes, and elders when He confirmed to them that He was the promised Messiah and the Son of God. For that confirmation they sought His death:

> And the high priest arose and said to Him, "Do You answer nothing? What is it these men testify against You?" But Jesus kept silent. And the high priest answered and said to Him, "I put You under oath by the living God: Tell us if You are the Christ, the Son of God!" Jesus said to him, "It is as you said. Nevertheless, I say to you, here after you will see the Son of Man sitting at the right hand of the Power, and coming on the clouds of heaven." (Matthew 26:62-64)

After His resurrection, Jesus encountered the apostle Thomas and showed him the wounds from His crucifixion. At this, Thomas confesses Jesus as Lord and God (John 20:26-29). Thomas's confession is similar to that of Simon Peter, when Jesus asked, "'Who do men say that I, the Son of Man, am?' So they said, 'Some say John the Baptist, some Elijah, and others Jeremiah or one of the prophets.' He said to them, 'But who do you say that I am?' Simon Peter answered and said, 'You are the Christ, the Son of the living God'" (Matthew 16:13-16).

Again, after His resurrection,

> Jesus Himself stood in the midst of them, and said to them, "Peace to you." But they were terrified and frightened, and supposed they had seen a spirit. And He said to them, "Why are you troubled? And why do doubts arise in your hearts? Behold My hands and My feet, that it is I Myself. Handle Me and see, for a spirit does not have flesh and bones as you see I have." When He had said this, He showed them His hands and His feet. But while they still did not believe for joy, and marveled, He said to them, "Have you any food here?" So they gave Him a piece of a broiled fish and some honeycomb. And He took it and ate in their presence.
>
> Then He said to them, "These are the words which I spoke to you while I was still with you, that all things must be fulfilled which were written in the Law of Moses and the Prophets and the Psalms concerning Me." And He opened their understanding, that they might comprehend the Scriptures. Then He said to them, "Thus it is written, and thus it was necessary for the Christ to suffer and to rise from the dead the third day, and that repentance and remission of sins should be preached in His name to all nations, beginning

> at Jerusalem. And you are witnesses of these things. Behold, I send the Promise of My Father upon you; but tarry in the city of Jerusalem until you are endued with power from on high." (Luke 24:36-49)

In Mark 16:12-14, the eleven apostles are rebuked by the resurrected Jesus for not believing two of the disciples who had seen Him: "After that, He appeared in another form to two of them as they walked and went into the country. And they went and told it to the rest, but they did not believe them either. Later He appeared to the eleven as they sat at the table; and He rebuked their unbelief and hardness of heart, because they did not believe those who had seen Him after He had risen."

All four Gospels declare the resurrected Jesus. Why would there be copies only of altered or changed Scriptures without there being even one copy of the unaltered Scriptures? Wouldn't God preserve at least one of the unaltered Scriptures?

Even in the face of historical evidence, some Muslims continue to deny the crucifixion and resurrection of Jesus the Christ, for to accept that teaching from the Word of God means that the Qur'an tells a different story. But to misquote and deny the Scriptures as Deedat does is intellectually dishonest, and he is practicing deception.

Eternal Destiny

Muslims teach that there are two destinies for all humankind that will be determined at the final great day of judgment: paradise or hell. Only true Muslims will be able to cross over a bridge to paradise. All others will fall off the bridge in their attempt to reach paradise and will land in the fires of hell. Only Allah knows who are worthy to reach paradise with all of its sensual pleasures. Wine, pure virgin companions, gardens, streams and rivers, lands of milk and honey, and a life of ease wait those who have strived to death in Jihad or those who have done more righteous deeds than bad (sura 53:31): "Yea, to Allah belongs all that is in the heavens and on earth: so that He rewards those who do evil, according to their deeds, and He rewards those who do good, with what is best."

Paradise

As I researched Islam, I found out that paradise had gardens with rivers underneath, fruit trees fed from the streams of clear water, and companions pure, virgins and holy:

> But give glad tidings to those who believe and work righteousness, that their portion is Gardens, beneath which rivers flow. Every time they are fed with fruits there from, they say: "Why, this is what we were fed with before," for they are given things in similitude; and they have therein companions pure (and holy); and they abide therein (for ever)" (sura 2:25)

> Fair in the eyes of men is the love of things they covet: Women and sons; Heaped-up hoards of gold and silver; horses branded (for blood and excellence); and (wealth of) cattle and well-tilled land. Such are the possessions of this world's life; but in nearness to Allah is the best of the goals (To return to). Say: Shall I give you glad tidings of things Far better than those? For the righteous are Gardens in nearness to their Lord, with rivers flowing beneath; therein is their eternal home; with companions pure (and holy); and the good pleasure of Allah. For in Allah's sight are (all) His servants (sura 3:14-15)

> But those who believe and do deeds of righteousness, We shall soon admit to Gardens, with rivers flowing beneath, their eternal home: Therein shall they have companions pure and holy: We shall admit them to shades, cool and ever deepening (sura 4:57)

> But those who believe and work righteousness, and humble themselves before their Lord, They will be companions of the gardens, to dwell therein for aye! (sura 11:23)

> (Here is) a Parable of the Garden which the righteous are promised: in it are rivers of water incorruptible; rivers of milk of which the taste never changes; rivers of wine, a joy to those who drink; and rivers of honey pure and clear. In it there are for them all kinds of fruits; and Grace from their Lord. (Can those in such Bliss) be compared to such as shall dwell for ever in the Fire, and be given, to drink, boiling water, so that it cuts up their bowels (to pieces)? (sura 47:15)

Much of sura 55 also speaks of the gardens, fruit trees, virgin maidens, brocade-covered sofas, and streams of waters.

The Day of Judgment

Judgment day is central in Islam and is something to be feared, because only Allah knows a person's eternal destiny. Sura 17:13-14 is descriptive of that day: "Every man's fate We have fastened on his own neck: On the Day of Judgment We shall bring out for him a scroll, which he will see spread open. (It will be said to him:) 'Read thine (own) record: Sufficient is thy soul this day to make out an account against thee.'"

Only at that time will a person, according to that sura and others, know what the record of his or her life will reveal.

By contrast, the God of the Bible wants you to know now where you are going to be eternally (1 John 5:11-13): "And this is the testimony: that <u>God has given us eternal life</u>, and this life is in His Son. He who has the Son has life; he who does not have the Son of God does not have life. These things I have written to you who believe in the name of the Son of God, <u>that you may know</u> that you have eternal life, and that you may continue to believe in the name of the Son of God."

Did you grasp the significance of those verses from the Bible, which is God's eternal, unchangeable Word? That is completely different from the Qur'an. How can they both be true?

To say the Bible has been altered or corrupted has no evidential foundation. That belies the prophet Muhammad's striking statements in the Qur'an that good Muslims must go to the books of the Jews and the Christians because they are the Word of God given to them, and Muslims can learn from them. It contradicts the Qur'an and traditions where Muhammad says the Bible has been corrupted.

Does the Qur'an Have Internal Contradictions?

Numerous internal contradictions are supposedly explained away by "divine abrogation" (changing of previously revealed truth). Important differences with the Bible are explained away by claiming the Bible has been corrupted or altered, but is this being intellectually honest? Let's look at some internal contradictions in the Qur'an.

<u>*Who Revealed the Qur'an?*</u>

There are four accounts in the Qur'an that relate how Muhammad received his revelations.

We are told that Muhammad was visited by Allah in the form of a man and that Muhammad saw him (suras 53:2-18; 81:19-24).

Next we are told that the Holy Spirit came to Muhammad: "Say, the Holy Spirit has brought the revelation from thy Lord in Truth, in order to strengthen those who believe, and as a Guide and Glad Tidings to Muslims" (suras 16:102; 81:19-24); "Verily this is a Revelation from the Lord of the Worlds: With it came down the spirit of Faith and Truth To thy heart and mind, that thou mayest admonish" (sura 26:192-94).

In sura 15:6 we are told the angels came down to Muhammad.

The most popular view held by Muslims is that the angel Gabriel revealed the Qur'an to him: "Say: Whoever is an enemy to Gabriel for he brings down the (revelation) to thy heart by Allah's will, a confirmation of what went before, and guidance and glad tidings for those who believe " (sura 2:97).

Muslims teach that Allah is transcendent and people cannot reach up into his presence; Allah does not physically lower himself to the human realm. So isn't it unthinkable and contradictory to Islamic doctrine that Allah would take the form of a man and come down and speak to Muhammad?

Noah and the Flood

Another example of internal contradiction within the Qur'an is found in sura 11, which relates the events of Noah and the flood. According to one account, one of Noah's sons, because of his unrighteous and rebellious conduct, perished in the flood; however, in another portion of the Qur'an, the son doesn't perish (suras 11:42-46; 21:76).

If the Qur'an is pure Arabic and the exact revelation of the Mother Book in heaven, why would it be contradictory?

Also, in sura 11:42 the ark of Noah comes to rest on Mount Judi. The biblical account states the ark came to rest on Mount Ararat. Wouldn't these significant contradictions cause one to wonder why Allah would be so confused? Once again I must ask, was not the Old Testament written long before the Qur'an, and according to the Qur'an, God will not allow His Word to be altered or changed? Muhammad told Muslims to go to the Book of the Jews for confirmation of the Qur'an. The Book of the Jews was the same Old Testament in Muhammad's day that we have today.

Reliability of Historical Events

Samaritans Led Israel Astray

If it is declared to be the eternal Word of Allah, shouldn't the Qur'an be 100 percent correct when it comes to history?

With regard to the children of Israel and their worship of the golden calf at Mount Sinai, Allah said (sura 20:85) said:

> "We have tested thy people in thy absence: the *Samiri* has led them astray." So Moses returned to his people in a state of indignation and sorrow. He said: "O my people! did not your Lord make a handsome promise to you? Did then the promise seem to you long (in coming)? Or did ye desire that Wrath should descend from your Lord on you, and so ye broke your promise to me?" They said: "We broke not the promise to thee, as far as lay in our power: but we were made to carry the weight of the ornaments of the (whole) people, and we threw them (into the fire), and that was what the *Samiri* suggested." Then he brought out (of the fire) before the (people) the image of a calf: It seemed to low: so they said: This is your god, and the god of Moses, but (Moses) has forgotten! Could they not see that it could not return them a word (for answer), and that it had no power either to harm them or to do them good?

Samiri refers to the Samaritans, saying that they led astray the people of Israel during the exodus and were responsible for producing the golden calf. The problem, however, is that the Samaritans didn't exist until 722 BC, hundreds of years after the exodus (66a).

Crucifixion at the Time of Pharaoh

Sura 7:123-24 claims that Pharaoh would carry out crucifixion as a means of punishment, even though history claims crucifixion was a form of execution invented by the Romans hundreds of years later. Nothing in Egyptian historical records would indicate crucifixion was practiced by the pharaohs of Egypt. Would Allah reveal erroneous information regarding historical facts?

Alexander the Great

Another historical area of confusion pertains to Alexander the Great, who is called Zul-qarnain in the Qur'an. Here's what has been recorded (sura 18:83-98):

> They ask thee concerning Zul-qarnain. Say, "I will rehearse to you something of his story." Verily We established his power on earth, and We gave him the ways and the means to all ends. One (such) way he followed, Until, when he reached the setting of the sun, he found it set in a spring of murky water: Near it he found a People: We said: "O Zul-qarnain! (thou hast authority,) either to punish them, or to treat them with kindness." He said: "Whoever doth wrong, him shall we punish; then shall he be sent back to his Lord; and He will punish him with a punishment unheard-of (before). But whoever believes, and works righteousness, he shall have a goodly reward, and easy will be his task as We order it by our Command." Then followed he (another) way, Until, when he came to the rising of the sun, he found it rising on a people for whom We had provided no covering protection against the sun. (He left them) as they were: We completely understood what was before him. Then followed he (another) way, Until, when he reached (a tract) between two mountains, he found, beneath them, a people who scarcely understood a word. They said: "O Zul-qarnain! the Gog and Magog (People) do great mischief on earth: shall we then render thee tribute in order that thou mightest erect a barrier between us and them?" He said: "(The power) in which my Lord has established me is better (than tribute): Help me therefore with strength (and labour): I will erect a strong barrier between you and them: Bring me blocks of iron." At length, when he had filled up the space between the two steep mountain-sides, He said, "Blow (with your bellows)." Then, when he had made it (red) as fire, he said: "Bring me, that I may pour over it, molten lead." Thus were they made powerless to scale it or to dig through it. He said: "This is a mercy from my Lord: But when the promise of my Lord comes to pass, He will make it into dust; and the promise of my Lord is true."

The passage makes the claim that Allah gave Zul-quarnain (Alexander the Great) the power to travel to the most western part of the flat earth to a miry fount where the sun sets every evening. Are we supposed to believe that the sun sets in a miry fount?

The passage says that Alexander then took a route until he found where the sun rose on a people to whom Allah had given no shelter from it, and then he followed a route until he came to a place between two mountains, where he found a people who scarcely could understand a language. This entire passage contradicts well-established historical facts:

> History says Alexander the Great never made such a trip.
>
> Science says the sun doesn't travel around the earth.
>
> The sun is one million times larger than earth and cannot orbit around the earth.
>
> The sun does not set in a miry fount in the distant west of a flat earth.
>
> The earth is not flat.
>
> The sun does not rise in the distant east of the flat earth.

In addition, Muslims say Alexander was a Muslim; however, he was a pagan who lived before the time of Muhammad. Muslims also say Alexander lived to be an old man, but he died at age thirty-three.

A Flat Earth

Several portions of the Qur'an say that the earth is flat: "And the earth We have spread out (like a carpet); set things in due balance" (sura 15:19). However, a carpet has length and width and is not a sphere, as the earth is. The Qur'an also teaches that the mountains are set to balance the flat earth and keep it from moving up and down.

Two other texts speak of the earth as being flat: "And when the earth is flattened out" (sura 84:3), but how can the earth be stretched out to a flat configuration? Sura 43:10 says, "(Yea, the same that) has made for you the earth (like a carpet) spread out, and has made for you roads (and channels) therein, in order that ye may find guidance (on the way)." Again, a carpet is flat (81a)! Wouldn't you find it hard to believe that the Creator God would lead people astray with such erroneous concepts? God's messengers must be 100 percent correct when they say they have a message from God. If not, they are false prophets.

Was Muhammad the First Muslim?

The Qur'an says in sura 39:12, "And I am commanded to be the first of those who bow to Allah in Islam," This means that Muhammad was the first Muslim. However, the Qur'an says in other suras that others who preceded Muhammad who were Muslims (sura 3:52): "When Jesus found Unbelief on their part He said: 'Who will be My helpers to (the work of) Allah?' Said the disciples: 'We are Allah's helpers: We believe in Allah, and do thou bear witness that we are Muslims.'" Who then was the first Muslim? Was it Muhammad, or Jesus, or his disciples, or earlier Old Testament characters?

Teachings about Family

In some suras of the Qur'an, Muslims are told to be kind to their parents, and in others they are told not to befriend them. For instance:

> (We enjoined man to show kindness to his parents, for with much pain his mother bears him, and he is not weaned before he is two years of age. We said: "Give thanks to Me and to your parents. To me shall all things return. But if they press you to serve besides Me deities you know nothing of, do not obey them. Be kind to them in this world, and follow the path of those who turn to Me. To Me you shall return, and I will declare to you all that you have done.") (sura 31:14-15; cf. sura 29:8)

> Believers, do not befriend your fathers or your brothers if they choose unbelief in preference to faith. Wrongdoers are those that befriend them. Say: "If your fathers, your sons, your brothers, your wives, your tribes, the property you have acquired, the merchandise you fear may not be sold, and the homes you love, are dearer to you than God, His apostle and the struggle for His cause, then wait until God shall fulfill His decree. God does not guide the evil-doers." (sura 9:23-24, N. J. Dawood translation; emphasis added)

More than one hundred internal contradictions are recorded at "Koran contradictions/Koran-the ultimate truth," (website), with detailed explanations of the contradictions. I have related only a few, which I feel is all that is necessary in this book. Why would Allah reveal contradictory statements? Muslim teachers attempt to explain these contradictions with the doctrine of abrogation, as noted in sura 2:106: "None of Our revelations do We abrogate or cause to be forgotten, but We substitute something better or similar: Knowest thou not that Allah Hath power over all things?" The difficulty of this doctrine is why Allah would give contradictory revelations without saying which is the correct revelation. Which of the revelations is repealed or destroyed? Is Allah the God of confusion? Must we assume that the latter suras must take precedence over earlier suras?

Contradictions Between the Qur'an and the Bible

It is interesting to note that many portions of the Qur'an have stories similar to those that are recorded in the Bible, but some of the characters and happenings are different.

How Long Was Zachariah Speechless?

This portion of the Qur'an contradicts the biblical account of the events surrounding the coming birth of John the Baptist (sura 3:38-41):

> There did Zakariya pray to his Lord, saying: "O my Lord! Grant unto me from Thee a progeny that is pure: for Thou art He that heareth prayer!" While he was standing in prayer in the chamber, the angels called unto him: "(Allah) doth give thee glad tidings of Yahya, witnessing the truth of a Word from Allah, and (be besides) noble, chaste, and a prophet, of the (goodly) company of the righteous." He said: "O my Lord! How shall I have a son, seeing I am very old, And my wife is barren?" "Thus," was the answer, "Doth God accomplish what He willeth." He said: "O my Lord! Give me a Sign!" "Thy Sign," was the answer, "Shall be that thou shalt speak to no man for three days but with signals. Then celebrate the praises of thy Lord again and again, and glorify Him in the evening and in the morning."

The Qur'an says Zachariah would not speak for three days, but the Bible says that Zachariah could not speak during Elizabeth's pregnancy and until the time of their son John's circumcision (Luke 1:59-66):

> So it was, on the eighth day, that they came to circumcise the child; and they would have called him by the name of his father, Zacharias. His mother answered and said, "No; he shall be called John." But they said to her, "There is no one among your relatives who is called by this name." So they made signs to his father what he would have him called. And he asked for a writing tablet, and wrote, saying, "His name is John." So they all marveled. Immediately his mouth was opened and his tongue loosed, and he spoke, praising God. Then fear came on all who dwelt around them; and all these sayings were throughout all the hill country of Judea. And all those who heard them kept them in their hearts, saying, "What kind of child will this be?" And the hand of the Lord was with him."

Isn't it significant that Luke, who was living at the time of these events, would have obtained a firsthand report from those involved that is consistent with the other Gospels? Look at Luke's opening of his Gospel (Luke 1:1-4):

> Inasmuch as many have taken in hand to set in order a narrative of those things which have been fulfilled among us, just as those who from the beginning were eyewitnesses and ministers of the word delivered them to us, it seemed good to me also, having had perfect understanding of all things from the very first, to write to you an orderly account, most excellent Theophilus, that you may know the certainty of those things in which you were instructed.

Read the entire book of Luke, and you will find his writings to be consistent with the events of those days. He confirmed his writings with those who were there and had witnessed the events.

The Family Tree of Mary the Mother of Jesus

Another difference comes about in the genealogy of Mary. The Old Testament tells us that Jesus would come from the tribe of Judah, the seed of David. The Bible traces the family tree for Mary's family and for Joseph's.

Matthew 1:1-17 records the genealogy from Abraham down to Joseph. Jewish family trees followed the father's lineage. Luke 3:23:38 records the genealogy starting with Joseph back to Adam; however, Luke is really tracking the lineage of Mary, through her earthly ancestors. Both of these genealogies trace back through David, just as prophecies in the Old Testament promised that the Messiah would come from the tribe of Judah, the root of David. Micah 5:2 says, "But you, Bethlehem Ephrathah, though you are little among the thousands of Judah, yet out of you shall come forth to Me the One to be Ruler in Israel, Whose goings forth are from of old, from everlasting." This text speaks prophetically about the first coming of Jesus, when He was rejected by His people. It also refers to His second coming and future reign as the King of kings who will rule from Jerusalem during the millennium. Also, that verse tells of the Messiah as an eternal person. Look at what Revelation 5:5 states, referring to Jesus: "But one of the elders said to me, 'Do not weep. Behold the Lion of the tribe of Judah, the Root of David, has prevailed to open the scroll and to loose its seven seals."

Evidence is overwhelming throughout the Old Testament that Jesus the Messiah would come through the lineage of David, whose lineage is traced back through Jesse his father, through Judah, Jacob, Isaac, Abraham, and all the way back to Shem, who is one of the sons of Noah. Also, the Bible traces Noah's ancestry back to Adam. These family trees are no accident of Scripture but are important evidences linked to the prophecies of the Bible. God's Word doesn't leave us in the dark. The entrance of God's Word brings light.

An entire sura in the Qur'an is named for the Virgin Mary. How does the Qur'an relate the lineage of Mary the mother of Jesus (18b)? "At length she brought the (babe) to her people, carrying him (in her arms). They said: 'O Mary! truly an amazing thing hast thou brought! O sister of Aaron! Thy father was not a man of evil, nor thy mother a woman unchaste!'" (sura 19:27-28). This sura is declaring that Mary is a sister of Aaron, who was a brother of Moses. This declaration has both Muslims and non-Muslims very confused.

It is true that Miriam was the sister of Moses, and that Mary is the name for Miriam in the New Testament; however, the time from the days of Moses and Aaron to Mary the mother of Jesus covered approximately fifteen hundred years. Some Muslims, in an attempt to alleviate the confusion, teach that Miriam the sister of Aaron was kept inanimate (asleep or in a coma) until the time of Christ and became the mother of Jesus. This is further complicated when the Qur'an mentions Mary as the offspring of Imran (sura 3:35): "Behold! a woman of 'Imran said: 'O my Lord! I do dedicate unto Thee what is in my womb for Thy special service: So accept this of me: For Thou hearest and knowest all things.'"

('Imran is the Arabic form of the Hebrew Imram, who was the father of Moses, Aaron, and Miriam.)

Sura 66:12 says, "And Mary the daughter of 'Imran, who guarded her chastity; and We breathed into (her body) of Our spirit; and she testified to the truth of the words of her Lord and of His Revelations, and was one of the devout (servants)." In that sura Mary is called a daughter of Imran. It would appear that Muhammad must have had exposure to the biblical stories of Moses' sister Miriam, who would be called Maryam in Arabic, and the story of Mary, the mother of Jesus, who in Arabic would also be called Maryam.

Imram's ancestry is traced back to Levi, one of the twelve sons of Jacob (Israel). From the tribe of Levi came all the priests who served in the tabernacle in the wilderness and the temple in Jerusalem. God ordained that the Levites would have that responsibility, but He also ordained that Jesus would come from the tribe of Judah.

God, speaking to Abraham in Genesis 12:3, tells him that through him all the families of the earth would be blessed. He was speaking of the Messiah who would come, which was confirmed and fulfilled in Matthew 1:1, "The book of the genealogy of Jesus Christ, the son of David, the son of Abraham." This passage of Scripture is explicit that the human lineage of Jesus is from Abraham through David. Jesus was born of the Seed of the woman. This was first prophesied in Genesis 3:13-15:

> And the LORD God said to the woman [Eve], "What is this you have done?" The woman said, "The serpent deceived me, and I ate." <u>So the LORD God said to the serpent</u>: "Because you have done this, You are cursed more than all cattle, And more than every beast of the field; On your belly you shall go, And you shall eat dust All the days of your life. And I will put enmity Between you and the woman, And between your seed and <u>her Seed</u>; He shall bruise your head, And you shall bruise His heel."

"Her Seed" speaks about the Messiah, Jesus, who was to be born within the womb of the Virgin Mary, and that Seed would confront and defeat the evil forces in the spiritual warfare of the cross and of victory over death through the resurrection. Therefore the lineage of Mary and the holy Child from her womb would have to be from David, and that is what the genealogy in Matthew carefully portrays. How could Mary and the Christ child's lineage come through the house of Imram, whose lineage is from Levi, when it is prophesied to be through Judah?

According to the Qur'an, regarding the revelations that there should not be differences between the revelations in the Bible and in the Qur'an (sura 2:136): "Say ye: 'We believe in Allah, and the revelation given to us, and to Abraham, Isma'il, Isaac, Jacob, and the Tribes, and that given to Moses and Jesus, and that given to (all) prophets from their Lord: We make no difference between one and another of them: And we bow to Allah (in Islam)." But there are many!

Genesis 11:27 says Terah was Abraham's father, the Qur'an says Azar was Abraham's father (sura 6:74).

Exodus 2:5 says that Pharaoh's daughter adopted Moses, while the Qur'an says it was Pharaoh's wife (sura 28:8-9).

The Quran says Ishmael was to be sacrificed by his father Abraham rather than Isaac (sura 37:100-103). In the biblical record (Genesis 22:1-18), Abraham is told to go to the land of Moriah, a place that was mountainous; the Ka'aba in Mecca, where the Qur'an says Abraham built the altar to sacrifice Ishmael, is not. The Bible says the place where Abraham made the altar was later referred to as "In the Mount of the LORD it shall be provided." This undoubtedly referred to the Mount of the Lord, where Solomon's temple was located in Jerusalem. Notice also that the Angel of the Lord referred to Isaac as Abraham's only son, because God recognized Isaac as the only son of promise through whose lineage the Messiah would come (Genesis 17:18-21).

Additional Contradictions

Additional contradictions can be found by obtaining the reference materials that are listed at the end of this book. What I have shared is sufficient evidence to show there are meaningful differences and historical inaccuracies. How can the Qur'an and the Bible both be the truth? Can proven historical facts be changed? God doesn't change history. He sees that it is recorded in His Word and preserves it unchanged. Since the Bible is the Word of God and predates the Qur'an, it takes precedence. The history, geography, and the prophecy of the Bible have been tested for centuries by critics and will always survive their attacks because truth always prevails against false claims.

My desire in researching and presenting these writings is to be honest, for to be otherwise would be to deceive myself and others. God forbid that this would be the case.

What has been written will undoubtedly cause some readers to be deeply agitated because of what they have been previously taught, and they may find it difficult to put that aside and believe what has been presented. Some closed their minds before they began to read what has been written. Some will look at what has been presented, will ponder the material, and will realize that what the

Qur'an declares and what the Bible says are contradictory, and difficult choices will have to be made.

If the Qur'an and Islam are true, then my eternal destiny will be paradise, because the Qur'an says a Christian who follows the *Injil* is on the right path. If, however, you are following Islam, and if the Bible and Christ are the way, then you will be separated from the Creator God forever, and you will be a lost soul forever. You must choose. Whatever your choice, you are responsible before God for your decision. God doesn't ordain people to hell. The Scripture says, "The Lord is not slack concerning His promise, as some count slackness, but is longsuffering toward us, not willing that any should perish but that all should come to repentance" (2 Peter 3:9). The Lord waits longingly for you to repent of the sin of unbelief, to turn to Him, and to acknowledge Him as your Lord and Savior. His coming to earth, His life, His death, and His resurrection were for you. He loves you.

In closing, let these Scriptures speak to your God-given conscience and to the soul and spirit of your inner person, the real you. In 1 John 4:20-21, we read, "If someone says, 'I love God,' and hates his brother, he is a liar; for he who does not love his brother whom he has seen, how can he love God whom he has not seen? And this commandment we have from Him: that he who loves God must love his brother also." Further, 1 John 5:1 says, "Whoever believes that Jesus is the Christ is born of God, and everyone who loves Him who begot also loves him who is begotten of Him."

Do you have deep within you real joy and peace regardless of the circumstances of life? Or do you live in fear? Listen to what Jesus says in John 14:27: "Peace I leave with you; my peace I give to you; not as the world gives do I give to you. Let not your heart be troubled, neither let it be afraid."

His gift of peace is peace with Him that will last forever. The choice is yours. You decide.

Chapter 5

Christianity: An Overview of the Bible

In the family home in which I grew up with eleven other children, we had a special table in the breakfast nook where we ate most of our meals. That table was unique. My father had designed it and had built it with bench seats on three sides. It had a hinged, drop-down leaf on each side that was spring-loaded, and before setting the table the two leaves were snapped into place. When everyone was seated, my father would give thanks for the food, after which there was a scramble of passing the plates of food and the ensuing family tiffs over someone taking too much. But my father would make an end to these disputes quickly. His piercing look was usually enough. When the leaves were down, it made it easier to clean the floor around the table and benches after eating.

After the meal, we all had to listen carefully as my dad read, or asked someone to read, a portion of the Bible before we were released from the table. We had other things on our minds, like getting to the neighborhood ball field in the empty lot. If my dad thought we had other things on our mind and weren't listening to what was being read, he would stop abruptly and ask one of us, "What were the last words?" If you couldn't recall he would say rather sternly, "You weren't listening, were you?" My father loved God, loved us, and had a deep respect for the Bible.

What about that Bible? Is the holy Bible unique above all other books ever written? Even more importantly, is the Bible the inspired Word of the Creator God? Is it the only, final, absolute authority concerning faith? Is the Old Testament that we have today the same Bible Jesus referred to? Can we be assured that it has not been changed or corrupted?

If the answers to these questions are yes, then it is not a matter of intolerance of other faiths or being bigoted but our duty to share with others the importance of its revelations. If the answers to these questions are no, then we do not have to answer to the Bible's message and its mandates.

I don't know how many times, as I'm sitting across from a small group of inmates, that I have asked, "Where can we go for a source of truth?" Usually someone will get around to pointing at a Bible, or saying, "The Bible." I then ask them, "Why do we go to the Bible?" Often I'll get many different answers; some will say because it is the truth, or it says it is inspired by God. I'll say that other books claim to be inspired by God, but does that mean they are? Some will say it takes faith, but do you want to put your faith in something that may not be true? But eventually someone will say, "Because it's the Word of God." I'll ask, "How do you know it's the Word of God?" If a person hasn't given much thought to that question it's difficult to answer. It's then that I will say, "Would you like me to share with you why I believe the Bible is the Word of God?" Maybe these views will be of some help to you as well.

First, I am thankful to God for the centuries of work of Israel's scribes. The tribes of Israel were chosen by God to be an example to the nations through a relationship with God that would prove their love for Him by keeping His commandments. The scribes preserved the Hebrew Scriptures by means of a system of meticulously copying texts onto scrolls. Thoroughly trained scribes guaranteed their repetitive accuracy. Without this ordained method of preservation, there would be no authentic writings of the revelations from the Creator God.

Problems arose when the people of Israel, instead of being faithful, rebelled against God and His Word. They turned this special relationship into a legalistic religious system. When the Messiah finally appeared hundreds of years later, the religious leaders didn't recognize Him, because they were wrapped up in the traditions developed by their rabbis. In fact, when Jesus the Messiah came and they refused to accept Him, He told them to search the Scriptures (the Old Testament), because they thought they had eternal life, but eternal life involves Him: "You search the Scriptures, for in them you think you have eternal life; and these are they which testify of Me" (John 5:39).

For them to deny Jesus as the Messiah, the Son of God, was to miss eternal life. Jesus had confidence in the preserved Scriptures in use at that time. He evidently didn't think they had been corrupted or changed. If they had been corrupted or changed, they would have to have been changed before Jesus' day, because the Scriptures of Jesus' day were the same as those on the Dead Sea Scrolls found in the caves at Qumran.

Evidence of the scribes' careful work was brought to light when the Dead Sea Scrolls, dating back to 150 years before Christ's birth, were found in 1947. Some additional scrolls were found later in nearby caves. The scrolls were undoubtedly sealed in water pots and hidden to keep them from being destroyed by the Romans, who ruled Israel at that time. The scrolls probably were hidden before AD 70, when the Romans destroyed the temple in Jerusalem and exiled most of the Jews from their homeland. Those scrolls verify that the present-day Hebrew Scriptures are accurate reproductions. Portions of every book of the Old Testament, with the exception of the book of Esther, were discovered among the scrolls. Should we believe this preservation of age-old Scriptures is coincidental, or the hand of the sovereign God?

The discovery of those scrolls is significant in light of the current-day unfolding of the prophetic Scriptures involving Israel and the nations of the world. Much of what happened concerning the first coming of Jesus Christ about two thousand years ago, and what is happening in Israel today, was foretold in the Word of God hundreds of years before those prophetic events came to pass.

Another significant thing is the preservation of Jewish identity down through the ages, the promises to Israel and to the descendants of Ishmael that have come to pass, and the prophecies that will still come to pass. All are evidences of God's hand in all of these predictions.

Second, there is no question that the Scriptures are accurate when it comes to its history. The history of the surrounding Gentile nations and Israel is recorded in the Hebrew and the Greek Scriptures, written over fourteen hundred to fifteen hundred years by about forty different writers. The accounts never contradict one another historically or otherwise. Wouldn't that in itself be a human impossibility?

The Greek New Testament was written near the end of that period (around fifty to one hundred years after the birth of Christ) by Jewish apostles who were chosen by Jesus. For three and a half years, He ministered among the people and taught His apostles. They were eyewitnesses who recorded what the Holy Spirit brought to their remembrance of what they had observed and heard from Jesus during His earthly ministry. They witnessed His death, burial, resurrection, and ascension. Yet the apostles do not contradict each other or the Old Testament.

The Old and the New Testaments complement each other, even though there is a time span of four hundred years between the two. In fact, Jesus, speaking to His apostles, foretold when and how the New Testament would be written: "But the Helper, the Holy Spirit, whom the Father will send in My name, He will teach you all things, and bring to your remembrance all the things I have said to you" (John 14:26). For what purpose? So that they might record all of the important words and works of Jesus as the Way to the Father in heaven.

It has been reported that there are more than one thousand cross references within the Old and New Testament that are 100 percent internally consistent. Could such consistency be human in origin, especially considering the forty writers involved? Could this happen without a superior Intelligence? Could this possibly be divine inspiration? Answering yes to those questions is of the utmost importance!

Third, there is no question regarding the accuracy of geography in the Scriptures and the science of the Bible. For the last two hundred years or more, secular archaeologists and persons of various faiths have used the Scriptures to locate places for their diggings. Some of those digs have uncovered important historical biblical locations, such as the stable in Bethlehem, the synagogue in Capernaum, the apostle Peter's house in Capernaum, Jacob's well at Sychar, the pool of Siloam, and the tomb of Lazarus. Artifacts found in the digs in the Mideast consistently verify the accuracy of the geography and history of the Bible.

Touching on the science of the Bible, it becomes apparent that human wisdom at the time the Bible was written was not the same wisdom revealed in the Bible. The science of humans took some two thousand to three thousand years to catch up to the revealed Word of God.

Today we know that the ocean floors have deep valleys, tall mountains, and underground springs, but at the time of the recorded Scripture, and for thousands of years after, the general thinking was that the ocean floor was smooth and bowl-shaped. Also, people believed that the oceans were fed their waters by rivers and rain. But what does the Bible have to say about how the oceans were fed? How did King David know there were channels in the seas unless the Spirit of God revealed this to him: "Then the channels of the sea were seen, the foundations of the world were uncovered" (2 Samuel 22:16)?

When Job was questioned by God, one of the questions reveals that the sea has springs: "Have you entered the springs of the sea? Or have you walked in search of the depths?" (Job 38:16).

Jonah, while he was in the belly of the great fish, has this revealed to him: "I went down to the moorings of the mountains; the earth with its bars closed behind me forever" (Jonah 2:6).

How did Moses know about fountains of the deep unless he had this revealed to him by the Holy Spirit? "In the six hundredth year of Noah's life, in the second month, the seventeenth day of the month, on that day all the fountains of the great deep were broken up, and the windows of heaven were opened" (Genesis 7:11).

Solomon could write about the fountains only if he had received divine inspiration: "When He established the clouds above, when He strengthened the fountains of the deep" (Proverbs 8:28) (14b).

Fourth, the relevance and the specific, detailed accuracy of the prophetic messages concerning the Messiah, humankind, and the nations that are revealed in the Scriptures are of primary importance. These prophecies are not general statements of trends but predict specific details and the particular persons and peoples involved.

Biblical prophecy has been of great interest to me since I was a young lad and has convinced me that only a source of intelligence other than human could have inspired the Scriptures. It's in this area of Scripture that I would like to share with you in greater depth and give proof texts from the Scriptures. Proof texts are important when they are combined or compared with other proof texts, especially when the context surrounding the proof text is considered. Consider this portion of God's Word: "All Scripture is given by inspiration of God, and is profitable for doctrine, for reproof, for correction, for instruction in righteousness" (2 Timothy 3:16). All of the Bible is inspired by God. Therefore we can depend on its accuracy and the preservation of the Hebrew and Greek Scriptures. Jesus tells us that if we hear Him, we must hear His apostles as well: "He who hears you hears Me, he who rejects you rejects Me, and he who rejects Me rejects Him who sent Me" (Luke 10:16). If a valid translation of the Bible is truly the Word of God, then we cannot set it aside and ignore its teachings. Too much is at risk.

But at this point an overview of the Old Testament Scriptures will be helpful. Then we will look at the major prophetic events facing Israel and other nations of the world. Most important are the prophecies about the promised Messiah and His impact on humankind.

Overview of the Old Testament

God the divine Architect created the world and people within a specific time frame, including the making of Man (Adam) and Woman (Eve); the introduction of Lucifer (Satan), who deceives Adam and Eve leading to the fall of man; the fall, which brings the curse of sin and extreme wickedness arising among humankind and leads to Noah and the flood and its catastrophic effect on the earth; the population explosion after the flood, the ensuing wickedness, the confusion resulting from God's decision to give people different languages, and the dispersing of those language groups to various parts of the earth.

Abraham appears on the scene. God makes promises to Abraham for his son Ishmael and promises to and through Abraham's son Isaac. Those promises tell about the coming of a Messiah/Savior; Abraham's descendants Isaac, Jacob, and Joseph lead to the people of Israel going to Egypt and ultimately into oppression and bondage under the Egyptians for four hundred years. During these four hundred years, Israel's population grows to more than 1,500,000 people and is of great concern to the pharaohs of Egypt.

Moses appears to deliver Israel from Egypt to the promised land; however, after their miraculous deliverance, their unbelief means that they wander in the wilderness for forty years. After this Israel conquers the unredeemable people inhabiting the promised land; under God, judges rule the land, but Israel wants a king, as is the case among the nations surrounding them. This is an insult to God's leadership, but God gives them their desires and Saul is anointed as the first king of Israel, followed by David and David's son Solomon.

Solomon rules the kingdom of Israel with great wisdom and splendor, and after his death the kingdom is divided, with ten tribes located in the north and two tribes in the south. Many evil kings rule in the northern kingdom and some in the southern. Israel during its many spiritual and economic ups and downs is warned by the prophets; God sends the prophets to warn Israel to repent and turn back to God. Israel as a nation repeatedly disregards the warnings and kills some of the prophets. As a consequence, Israel is finally sent into captivity and is dispersed throughout the nations of the world, with only a remnant left in Israel. This closes the Old Testament Scriptures.

Then there are four hundred years of silence, from the last of the prophets sent by God until the birth of the promised Messiah. This overview covered about four thousand years of God's conditional and unconditional covenants with Israel and the Gentile nations of the world.

Expanding the Overview

The Bible opens with the book of Genesis, which reveals God's vocal expressions in the act of creation. "In the beginning God created the Heavens and the Earth." At that beginning God brought into existence space, matter, energy, time, and all the angelic beings. Then God called light to appear, and this ended the first day. In the next five days, the remainder of creation is accomplished in a sequence that many scientists agree is the only time frame and sequence that would sustain life.

When the Pentateuch, the first five books of the Bible, was written, how could Moses, who lived hundreds of years after the creation, devise and record this correct order of creation? Would the account not suggest that a divine Maestro orchestrated this process of creation and revealed its order to Moses?

Genesis tells us that God, in His orderly, well-designed creative process, made man in His image according to His likeness, thus enabling man to have fellowship with Him. We read in Genesis 1:26, "Then God said, 'Let Us make man in Our image, according to Our likeness; let them have dominion over the fish of the sea, over the birds of the air, and over the cattle, over all the earth and over every creeping thing that creeps on the earth.'" Notice this early revelation of "Us" and "Our," indicating a plurality within the creative process and God's placing man in the role of ruling over this superb creation.

If you read Genesis 3:22, you will discover that the Lord God said, after Adam and Eve ate of the tree of the knowledge of good and evil, "Man has become like one of Us, to know good and evil. And now lest he put out his hand and take of the tree of life, and eat, and live forever . . . " Though God knows good and evil, because God knows everything, it is impossible for God, due to His righteous character, to choose or do evil, but that was not so for Adam and Eve. They could choose evil when offered good or evil, because even though they were made in the image of God, they were not God. God knew this, and I believe that is the reason God wanted Adam and Eve to obey Him and not eat of the tree of the knowledge of good and evil. But because they disobeyed God, they were sinners and could live forever in that condition if they took fruit from the tree of life. Consider this: The tree was there to test man. If man wouldn't obey God, would that be a good relationship?

So to prevent this eternally sinful existence, God would have to expel man from the garden. Notice this expulsion is again an example of God's grace by sparing man from an endless existence of a degrading, sinful life, encountering all that the disabilities and disease of sin would bring without the possibility of restoration. The intimacy of the earlier relationship and fellowship that Adam and Eve had with God was now nonexistent due to the barrier of sin. God's holy character cannot tolerate a sinful relationship.

Some people wonder why God didn't prevent Adam and Eve from taking of the forbidden fruit and save all this misery, but that would mean man would have to be programmed without the attributes of God. Mankind would not have a choice or be a free agent. He would be a robot. Mankind needed to have the attributes of God to have a meaningful relationship with God that could be built on the principles of trust, loyalty, and love. That kind of relationship is essential for a person-to-person fellowship as well. You can't force people to love you. Try to do that and you will have nothing but strife. If people can't trust one another they will have a rocky relationship, and if there is no loyalty it is difficult to love others.

Being made in God's image and likeness gave us some of His attributes, such as speech, sight, taste, emotions, hearing, mobility, free will, and intellect, with the power to reason and make choices. However, God has all these attributes with perfection. Again, God did not make us robots. And because we are not robots and have the intellect and power to reason, man has been able to use those creative gifts to accumulate knowledge over the years, and use that knowledge to develop technology for good. This technology is so evident in society today. The flip side of this is that mankind can also be devious and do great evil with knowledge. Just look at the technology involved in weapons of war.

The difference between God's attributes and ours is that God uses His attributes for ultimate good. Because we have free will, we can choose to believe or not to believe God. A loving relationship with God cannot be obtained by force; it requires freedom of choice. God gives great latitude to man, within the realm of God's eternal purposes and plans.

Once God molded man in His image, we read, "God breathed into the nostrils of man the breath of life and man became a living soul" (Genesis 2:7). With this final act of initiating human life at this stage of creation, God rested, meaning He ceased from His creative work, and for man's sake God instituted the seventh day as the Sabbath or a day of rest, when people cease from their six days of daily routine.

Everything, except for Adam, was brought into existence through God's spoken Word. Then God exclaimed, "It is good, it is very good." Isn't it interesting that God didn't speak Adam into existence like everything else, but made his body from the soil of the earth, soil that had been previously created? The word for "dirt" is derived from the Hebrew word for Adam.

Isn't it also significant that our bodies, scientists say, contain the same chemicals found in the earth? Did this happen by chance? How could Moses have known this if God didn't relate it to him, the man God chose to reveal the first five books of the Old Testament? Would Moses concoct such a story that man was made from the dirt of the earth?

Adam and Eve were then placed in the Garden of Eden with all of their needs met through God's provision. It was in the Garden of Eden that Adam and Eve could have had a perfect existence, but they fell for the deceitfulness of the Serpent (Lucifer/Satan).

God had created Lucifer as a powerful spirit being high in the hierarchy of the heavenly hosts. Lucifer wasn't satisfied with worshiping and obeying God. Lucifer wanted to have the highest place in the throne room of heaven. He wanted the angels of the heavenly realm to bow down to him. This act of defiance toward God ended with Lucifer being cast out of God's holy sanctuary. Lucifer no longer had the right to be there. We read in Isaiah 14:12-15:

> How you are fallen from heaven,
> O Lucifer, son of the morning!
> How you are cut down to the ground,
> You who weakened the nations!
> For you have said in your heart:
> "I will ascend into heaven,
> I will exalt my throne above the stars of God;
> I will also sit on the mount of the congregation
> On the farthest sides of the north;
> I will ascend above the heights of the clouds,
> I will be like the Most High."
> Yet you shall be brought down to Sheol,
> To the lowest depths of the Pit.

Adam and Eve, rather than believe and obey God, listened to Satan. He tempted Eve by questioning whether God meant what He had said, and finally openly defying what God had told Eve: "but of the tree of the knowledge of good and evil you shall not eat, for in the day that you eat of it you shall surely die" (Genesis 2:17).

Adam and Eve disregarded God's warning, and through their disobedience sin entered the world. With that fall both spiritual and physical death were introduced into the annals of time. Once man had sinned, death was its consequence, and death is a constant daily reality to all humankind.

Death does not mean cessation of existence but separation from the prior state. The day Adam and Eve ate of the fruit of the forbidden tree they experienced immediate spiritual death; also, that prior intimate fellowship they had with God ceased. In addition, the process of physical death began, as they now had mortal bodies subject to corruption and disease, just as we all have today. Adam lived 930 years, but he did die.

Adam's sin also brought a curse on the cosmos. By disobeying God and obeying Satan, Adam lost his rule over the earth and came under the kingdom of darkness ruled by Satan and the fallen angels. Death came as a result of Adam's sin, and since all of mankind came from Adam, all of us are inheritors of the sin nature. Psalm 51:5 declares, "Behold, I was brought forth in iniquity, and in sin my mother conceived me."

At birth, a human already has a sin nature. If humans were born sinless after Adam, that means they would be perfect. Then why wouldn't some stay perfect? Everyone sins because each of us has a sin nature. We don't become sinners; we are sinners who can become addicted to sin. Often it is difficult for people to accept the fact they are sinners according to God's standards, and therefore they establish their own righteousness and standards apart from God, even denying there is a God.

God's Word in Psalm 14:1 says, "The fool has said in his heart, 'There is no God.' They are corrupt, they have done abominable works, there is none who does good." Romans 3:23 adds, "for all have sinned and fall short of the glory of God." God's perfect law is the Ten Commandments, and no one can keep those commandments. The breaking of one law proves imperfection; therefore, all are sinners and desperately need God's loving offer of peace and forgiveness.

How can we ever make amends for the multitude of our sins? By feeling sorry for all of our failed promises to do better, or by our feeble efforts to achieve righteousness on our own? God's Word specifically states that without the shedding of blood there is no forgiveness! In the Garden of Eden, God took the life of an animal to make a covering for naked Adam and Eve. That was the first blood sacrifice.

Even after being evicted from the garden, mankind went on, without fear of God, to murder and to increasing depths of evil, up to a point that God couldn't stand where man was heading and destroyed all life on earth with a flood. Only righteous Noah and his family were spared. Again, after the judgment waters of the flood, humankind went its own way rather than seek after God. People ignored God and became involved in building the Tower of Babel in the geographical area of Babylon, located in today's Iraq. They were one society of people with a common language trying to establish their own reputation. To prevent mankind from turning into a community of increasingly gross evil, God confused their language and dispersed the different language groups throughout the earth. All of this is related in the first eleven chapters of Genesis.

In Genesis 12, God visits Abram, and Abram is told to leave his home in Ur (in modern-day Iraq) of the Chaldeans and proceed to Canaan. Abram, later called Abraham, folded up his tents and took off for the promised land believing God would perform what He promised.

The Lord God (Yahweh-Elohim) made covenants and promises to Abraham. These promises would have not only immediate and long-range blessings but also future problems for him and his descendants. He would also be the father of many nations:

> When Abram was ninety-nine years old, the LORD appeared to Abram and said to him, "I am Almighty God; walk before Me and be blameless. And I will make My covenant between Me and you, and will multiply you exceedingly." Then Abram fell on his face, and God talked with him, saying: "As for Me, behold, My covenant is with you, and you shall be a father of many nations. No longer shall your name be called Abram, but your name shall be Abraham; for I have made you a father of many nations. I will make you exceedingly fruitful; and I will make nations of you, and kings shall come from you. And I will establish My covenant between Me and you and your descendants after you in their generations, for an everlasting covenant, to be God to you and your descendants after you. Also I give to you and your descendants after you the land in which you are a stranger, all the land of Canaan, as an everlasting possession; and I will be their God." (Genesis17:1-8)

We see much of this fulfilled today through Abraham's descendents: from Ishmael came twelve kings; from Jacob the twelve tribes of Israel; and from Esau the nation of Edom. Through Abraham's nephew Lot came the Moabites. All of these nations geographically surrounded the twelve tribes of Israel at that time, and it is evident their relatives still surround the epicenter, Jerusalem, wanting what was promised to Israel.

Throughout the Old Testament God challenged Israel, His chosen people, to have a faith-obedience relationship with Him, and as a result God would bless them mightily. Some of God's covenants were conditional they set out conditions that had to be met by Abraham and his descendants. Some were unconditional God promised He would fulfill them regardless of the faithfulness of Israel. The Hebrew Scriptures have to do primarily with the nation Israel, its people, and the prophesied coming of the Messiah.

God's covenant with Abraham and his wife Sarah was that they would have a son of promise, which was Isaac by a miraculous birth. Sarah was past childbearing age when she gave birth to Isaac. Later, Isaac married and had a son, Jacob, through whom the twelve tribes appear as part of God's program for Israel. Ishmael was not the son of promise, because he was not the son of Sarah and Abraham, to whom the promise was made, but the son of Abraham and Hagar, who was Sarah's Egyptian handmaid. Ishmael, however, would go on to be the father of many nations.

God's dealing further with Abram is related in Genesis 15:13-16, where we read, "Then He said to Abram: 'Know certainly that your descendants will be strangers in a land that is not theirs, and will serve them, and they will afflict them 400 years. And also the nation whom they serve I will judge; afterward they shall come out with great possessions. Now as for you, you shall go to your fathers in peace; you shall be buried at a good old age. But in the fourth generation they shall return here, for the iniquity of the Amorites is not yet complete.'" The resident Amorites of Canaan were very sinful, refusing to repent of their sin, not seeking the living God but worshiping idols. They finally reached such a degrading level of sin that it brought on God's judgment, resulting in their destruction.

God told Abraham that his descendents would be servants in a foreign land for four hundred years. But God would judge that foreign nation for its cruelty and oppression, and when Abraham's descendents left, they would do so with great possessions. This prophecy was fulfilled when Jacob and his family were spared the famine in Canaan by going to Egypt, where Jacob's son Joseph, through God's miraculous intervention, had been placed second in command to Pharaoh. Eventually Israel became slaves to the Egyptian pharaohs, and some four hundred years later the exodus took place after all the miracles and plagues performed by God through Moses and Aaron.

The last of the miraculous signs was the plague, slaying all of the firstborn in the households of those who did not provide the sacrificial lamb. Just killing the lamb was not sufficient. The blood of the lamb had to be applied to the lintel and the doorposts of the house. This required an act of faith. When the Lord saw the blood, He would pass over that household and the lives of the firstborn would be spared. This Passover is celebrated each year in most Jewish households, thus remembering the deliverance from the cruel bondage their ancestors experienced in Egypt.

After the miraculous deliverance through the Red Sea, Moses led the people toward Sinai, where the twelve spies were sent into the promised land. They came back with a negative report of giants in the land, except for Joshua and Caleb. Because they didn't believe that God was able to take care of the giants, Israel wandered through the wilderness for forty years, until all of the generation that came out of Egypt died in the wilderness. However, Joshua and Caleb were spared.

In their wanderings Israel came to Mount Sinai, where the Ten Commandments were given. Also, instructions were given to Moses for the building of the portable tabernacle. This tabernacle would confirm God's presence by leading Israel with a cloud by day and a pillar of fire by night. All through the wilderness wanderings in the Sinai, God was leading and providing for Israel, even with all of their complaining and rebellion. By the way, there were no shoe salesmen during the forty-year sojourn in the wilderness, because the Israelites' sandals never wore out. With the God of the Bible everything is possible.

After this purging in the wilderness, it was time for Israel to enter the promised land; however, because of two incidents of unbelief, Moses was not allowed to enter.

Joshua then took over as God's leader of the people. Under Joshua's leadership, the corrupt Canaanites were partially removed from the promised land. The land was then divided between the twelve tribes, but because Israel did not complete what God required of them to rid the land of their enemies they were harassed by those who were left . . . and are even today. This continued to cause Israel no end of problems, both spiritually and physically. Disobedience always has its consequences, as Judges 2:1-3 shows:

> Then the Angel of the LORD came up from Gilgal to Bochim, and said: "I led you up from Egypt and brought you to the land of which I swore to your fathers; and I said, "I will never break My covenant with you. And 'you shall make no covenant with the inhabitants of this land; you shall tear down their altars.' But you have not obeyed My voice. Why have you done this? Therefore I also said, 'I will not drive them out before you; but they shall be thorns in your side, and their gods shall be a snare to you."

Over time the people forget their covenant with God and served the idols of Baal, who was the god of the foreigners. God appointed judges in Israel who were to carry out justice among the people. Even with all their rebellion God called Israel His treasured possession. Disobeying His commandments turned many of the people to false gods and idolatry. God never intended for people's lives to be controlled by religious ritual and the worship of inanimate idols. Israel's cycles of idolatry and repentance brought on spiritual and economic ups and downs during this four-hundred- year period of the judges.

Near the end of these four hundred years, the people of Israel went to Samuel, the last judge and the first prophet. They wanted to be like the surrounding nations and have a king. This was in essence a rejection of Yahweh (Jehovah) as their King, especially after all God had done for them. The people said to Samuel:

> "Look, you are old, and your sons do not walk in your ways. Now make us a king to judge us like all the nations."
>
> But the thing displeased Samuel when they said, "Give us a king to judge us." So Samuel prayed to the LORD. And the LORD said to Samuel, "Heed the voice of the people in all that they say to you; for they have not rejected you, but they have rejected Me, that I should not reign over them. According to all the works which they have done since the day that I brought them up out of Egypt, even to this day—with which they have forsaken Me and served other gods—so they are doing to you also. Now therefore, heed their voice. However, you shall solemnly forewarn them, and show them the behavior of the king who will reign over them." (1 Samuel 8:5-9)

The people wanted Saul to be their first king, and Samuel anointed him as such, but Saul, through self-centered actions, disobeyed and displeased God. So, David was anointed to take Saul's place as the future king of Israel. King David reigned for forty years. David, through an intimate covenant relationship with God, established a powerful, flourishing kingdom.

All of this is being told because King David, of the tribe of Judah and ruling from the city of Jerusalem, began carrying out a major role in Hebrew history. This set the divine stage for the coming Messiah, the son of Abraham, the son of David to be born hundreds of years later in Bethlehem of Judea, as prophesied in Micah 5:2: "But you, Bethlehem Ephrathah, though you are little among the thousands of Judah, yet out of you shall come forth to Me the One to be Ruler in Israel, whose goings forth are from of old, from everlasting."

This verse refers to the prophesied first coming and the yet-to-be-fulfilled second coming of Christ Jesus, the Alpha and the Omega, who will ultimately be recognized as the King of kings and the Lord of lords. This Jesus, the son of David, was rejected at His first coming, but this will not be so at His second coming. Notice too this Scripture, besides being prophetic, tells that the One (Jesus) to be the coming ruler of Israel at His second appearance on earth is from old, from everlasting, or the eternal Jehovah.

King David, out of deep gratitude to the Lord, wanted to build a temple for God. However, God said a son of David would erect the temple. That son was Solomon, who built a marvelous temple that housed the ark of the covenant. This temple evidenced God's presence in the Holy of Holies, the room behind the veil that separated that Holy of Holies from the Holy Place.

Solomon as king started out well but finished poorly by setting up altars to the various idol gods worshiped by his many foreign wives. God had forbidden the marrying of foreign wives. God proposes what's best for us, and when we are disobedient we and others suffer the consequences.

After Solomon's death the nation of Israel was divided into a northern kingdom called Israel, made up of ten tribes whose capital was Samaria. A southern kingdom, called Judah, was comprised of two tribes, Judah and Benjamin, and its capital was Jerusalem. During this time of the reign of the kings, which was for 457 years, there appeared many prophets of the Lord. The prophets were inspired by the Holy Spirit with messages from God telling Israel's leaders and people to repent so they would be spared from harsh judgments. Israel generally ignored the prophets, disrespecting them and killing many of them. Several of the prophets' messages were related to events at that time, but other prophecies concerned Israel's future and the coming of the Messiah.

The Lord was very displeased with the sinful actions of the ten tribes of the north, and about 720 BC the Lord began the chastening process by sending them into exile at the hands of the Assyrians; from there they were dispersed. The dispersed were replaced with Gentile rulers in the northern kingdom. This is recorded in 2 Kings 17.

Judah had God-fearing kings, but some of them were evil, like most of those of the northern kingdom. In 586 BC, the king and people of Judah were taken captive by King Nebuchadnezzar and brought to Babylon. Seventy years later, in 516 BC, Cyrus the Great allowed many Jews to return to Jerusalem and provided them with the necessary materials to repair Solomon's temple and the falling walls of Jerusalem. This return was prophesied by Jeremiah: "For thus says the Lord: After seventy years are completed at Babylon, I will visit you and perform My good word toward you, and cause you to return to this place" (Jeremiah 29:10).

From this point on, Israel was under the control of the world powers of Babylon, Persia, Greece, and the Roman Empire in that succession, just as the prophets had said. For about four hundred years, until the birth of Jesus, God sent no prophets with messages to Israel. This four-hundred-year period is often referred to as the "silent years."

However, during these four hundred years of silence, the Hebrew Scriptures were translated into the Greek language, and that translation was called the Septuagint. During those four hundred years, and into the era of Christ and His disciples, Greek became the universal language, even though at that time the Romans controlled the Holy Land.

Historians have recorded that in AD 70, the temple in Jerusalem was destroyed. Not one stone was left on top of another, just as Jesus had prophesied: "Then as He went out of the temple, one of His disciples said to Him, 'Teacher, see what manner of stones and what buildings are here!' And Jesus answered and said to him, 'Do you see these great buildings? Not one stone shall be left upon another, that shall not be thrown down'" (Mark 13:1-2). After that time, the temple sacrifices ceased. Later the Jews were dispersed from the Holy Land by the Romans and forced to live in foreign lands for about eighteen hundred years.

In 1948, Israel was recognized as a nation by the United Nations, and the Jewish people begin returning in large numbers from the north (Russia) and other countries to their promised land. Currently, for the first time since the dispersion, there are more Jewish people in Israel than in any other country of the world. In spite of the way things are shaping up in the Middle East today (terrorism, anti-Israel sentiment from many nations around the world, chaos, and continued unrest), there will be a short period of peace brought about by a powerful, charismatic world leader. But there is more to come. Some perilous times are on the horizon.

God's prophetic Word tells us that in the last days the Jewish people will return to the promised land not believing that the Messiah had come. It will be different at the second coming of Christ, which will occur at the end of the seven-year period of the great tribulation. (This tribulation is referred to in the prophetic Old Testament Scriptures and in the New Testament book of Revelation.) During the last half of the seven-year period, there will be troublous times for Israel and the world. Those Israelis remaining in Israel at the end of the great tribulation will face the threat of a battle brewing in Armageddon. There will be armies of millions gathering there to annihilate Israel; Israel will and can be rescued only by the Messiah, who comes with power and great glory.

Israel will recognize the Messiah as the One whom they had pierced and who was hung on a cross. It is then that Israel will be saved and made secure in the land they were promised. Establishing His earthly kingdom, the Messiah Jesus will reign for one thousand years with Jerusalem as the world capital. From that city, the Messiah, who is the King of kings, will rightfully rule over all the nations.

A lot is happening in the world today to bring this about. These are perilous and chaotic times, especially in the Middle East, as we see events unfolding leading to the fulfillment of biblical prophecy.

What a history of God's chosen people! But there is more prophecy in Israel's future that must come to pass. Israel will be duped by a false messiah, who will really be Antichrist. Through his charisma and powerful rule over the leaders of the ten kingdoms of the world, he will control awesome military power that allows Israel to experience a short period of peace. This short time of peace is followed by the prophesied great tribulation that comes on Israel and the rest of the world.

Just open the book of Revelation to chapter 6 and read through chapter 19. The specific and graphic language describes the horrible events of that period. At the end of that tribulation period, Jesus, the Lord of lords, comes in power and great glory and destroys the nations that are amassing in the plains of Meggido with the intent to annihilate Israel. Jesus the Messiah comes to Israel's timely rescue. Those are some of the events written in the prophecies of the Old and New Testaments that surround the Messiah's second coming.

Significant Prophecies of the Old Testament

Now, let's look at some of the Old Testament and examine some of the fulfilled prophecies concerning the first coming of Jesus the Messiah.

It is important to remember that when a prophet makes a prediction (prophecy) and it doesn't come to pass, then that prophet is a false prophet, and the rest of that person's teaching or prophecies must be brought into question:

> "But the prophet who presumes to speak a word in My name, which I have not commanded him to speak, or who speaks in the name of other gods, that prophet shall die. And if you say in your heart, 'How shall we know the word which the LORD has not spoken?' when a prophet speaks in the name of the LORD, if the thing does not happen or come to pass, that

> is the thing which the LORD has not spoken; the prophet has spoken it presumptuously; you shall not be afraid of him." (Deuteronomy 18:20-22)

This is an important declaration and needs to be embraced, especially when you put this test to the many prophets of the past and present who have led many astray with false prophecies.

God's Word must be true in all aspects or it cannot be trusted at all. The prophecies concerning the first coming of the Messiah Jesus were all fulfilled with precise detail and accuracy. The prophecies in the Word of God are specific in their declaration and will always come to pass. It is because of this sure word of prophecy that we can depend on the other promises of God in His Word. Not the smallest detail will be overlooked.

It is reported that there are more than three hundred prophecies in the Hebrew Scriptures regarding the Messiah. ("Messiah" is translated "Christ" in the English New Testament.) More than one hundred of those prophecies were fulfilled through the first coming of Jesus the Christ. Remember when reading these prophecies that there is at least a minimum of four hundred years from the date prophesied to the fulfillment. Some of those one hundred prophecies are outlined as follows:

Prophecy in the Old Testament	Subject	Fulfillment in the New Testament
Micah 5:2, "But you, Bethlehem Ephrathah, though you are little among the thousands of Judah, yet out of you shall come forth to Me the One to be Ruler in Israel, whose goings forth are from of old, from everlasting."	the Messiah's birthplace	Matthew 2:1, "Now after Jesus was born in Bethlehem of Judea in the days of Herod the king"
Isaiah 7:14, "Therefore the Lord Himself will give you a sign: Behold, the virgin shall conceive and bear a Son, and shall call His name Immanuel." ("Immanuel" means God with us.")	the virgin birth of Messiah	Luke 1:26-31, "Now in the sixth month the angel Gabriel was sent by God to a city of Galilee named Nazareth, to a virgin betrothed to a man whose name was Joseph, of the house of David. The virgin's name was Mary. Then the angel said to her, 'Do not be afraid, Mary, for you have found favor with God. And behold, you will conceive in your womb and bring forth a Son, and shall call His name JESUS.'"

Prophecy in the Old Testament	Subject	Fulfillment in the New Testament
Isaiah 9:6, "For unto us a Child is born, unto us a Son is given; and the government will be upon His shoulder. And His name will be called Wonderful, Counselor, Mighty God, Everlasting Father, Prince of Peace."	Messiah's titles and His future coming to rule over Israel during the kingdom age	Luke 1:30-33, "Then the angel said to her, 'Do not be afraid, Mary, for you have found favor with God. And behold, you will conceive in your womb and bring forth a Son, and shall call His name JESUS. He will be great, and will be called the Son of the Highest; and the Lord God will give Him the throne of His father David. And He will reign over the house of Jacob forever, and of His kingdom there will be no end.'"
Isaiah 53:3, "He is despised and rejected by men, a Man of sorrows and acquainted with grief. And we hid, as it were, our faces from Him; He was despised, and we did not esteem Him."	Messiah would come and be rejected	John 1:11, "He came to His own, and His own did not receive Him." Luke 23:18, "And they all cried out at once, saying, 'Away with this Man, and release to us Barabbas.'"
Isaiah 53:8, "For He was cut off from the land of the living; for the transgressions of My people He was stricken." Daniel 9:26, "And after the sixty-two weeks Messiah shall be cut off, but not for Himself." Isaiah 53:12, "Because He poured out His soul unto death"	Messiah would be killed by the people of that day	Luke 23:33, "And when they had come to the place called Calvary, there they crucified Him, and the criminals, one on the right hand and the other on the left." John 19:30, "So when Jesus had received the sour wine, He said, 'It is finished!' And bowing His head, He gave up His spirit."
Psalm 45:6-7, "Your throne, O God, is forever and ever; a scepter of righteousness is the scepter of Your kingdom. You love righteousness and hate wickedness; Therefore God, Your God, has anointed You with the oil of gladness more than Your companions." Psalm 102:25-27, "Of old You laid the foundation of the earth, and the heavens are the work of Your hands. They will perish, but You will endure; yes, they will all grow old like a garment; like a cloak You will change them, and they will be changed. But You are the same, and Your years will have no end."	Messiah is anointed and eternal	Hebrews 1:8-12, "But to the Son He says: 'Your throne, O God, is forever and ever; a scepter of righteousness is the scepter of Your kingdom. You have loved righteousness and hated lawlessness; Therefore God, Your God, has anointed You with the oil of gladness more than Your companions.'" And: "You, Lord, in the beginning laid the foundation of the earth, and the heavens are the work of Your hands. They will perish, but You remain; and they will all grow old like a garment; like a cloak You will fold them up, and they will be changed. But You are the same, and Your years will not fail."

Prophecy in the Old Testament	Subject	Fulfillment in the New Testament
Genesis 3:15, "And I will put enmity between you and the woman, and between your seed and her Seed; He shall bruise your head, and you shall bruise His heel."	Messiah is born from the seed of a woman	Galatians 4:4, "But when the fullness of the time had come, God sent forth His Son, born of a woman, born under the law."
Genesis 49:10, "The scepter shall not depart from Judah, nor a lawgiver from between his feet, until Shiloh comes; and to Him shall be the obedience of the people."	Messiah descends from Judah	Luke 3:33, "the son of Amminadab, the son of Ram, the son of Hezron, the son of Perez, the son of Judah"
Isaiah 40:3-5, "The voice of one crying in the wilderness: 'Prepare the way of the Lord; Make straight in the desert A highway for our God. Every valley shall be exalted And every mountain and hill brought low; The crooked places shall be made straight And the rough places smooth; The glory of the Lord shall be revealed, And all flesh shall see it together; For the mouth of the Lord has spoken.'"	Messiah's way is prepared by John the Baptist. These two passages indicate Jesus is Lord, and therefore Jehovah, the Creator God.	Luke 3:3-6, "And he went into all the region around the Jordan, preaching a baptism of repentance for the remission of sins, as it is written in the book of the words of Isaiah the prophet, saying: 'The voice of one crying in the wilderness: 'Prepare the way of the Lord; Make His paths straight. Every valley shall be filled And every mountain and hill brought low; The crooked places shall be made straight And the rough ways smooth; And all flesh shall see the salvation of God.'"
Zechariah 9:9, "Rejoice greatly, O Daughter of Zion! Shout, Daughter of Jerusalem! See, your king comes to you, righteous and having salvation, gentle and riding on a donkey, on a colt, the foal of a donkey."	Messiah's triumphant entry into Jerusalem riding on a colt	Mark 11:7-11, "Then they brought the colt to Jesus and threw their clothes on it, and He sat on it. And many spread their clothes on the road, and others cut down leafy branches from the trees and spread them on the road. Then those who went before and those who followed cried out, saying: 'Hosanna!' Blessed is He who comes in the name of the Lord!' Blessed is the kingdom of our father David that comes in the name of the Lord! Hosanna in the highest!" And Jesus went into Jerusalem and into the temple. So when He had looked around at all things, as the hour was already late, He went out to Bethany with the twelve."

Prophecy in the Old Testament	Subject	Fulfillment in the New Testament
Zechariah 11:12, "Then I said to them, 'If it is agreeable to you, give me my wages; and if not, refrain.' So they weighed out for my wages thirty pieces of silver."	Messiah was betrayed for thirty pieces of silver	Mark 26:14-15, "Then one of the twelve, called Judas Iscariot, went to the chief priests and said, 'What are you willing to give me if I deliver Him to you?' And they counted out to him thirty pieces of silver."
Isaiah 50:6, "I gave My back to those who struck Me, and My cheeks to those who plucked out the beard; I did not hide My face from shame and spitting."	Messiah was spat upon and struck	Matthew 26:67, "Then they spat in His face and beat Him; and others struck Him with the palms of their hands."
Isaiah 53:5, "But He was wounded for our transgressions, He was bruised for our iniquities; the chastisement for our peace was upon Him, and by His stripes we are healed."	Messiah's death for others	Romans 5:6-8, "For when we were still without strength, in due time Christ died for the ungodly. For scarcely for a righteous man will one die; But God demonstrates His own love toward us, in that while we were still sinners, Christ died for us."
Isaiah 53:12, "Therefore I will divide Him a portion with the great, and He shall divide the spoil with the strong, because He poured out His soul unto death, and He was numbered with the transgressors, and He bore the sin of many, and made intercession for the transgressors."	Messiah is crucified between two transgressors	Mark 15:27-28, "With Him they also crucified two robbers, one on His right and the other on His left. So the Scripture was fulfilled which says, 'And He was numbered with the transgressors.'"
Zechariah 12:10, "And I will pour on the house of David and on the inhabitants of Jerusalem the Spirit of grace and supplication; then they will look on Me whom they pierced. Yes, they will mourn for Him as one mourns for his only son, and grieve for Him as one grieves for a firstborn."	Messiah's side is pierced	John 19:34, "But one of the soldiers pierced His side with a spear, and immediately blood and water came out."
Psalm 16:10, "For You will not leave my soul in Sheol, Nor will You allow Your Holy One to see corruption." Psalm 49:15, "But God will redeem my soul from the power of the grave, for He shall receive me."	Messiah would be resurrected	Mark 16:6-7, "But he said to them, 'Do not be alarmed. You seek Jesus of Nazareth, who was crucified. He is risen! He is not here. See the place where they laid Him But go, tell His disciples—and Peter—that He is going before you into Galilee; there you will see Him, as He said to you.'"

Prophecy in the Old Testament	Subject	Fulfillment in the New Testament
Psalm 68:18, "You have ascended on high, You have led captivity captive; You have received gifts among men, even from the rebellious, that the Lord God might dwell there."	Messiah would ascend to the right hand of God the Father	1 Corinthians 15:4, "and that He was buried, and that He rose again the third day according to the Scriptures" Mark 16:19, "So then, after the Lord had spoken to them, He was received up into heaven, and sat down at the right hand of God." Ephesians 4:8, "Therefore He says: 'When He ascended on high, He led captivity captive, and gave gifts to men.'"

How could man be the author of all these prophecies so precisely fulfilled hundreds of years later? What would be the mathematical odds that several different men writing these prophecies over a period of several hundred years could foretell their outcome several hundred of years into the future with such exact detail? These prophecies are not general statements of trends that some call prophecies, but very specific descriptions within time frames in which the events will come to pass. The Scriptures could only be inspired by God, and therefore Jesus was who He said He was: "And now, O Father, glorify Me together with yourself, with the glory which I had with You before the world was" (John 17:5). God's Word declares in 1 John 4:12-16:

> No one has seen God at any time. If we love one another, God abides in us, and His love has been perfected in us. By this we know that we abide in Him, and He in us, because He has given us of His Spirit. And we have seen and testify that the Father has sent the Son as Savior of the world. Whoever confesses that Jesus is the Son of God, God abides in him, and he in God. And we have known and believed the love that God has for us. God is love, and he who abides in love abides in God, and God in him.

In the Old Testament we see all the prophetic promises of the coming Messiah revealing Him as Yahweh (Jehovah) the eternal God.

Jesus' References to Scripture and Prophecy

The Messiah Jesus, sinless in nature, frequently referred to the Old Testament Scriptures:

> Then He said to them, "O foolish ones, and slow of heart to believe in all that the prophets have spoken! Ought not the Christ to have suffered these things and to enter into His glory?" And beginning at Moses and all the Prophets, He expounded to them in all the Scriptures the things concerning Himself. (Luke 24:25-27)
>
> Then He said to them, "These are the words which I spoke to you while I was still with you, that all things must be fulfilled which were written in the Law of Moses and the Prophets and the Psalms concerning Me." (Luke 24:44)

In Luke 4:16-21, Jesus visits a synagogue and reads from Isaiah 61:16:

> So He came to Nazareth, where He had been brought up. And as His custom was, He went into the synagogue on the Sabbath day, and stood up to read. And He was handed the book of the prophet Isaiah. And when He had opened the book, He found the place where it was written:
>
> > "The Spirit of the LORD is upon Me,
> > Because He has anointed Me
> > To preach the gospel to the poor;
> > He has sent Me to heal the brokenhearted,
> > To proclaim liberty to the captives
> > And recovery of sight to the blind,
> > To set at liberty those who are oppressed;
> > To proclaim the acceptable year of the LORD."
>
> Then He closed the book, and gave it back to the attendant and sat down. And the eyes of all who were in the synagogue were fixed on Him. And He began to say to them, "Today this Scripture is fulfilled in your hearing."

This portion of Scripture indicates that Jesus was reading from the Old Testament, and it had to be a correct manuscript from the original writings or Jesus would not have used it. There have been no changes to the Hebrew Old Testament since that day Jesus read from it. For Jesus to have read from an altered or corrupted text would have been a violation of His sinless character. None of the so-called Christian religions or Islam would refute the sinless nature of Jesus, but they uphold that teaching.

Note Jesus speaking in John 5:39: "You search the Scriptures, for in them you think you have eternal life; and these are they which testify of Me." And in Matthew 5:18, He says, "For assuredly, I say to you, till heaven and earth pass away, one jot or one tittle will by no means pass from the law till all is fulfilled."

Future prophecies will be fulfilled, because Jesus said they would. Notice, for example, Deuteronomy 9:10: "Then the Lord delivered to me [Moses] two tablets of stone written with the finger of God, and on them were all the words which the Lord had spoken to you on the mountain from the midst of the fire in the day of the assembly."

God's words to Moses and Israel are not lost or without purpose: "Jesus answered and said to them, 'You are mistaken, not knowing the Scriptures nor the power of God'" (Matthew 22:29). Jesus is saying that if you don't know the Scriptures, how will you know God's power in all of its aspects?

It's important to understand that all other prophets were sinners. Only Jesus was perfect in all aspects of His person. Only God is perfect and cannot sin. Muhammad even admitted in the Qur'an that he was sinful. Muhammad and the prophets were born of the seed of a man and a woman, while Jesus was born of the Seed of the virgin Mary. This Seed was fertilized by the unlimited power and the Word of the Holy Spirit. Jesus was sinless in His humanity, and because He was the only begotten Son of God, He was sinless in His everyday life on earth.

Not one person can claim to be righteous or sinless: not Charles Taze Russell, not Joseph Smith, not Muhammad. Only Jesus is sinless and righteous. Doesn't that alone make Him unique? All have died, and only Jesus arose from the dead, is alive today, and is seated at the right hand of the Father in heaven.

God will *never* go against His principles, nor does He change truth, because He is truth, and His truth is eternal; therefore He could only speak the truth. He would never reveal untruths. He couldn't. He would never disobey His laws, because His righteousness and justice would never permit it. Doesn't that sound like Jesus? To be otherwise would defile His character. He would not be sinless and therefore could not be depended on. His promises could not be trusted.

Jesus was who He said He was: the Son of Man and the Son of God. His twelve apostles, all the disciples of Jesus' day, and millions on millions of people since that time have found Him to be all that the Bible says He is. He is our Lord and Savior who will come again. It may be sooner than you think! Dear friend, be ready for His coming. To not do so is to not believe the offer and the warning of God's Word. Continued unbelief is the unpardonable sin.

New Testament Overview

It becomes apparent, as you go through the opening four books of the New Testament, the Gospels, that they tell of Jesus' birth, His ministry (primarily to Israel), His miracles, His death, and His resurrection. After His resurrection, He ministered to his apostles and disciples. The Gospels end with the commission to Jesus' disciples to carry the message of Good News to the ends of the earth, to every person.

The Gospels are followed by the book of Acts, which tells of Jesus' last days on earth before ascending into the clouds of heaven, which was observed by His apostles. Before His ascension, Jesus tells His disciples to expect the coming of the Holy Spirit as He had promised. This would happen on the day of Pentecost. (This was a Jewish holy day and part of the Feast of Weeks.) We read about Pentecost in the early chapters of the Acts of the Apostles.

At Pentecost, the apostles not only receive evidence of the coming of the Holy Spirit but also are indwelled by Him. They are at that time empowered to carry on the task of proclaiming the gospel to the Jews first, in and around Jerusalem; then Judea and Samaria; and then to the uttermost ends of the earth. When you think about it, this did happen.

During Pentecost, many Jews, literally thousands, repented of their past traditions and religious ritual to accept Jesus as the Messiah and the rightful heir to the throne of David. However, the religious leaders and most of the nation of Israel rejected Jesus as the Messiah, and that continues today. However, a remnant of Jews currently recognizes Jesus as their Messiah.

When you go through the Acts of the Apostles, Saul appears on the scene as a persecutor of the church, but you will also read of his conversion and his calling to be an apostle to the Gentiles. But he became the apostle to the Gentiles only after reaching out to the Jews first. They turn deaf ears to the gospel of the grace of God, and since the Jews refuse to hear and repent, Paul turns to the Gentiles. The Gentiles, who are all the other people who are not Jews, listen and believe.

Let's elaborate a bit on this unique apostle, who was the great evangelist to his world and a pastor to the early churches. Before his conversion to become a Christian, Saul, who later became the apostle Paul, was authorized by the high priest and the elders in Jerusalem to go to Damascus and bring Christians back to Jerusalem as prisoners. During this trip, a bright light beamed down out of the heavens and stopped Saul in his tracks. I am sure he was frightened, especially when a voice from heaven cried out, "Saul, Saul, why are you persecuting me?" We read about this encounter in Acts 22:4-10:

> "I persecuted this Way to the death, binding and delivering into prisons both men and women, as also the high priest bears me witness, and all the council of the elders, from whom I also received letters to the brethren, and went to Damascus to bring in chains even those who were there to Jerusalem to be punished.
>
> "Now it happened, as I journeyed and came near Damascus at about noon, suddenly a great light from heaven shone around me. And I fell to the ground and heard a voice saying to me, 'Saul, Saul, why are you persecuting Me?' So I answered, 'Who are You, Lord?' And He said to me, 'I am Jesus of Nazareth, whom you are persecuting.'
>
> "And those who were with me indeed saw the light and were afraid, but they did not hear the voice of Him who spoke to me. So I said, 'What shall I do, Lord?' And the Lord said to me, 'Arise and go into Damascus, and there you will be told all things which are appointed for you to do.'"

When Jesus said Saul was persecuting Him, what was He talking about? The only conclusion you can come to is that Saul was persecuting Christians, who were members of the body of Christ, which is His church. All born-again believers are members of that body with Christ as the head. It is this oneness that makes such a unique relationship with Jesus Christ. It is so intimate that Jesus can feel the persecution of the members of His body. Didn't Jesus say, "I will build my church, and the gates of hell shall not prevail against it"? It is His church, and Saul, called to be an apostle to the Gentiles, was to play a major role as an ambassador in the building of Christ's church.

Although Paul was called to be an apostle to those who were not Jews, his first outreach was to those of his own people, the Jews. Paul confirms this order of outreach in Acts 1:16: "For I am not ashamed of the gospel of Christ, for it is the power of God to salvation for everyone who believes, for the Jew first and also for the Greek." Paul had a deep compassion for his countrymen, but when the Jews continued to reject the message of Jesus the Messiah, he turned his ministry to those outside of the Jewish religion.

Even today, as was prophesied, the Jewish people are returning to Israel, and, as predicted, are still rejecting Jesus as their Messiah. There will come a day when the nation of Israel will recognize and accept Jesus the Messiah, but only after great persecution and tribulation. The way things are happening in the Middle East today, it seems to be rapidly setting the prophetic stage for all of those still-to-be-fulfilled events found in the Bible. Only God knows the timing.

Here's an indication of coming events for Israel. The Bible says in Zechariah 1:14-18:

> So the angel who was speaking with me said to me, "Proclaim, saying, 'Thus says the LORD of hosts:
>
> > "I am exceedingly jealous for Jerusalem and Zion.
> > But I am very angry with the nations who are at ease;
> > for while I was only a little angry,
> > they furthered the disaster."
>
> Therefore thus says the LORD:
>
> > "I will return to Jerusalem with compassion;
> > My house will be built in it,"
> > declares the LORD of hosts,
> > 'and a measuring line will be stretched over Jerusalem.'
>
> Again, proclaim, saying, 'Thus says the LORD of hosts:
>
> > "My cities will again overflow with prosperity,
> > and the LORD will again comfort Zion
> > and again choose Jerusalem."'"

Joel Rosenberg writes, "This is good news. The God of Israel will neither sleep nor slumber. He is jealous for Jerusalem. He will defend His country, His city, and His people. But He expects us to do our part. And He promises in Genesis 12:1-3 that if we bless Israel, He will bless us" (75). In another web letter, Rosenberg writes:

> As I describe in my non-fiction book, *Epicenter*, Bible prophecies in the Old and New Testaments indicate that in the End Times, a Third Temple will be built on the Temple Mount in Jerusalem, the site where the First and Second Temples once stood. Skeptics and cynics have long dismissed such prophecies. Military officials, moreover, have long argued that a Jewish effort to build a new temple could unleash the fury of 1.3 billion Muslims and trigger an apocalyptic war in the epicenter.
>
> But a new poll in Israel finds a stunning 64% percent of Israelis—including 47% of secular Israelis—want to see the Third Temple built.
>
> The Hebrew Prophet Isaiah writes, "It will come about in the last days that the mountain of the house of the Lord will be established as the chief of mountains" and that "the nations will stream to it." (Isaiah 2:2)
>
> In Daniel 9:26-27, we read: "The Messiah will be cut off and have nothing, and `the people of the prince who is to come [the Anti-Christ] will destroy the city [Jerusalem] and the sanctuary [the Second Temple].... Even to the end [of days] there will be war; desolations are determined. And he [the Anti-Christ] will make a firm covenant with the many for seven years, but in the middle of that week, he will put a stop to sacrifice and grain offering [in a rebuilt End of Days Temple] and on the wing of abominations will come one who makes desolate."
>
> The Book of Revelation also confirms that a fully functional and operational Temple will be in place when the coming Tribulation begins (see Revelation 11).
>
> Jewish groups in Israel are already producing architectural plans to build the Third Temple, and making other preparations as well.
>
> It will happen for God's Word will never fall short in what is predicted. (82)

Continuing on, the Acts are followed by an inspired letter (epistle) to the Romans from Paul conveying the important message of justification by faith. Romans is followed by several Pauline letters to the churches telling of all that

Christians have in Christ but also admonishing Christians to walk the life of the faith. Paul's letters end with the letter to Philemon.

Next is the letter to the Hebrews, which opens with the glorious attributes of the Son of God and describes the high priestly office of Christ. Hebrews points out that the Old Covenant of the law was insufficient to bring about righteousness, while the New Covenant, through the once-for-all sacrifice of Jesus the Christ, is sufficient for all who are willing to accept Jesus by faith. These people are then considered righteous and are saved.

Then is a short epistle by James that conveys the message that just knowing about Jesus (I call it intellectual faith) will never bring godly works. We need the real faith that comes by accepting Christ Jesus as Lord and Savior and committing our life to Him. This will produce godly works through us, because the Holy Spirit will work in us, revealing and urging us to allow Christ to live His life in us. We have this new nature within us when we are born again: "I am crucified with Christ, never the less I live, yet not I but Christ lives in me, and the life I now live I live by the faith of the Son of God who loved me and gave Himself for me" (Galatians 2:20).

After James come two letters from the apostle Peter. The first letter is addressed specifically to the Jews, who had been dispersed to various regions of the world; Peter reminds them of all that they have as the elect of God. He tells them how to live before God and those in the world. He also talks about the suffering we go through and how to handle it. He gives words of encouragement to those who are elders or pastors in the church and tells them how to care for their charge as shepherds of the flock of God. It was Peter who was told by Jesus told to feed His lambs and care for His sheep:

> So when they had eaten breakfast, Jesus said to Simon Peter, "Simon, son of Jonah, do you love Me more than these?"
>
> He said to Him, "Yes, Lord; You know that I love You."
>
> He said to him, "Feed My lambs."
>
> He said to him again a second time, "Simon, son of Jonah, do you love Me?"
>
> He said to Him, "Yes, Lord; You know that I love You."
>
> He said to him, "Tend My sheep."
>
> He said to him the third time, "Simon, son of Jonah, do you love Me?" Peter was grieved because He said to him the third time, "Do you love Me?"
>
> And he said to Him, "Lord, You know all things; You know that I love You."

Jesus said to him, "Feed My sheep." (John 21:15-17)

The second letter from Peter tells about the false teachers who will confront the beloved of God. Peter encourages believers to not give up in the face of adversity, for a day of judgment is coming to spell the doom of those who ignore God's Word and teach false doctrines.

Peter's letters are followed by the writings from the apostle John, who experienced the love shown by Jesus to him. John's first letter relates the importance of abiding in Christ so that believers are able to continue in an intimate fellowship with Him. They are to keep that fellowship unhindered by confessing their sins and turning away from sin.

Here we find the great doctrine that God is love and we are to emulate that love of God. Indwelling every true believer is that love, power, and presence of the Spirit of Christ, which can be released or restrained. John also reminds believers to discern between the Spirit of truth and the spirit of error. He ends the letter by reminding us who believe in the name of the Son of God that this book was written so that we may know that we have eternal life. Isn't that assuring and comforting to know?

Following the first letter are the second and third letters of John. Those letters urge believers to obey Christ's commandments and beware of deceivers who are really Antichrist. Also, Christians are to imitate what is good, and not what is evil.

The next letter is from Jude, which is a short but powerful message that urges believers to contend for the faith and to watch out for those apostates who speak evil of what they do not comprehend. Those apostates do not listen to the Spirit of truth.

The New Testament closes with The Revelation of Jesus Christ, and this book primarily describes the events of the last days before the second coming of Jesus Christ. In Revelation, we find the prophetic pieces falling in line with the prophecies found in the books of the Old Testament. It is interesting that Genesis, the first book of the Bible, reveals Adam and Eve ousted from the paradise of Eden, and the last book, Revelation, reveals the restoration of paradise within the new heavens and the new earth, in which dwells righteousness.

That gave a brief overview of the New Testament. Now we will take a look at Christianity following the outline that was utilized for Jehovah's Witnesses, Mormonism, and Islam.

Chapter 6

Christianity: Its Source Document and Its Beliefs

In previous chapters, we surveyed the source documents and beliefs of Jehovah's Witnesses, Mormonism, and Islam. After reading an overview of the accounts of the Bible (chapter 5 in this book), we're ready to study the Bible as the source document of Christianity and to learn more about Christian beliefs.

The Bible

The Bible is the only source document of true Christianity. Even though there have been thousands of helpful books written by Christian scholars based on the Bible, the final authority for Christians is the Bible.

It has been my observation that when humans attempt to rewrite the Scriptures, add to them, subtract from them, or develop religious ritual and traditions that are inconsistent with the Bible, it opens the door to non-truths in these people's overall teaching. When an untruth is taught, more untruths have to be taught in an attempt to validate the first untruth. Those teachings lead people away from the truth found in the Word of God.

There are plenty of reasons given in the other sections of this book that would give credence to the Bible being the Word of the Creator God. The hundreds of prophetic revelations in the Bible, and that they have been fulfilled, should be enough to indicate that people could not have been the Bible's inspiration. The Bible had to be inspired by a higher Power. To Christians, that higher Power is the living Creator God. There is no possibility that man was the inspiration for the Bible. About forty writers wrote over fourteen hundred to fifteen hundred years and did not disagree with each other, but to the contrary, complemented each others' writings. These facts show that people could not have inspired the Bible. Only God would have been able to inspire the writers of Scripture, and that's why it is called the Word of God. The writer of Ecclesiastes 3:14 has some important inspired input: "I know that whatever God does, it shall be forever. Nothing can be added to it, and nothing taken from it. God does it, that men should fear before Him." This pertains particularly to His Word. Isaiah 40:8 adds, "The grass withers, the flower fades, but the word of our God stands forever."

When Jesus explains to His apostles that he will go back to His Father in heaven, He also tells them that the Holy Spirit will be with them and indwell them: "But the Helper, the Holy Spirit, whom the Father will send in My name, He will teach you all things, and bring to your remembrance all things that I said to you" (John 14:26). This is spoken to His chosen disciples, who were the apostles, and not to self-appointed apostles of later dates. So when John, who was the last apostle to be alive, wrote the last book of the Bible, Revelation, the writing of the Bible was concluded. The Bible was complete. Revelation 22 finishes with this warning: "For I testify to everyone who hears the words of the prophecy of this book: If anyone adds to these things, God will add to him the plagues that are written in this book; and if anyone takes away from the words of the book of this prophecy, God shall take away his part from the Book of Life, from the holy city, and from the things which are written in this book" (Revelation 22:18-19).

I shudder to think of what will happen to those who have changed or added to the Bible. It tells us of the dire consequences for disregarding the warning in the above verses, but unless you read the plagues outlined in Revelation you don't get the full picture. I have, and it will be awful, but worse than all of that is to be separated from God for all eternity in an existence of torment and remorse.

If we are intellectually honest, we must observe that the source documents of the other religions show internal inconsistency, have problems with contradictions, historical and prophetic inaccuracies, and retractions of or changes in what was previously written and originally considered divine revelation. Do you believe God would be the inspiration of such confusion, and is He so changeable?

Beliefs of Christianity

Creation

The Bible is specific pertaining to the time frame and the inclusiveness of all that was created. Before we turn to the book of Genesis to observe the order of creation, I would like to draw your attention to three verses in the New Testament: "In the beginning was the Word, and the Word was with God, and the Word was God. He was in the beginning with God. All things were made through Him, and without Him nothing was made that was made" (John 1:1-3).

There are some profound statements made in those three verses that at first glance seem to be difficult to comprehend; for instance, the Word was with God, and the Word was also God. Also the Word, who was God, was there from the beginning, and all things were created through Him. This will clear up as we unfold the creation acts and who is involved.

We can accept what the Bible says about creation or we can reject it, but we have no right to change what it says. So when it says in the beginning God created everything and rested from His creation, it means He created within a certain specific period time, space, energy, and matter, and everything in the universe today was part of that creation.

For centuries, there have been people who have theories regarding how everything came into existence. People have struggled, within their limited knowledge, to convince themselves that their hypotheses are scientific fact. The problem with their hypotheses is that the people were not there when creation happened, and they cannot duplicate creation, but whoever was there certainly should know how things were created.

I rather think that the revelation of creation in the book of Genesis came from the Creator God. Accepting this story of creation does require faith that is based on reliable history, accurate geography, and the sure word of prophecy. The mathematical odds and the laws of probabilities are so incredible that they put those fulfilled prophecies outside of human inspiration and wisdom. I believe God revealed just enough about creation in His Word so that humankind would have sufficient information to explain His and our existence but still would require faith, for Hebrews 11:6 declares, "But without faith it is impossible to please Him."

This would indicate that faith is the essential foundation for pleasing God. Believing what God says is very important to God. Not to do so is to make out God to be a liar. That's why true Christianity cannot accept evolution as the process for creation. It is contradictory to the explanation and time frame for creation in the Word of God.

There are Christians who subscribe to the "big bang" theory and a universe evolving over billions of years, but you have to use hypothetical expanded ages for the creation days in the book of Genesis to believe that. If you believe in the "big bang" concept, then you accept as fact that the dating of fossils to be millions of years ago would indicate that death was on the scene before Adam's time.

The Bible teaches that the curse of death came as a result of Adam's sin. Evolutionists holding to the "big bang" theory state that people could not have been around at the time of the fossils and the dinosaurs. According to them, there would have to be a separation of millions of years between the dinosaurs and the evolution of man. However, if you accept the flood of Noah's day with all of the cataclysmic events and unfathomable tons of water pressure over the face of the earth as the means for all the fossils' existence, then the Bible's creation record makes sense. The earth would be roughly six thousand years old, and the population numbers of today are mathematically understandable. If the universe evolved over billions of years before man came into existence and man has been around for a million years, as evolutionists claim, the population on earth today would be impossible.

There are scientists today, who are Christians, who accept the "old earth" theory of evolutionists that the universe has been evolving for 13 billion years, and some of these scientists agree that humankind has been in existence for 100,000 years. This means they accept the concept that death occurred prior to the time of the Garden of Eden. But Scripture records that death came into the world as a result of Adam disobeying God's command. Listen to what Jesus had to say to the Pharisees: "From the beginning of the creation, God 'made them male and female'" (Mark 10:6). Jesus says that Adam and Eve were there at the beginning of creation, not billions of years later.

Let's not forget that evolution is a hypothesis or conjecture and cannot be established as fact. Evolution takes a lot of faith to accept that which evolutionists cannot prove. The sad fact is that humanists promote evolution as a proven science in schools and universities and in television programs. They have no laboratory proof, so how can evolution be called provable science? It is only theory. The carbon dating and half-life formulas are based on theories that the timing of atoms of matter changing into atoms of another form of matter is always consistent over time, particularly when it comes to rock formation.

Couldn't there possibly be a short time in the fossil process due to outside intervention like the cataclysmic events and the pressures of the flood at Noah's time? In any event, the scientists were not there when matter and time came into existence, so how can they be positive about that dating process to determine the age of the universe? If the Bible is true, then their theories are just that: they are theories. The theories are not provable, and the Bible's explanation of creation is more plausible than that of the evolutionists, because God was there.

Whether people like to admit it or not, evolution is a religion, because it requires faith in an unorganized evolving of extraordinary complex structures by chance that also had to include a life force. Evolutionists believe all of this happened without any influence from a superior planner, who has the unique intelligence and power to bring about the first cause and the orderly design of such complex systems and structures. Believing this requires enormous faith. Do you really believe that out of chaos comes all the precision and order of the universe?

Look at the devastation and disorder brought about by an earthquake or a tsunami. Does it all come back into place without planning and orderly reconstruction by intelligent efforts? Is it even probable that the precise orbiting of all objects in the universe came into existence from a chaotic beginning such as the "big bang" hypothesis proposes? It truly is unproven conjecture that cannot be repeated in a laboratory.

There is a joke that a scientist challenged God that under the right laboratory conditions he could duplicate man out of soil. God said, "Go ahead. I would like to see this. Take as much time as needed. I can wait." So the scientist gathered up what he considered was the proper soil and was beginning to set up what he thought were the proper laboratory conditions when God interrupted him and told him to get his own dirt.

In Geneva, Switzerland, final stages of the world's most powerful particle accelerator are being completed at the Cern Center by the nations of the European Union. The purpose of this superaccelerator is to splinter atoms that will collide and will duplicate what happened nanoseconds after the big bang that supposedly was the beginning of the evolving universe and ultimately life.

It's interesting that the scientists involved have already determined that this project will be "the laboratory experiment" that will prove the big bang theory of how the universe came into existence. This theory, or better yet it should be described as a hypothesis, declares there was an extremely high compacted energy density from which the universe evolved by a sudden explosive expansion and simultaneous cooling. Will this experiment create another universe? If not, how does that experiment without duplicating the universe prove creation? Also, they are not starting with their own dirt!

This future experiment is a good example of theory based on presuppositions that will then be declared a fact of science. The reason this will be only a hypothesis is that human wisdom is always flawed and comes up short, especially when it disagrees with God's revelation of creation described in the opening book of the Bible. "In the beginning God created the heavens and the earth." In any event, where did the "high-energy density" come from to accommodate the big bang theory? Did it appear by chance?

There is good that comes out of scientific study, but when the results of those discoveries are distorted as evidence of how matter came into existence, it is presupposition and conjecture. It is a matter of stating as truth something that is substituted for reality. That is a practice Satan (the serpent) has been using since the beginning of time. It is my opinion that the theory of evolution that is being taught in the schools of America is a main reason for the problems of society today. If you are being taught the survival of the fittest without being accountable to a Creator God, then anything goes; God is not God, and we don't have to answer to Him. We set our own rules. To atheists, evolution is their way of attempting to explain the universe and life. What is biblical creation? What does the Genesis account have to say about the order of creation?

It is important to grasp the teaching of the early chapters of Genesis. Let's look at Genesis 1:1-31:

> In the beginning God created the heavens and the earth. The earth was without form, and void; and darkness was on the face of the deep. And the Spirit of God was hovering over the face of the waters.
>
> Then God said, "Let there be light"; and there was light. And God saw the light, that it was good; and God divided the light from the darkness. God called the light Day, and the darkness He called Night. So the evening and the morning were the first day.
>
> Then God said, "Let there be a firmament in the midst of the waters, and let it divide the waters from the waters." Thus God made the firmament, and divided the waters which were under the firmament from the waters which were above the firmament; and it was so. And God called the firmament Heaven. So the evening and the morning were the second day.

Then God said, "Let the waters under the heavens be gathered together into one place, and let the dry land appear"; and it was so. And God called the dry land Earth, and the gathering together of the waters He called Seas. And God saw that it was good.

Then God said, "Let the earth bring forth grass, the herb that yields seed, and the fruit tree that yields fruit according to its kind, whose seed is in itself, on the earth"; and it was so. And the earth brought forth grass, the herb that yields seed according to its kind, and the tree that yields fruit, whose seed is in itself according to its kind. And God saw that it was good. So the evening and the morning were the third day.

Then God said, "Let there be lights in the firmament of the heavens to divide the day from the night; and let them be for signs and seasons, and for days and years; and let them be for lights in the firmament of the heavens to give light on the earth"; and it was so. Then God made two great lights: the greater light to rule the day, and the lesser light to rule the night. He made the stars also. God set them in the firmament of the heavens to give light on the earth, and to rule over the day and over the night, and to divide the light from the darkness. And God saw that it was good. So the evening and the morning were the fourth day.

Then God said, "Let the waters abound with an abundance of living creatures, and let birds fly above the earth across the face of the firmament of the heavens." So God created great sea creatures and every living thing that moves, with which the waters abounded, according to their kind, and every winged bird according to its kind. And God saw that it was good. And God blessed them, saying, "Be fruitful and multiply, and fill the waters in the seas, and let birds multiply on the earth." So the evening and the morning were the fifth day.

Then God said, "Let the earth bring forth the living creature according to its kind: cattle and creeping thing and beast of the earth, each according to its kind"; and it was so. And God made the beast of the earth according to its kind, cattle according to its kind, and everything that creeps on the earth according to its kind. And God saw that it was good.

> Then God said, "Let Us make man in Our image, according to Our likeness; let them have dominion over the fish of the sea, over the birds of the air, and over the cattle, over all the earth and over every creeping thing that creeps on the earth." So God created man in His own image; in the image of God He created him; male and female He created them. Then God blessed them, and God said to them, "Be fruitful and multiply; fill the earth and subdue it; have dominion over the fish of the sea, over the birds of the air, and over every living thing that moves on the earth."
>
> And God said, "See, I have given you every herb that yields seed which is on the face of all the earth, and every tree whose fruit yields seed; to you it shall be for food. Also, to every beast of the earth, to every bird of the air, and to everything that creeps on the earth, in which there is life, I have given every green herb for food;" and it was so. Then God saw everything that He had made, and indeed it was very good. So the evening and the morning were the sixth day.

In the opening of John's Gospel we observed that the Word was God, and it was God the Word that created the heavens and the earth. Also in the first three verses of Genesis we find the Spirit of God is introduced as another person involved in the creation events. Thus we have God the Father, God the Word, and God the Spirit—not three separate gods but one God in three persons. At creation the Spirit is hovering or fluttering over the face of the waters.

The God of the Bible is awesome, when all He has to do is speak and it is. Notice how many times in this chapter the words "then God said" are used, and what God said came to pass. Notice too when it comes to man, God made man. He didn't speak man into existence but took the dirt of the earth and molded man in His image, as it is described in Genesis 2:4-7:

> This is the history of the heavens and the earth when they were created, in the day that the LORD God made the earth and the heavens, before any plant of the field was in the earth and before any herb of the field had grown. For the LORD God had not caused it to rain on the earth, and there was no man to till the ground; but a mist went up from the earth and watered the whole face of the ground. And the LORD God formed man

> of the dust of the ground, and breathed into his nostrils the breath of life; and man became a living being.

Everything you and I observe today was created during those six days. Scripture can't be any clearer when it says in Exodus 20:11, "For in six days the LORD made the heavens and the earth, the sea, and all that is in them, and rested the seventh day. Therefore the LORD blessed the Sabbath day and hallowed it." This Scripture is consistent with Genesis 1–2, in which the evening and the morning are a twenty-four-hour day and consistent with the solar system and seasons that God put into existence. If someone doesn't want to believe it, that is his or her privilege. Did God intend the Sabbath day to be more than twenty-four hours? It is my privilege and choice to believe that things didn't evolve over millions of years and that science, due to its limited knowledge, doesn't prove the Bible. It is my opinion that the Bible determines the validity of science. If science disagrees with the Bible, then it is science that is flawed, not the Word of the living God.

In this portion of Genesis you cannot help but see that God said, "Let Us make man in Our image, according to Our likeness." Who do you suppose "Us" and "Our" refers to?

The Bible teaches that God is Spirit, not *a* Spirit. God is Spirit and as Spirit therefore is everywhere at the same time, knows all that is going on, and is all powerful. God is fully manifested with all of the God attributes in three persons and is thus a Tri-unity. That Tri-unity is the "Us" and "Our" of Genesis and can only be the one God in three persons: the Father; the pre-incarnate Jesus, who is the Word of God; and the Holy Spirit, who hovered over the face of the waters.

Let's end this portion on creation by reading John 1:14: "And the Word became flesh and dwelt among us, and we beheld His glory, the glory as of the only begotten of the Father, full of grace and truth." This tells us that the Word, who is God, became a human being, and that human being is none other than the virgin-born Jesus. Anyone who says the Bible doesn't teach that Jesus is God in a human body is unwilling to accept what the Word of God says. More importantly, the Word, who is the pre-incarnate Jesus the Christ, is the Word that spoke into existence everything that exists today. The Creator put everything together in such a spectacular way. What the mind of the Creator conceived, He achieved by His spoken Word.

We saw that the Bible opens with, "In the beginning God created the Heavens and the Earth." This was when space, matter, energy, and time came into existence to make up the universe that accommodates all that God had planned for His unique creation.

Space has substance to it, allowing for occupation.

Matter occupies space and allows for the physical presence of objects.

Energy within matter can be altered to unleash power that can accomplish benefits from the altered state.

Time allows for everything to be kept in orderly sequence.

Hebrews 1:3 tells us that all of the above is held together by Jesus, who is "upholding all things by the word of His power."

This marvelous Creator/God made man in His image and likeness so man could enjoy a relationship with the Father, the Son, and the Holy Spirit. Humans, however, have devised their own concepts of deity. God desires a relationship with people, and humans want religion with all its incorporated activities of doing. They think that through their level of ritual and achievement they have earned acceptability from God.

I was in Old Delhi, India, visiting an active Hindu temple. As I walked around I observed a motto on the wall that caught my attention. It said, "Love is God." I thought to myself, *That's pretty good*, but as I thought about it, love isn't God, but rather God is love. The emphasis was in the wrong place. Man had twisted this to relegate God to a secondary place. Another motto said, "Truth is God." This Hindu view is consistent with a non-relational experience with the multitudes of the idol gods of its religion:

God's Perspective:	**Man's View**
Relationship is primary	Religion is primary
God is love	love is God
God is truth	truth is God
God is life	Life is God

It is difficult to get someone to believe who doesn't want to, even when that person is shown the truth from the Word of God. In essence, people say, "Don't confuse me with what the Bible teaches, for my mind is made up!"

God

No matter what you may have been taught or heard, Christians do not worship three separate gods. This is not taught in the Word of God. In fact, the Old and New Testaments teach there is only one God:

> we know that an idol is nothing in the world, and that there is no other God but one (1 Corinthians 8:4)

"Hear, O Israel: The LORD our God, the LORD is one!" (Deuteronomy 6:4)

In chapter 1 of this book, it was expressed that the word "one" in Deuteronomy 6:4 is the same word in Hebrew that is used when God declares that a man and woman through their marriage become one flesh, but they are still two people

Often times when I'm engaged in discussion with men in prison, the subject of the Trinity comes up. It's then that I like to use the illustration of water, ice, and steam, and ask, "What are they made of?" Invariably people will say, "Water." I'll say, "Sorry," and finally, often with prompting, the answer of "H_2O" will come out. The three forms, liquid, solid, or vapor, are all of the same essence, that is, H_2O.

I can take a cup of water and freeze it, let it thaw, and it becomes liquid again. I can take that same cup of water and make steam out of it, let it condense, and it becomes liquid again. That's because the essence and nature of water, ice, and steam in each of its three forms is H_2O. Similarly, the true nature, character, and essence of the Father, Jesus, and the Holy Spirit are the fullness of the one God in each of them. God is not divisible. The Bible says God is Spirit, not that God is *a* Spirit, and because He is Spirit He can be everywhere at the same time in all of His fullness. There is no question that Scripture teaches that the Godhood or the Godhead is a Tri-unity:

> *God the Father*
> elect according to the foreknowledge of God the Father, in sanctification of the Spirit, for obedience and sprinkling of the blood of Jesus Christ (1 Peter 1:2)
>
> *God the Son*
> Simon Peter, a bondservant and apostle of Jesus Christ, To those who have obtained like precious faith with us by the righteousness of our God and Savior Jesus Christ (2 Peter 1:1)
>
> looking for the blessed hope and glorious appearing of our great God and Savior Jesus Christ (Titus 2:13)
>
> who are Israelites, to whom pertain the adoption, the glory, the covenants, the giving of the law, the service of God, and the promises; of whom are the fathers and from whom, according

> to the flesh, Christ came, who is over all, the eternally blessed God. Amen. (Romans 9:4-5)
>
> *God the Spirit*
> But Peter said, "Ananias, why has Satan filled your heart to lie to the Holy Spirit and keep back part of the price of the land for yourself? While it remained, was it not your own? And after it was sold, was it not in your own control? Why have you conceived this thing in your heart? You have not lied to men but to God." (Acts 5:3-4)
>
> Do you not know that you are the temple of God and that the Spirit of God dwells in you? (1 Corinthians 3:16)

I believe the Scriptures teach the Father is in the Son and the Holy Spirit, the Son is in the Father and the Holy Spirit, and the Holy Spirit is in the Father and the Son. How can his be? Because God is one, each of the Tri-unity has the fullness of God in each, and each has functions and ministry that they do within the Godhead.

The Word of God is clear regarding all three persons of the Tri-unity. You must decide whether to accept or reject this teaching of the unadulterated, unchangeable, and everlasting Word of the living God. To deny this is to disclaim the one God of the Bible!

Christ Jesus

Without knowing who the biblical Jesus is, one will never be able to reconcile the major teachings of Christianity that are found in the Scriptures. Then who is this Jesus of Nazareth? What does the Bible teach regarding the titles and attributes of Jesus? He is

> the Alpha and the Omega (first and last; Revelation 1:8, 11; 22:13)
> the Lord of lords and King of kings (Revelation 19:16)
> the Lord of creation, who created everything (Colossians 1:15-18)
> the Lord of the hosts of heaven (Isaiah 47:4)
> the Word of God, who is God (John 1:1-3)
> the Messiah, the promised one (Daniel 9:25; John 2:41)
> the Word who was wrapped in a holy body, the man Jesus (John 1:14)
> the man of sorrows acquainted with grief (Isaiah 53)
> the great high priest, sympathizing with our weaknesses (Hebrews 4:15)

the intercessor for the members of His body the church (1 Timothy 2:5)
the one and only Savior for humankind (John 14:6)
the lover of our souls (John 3:16)
the rock (1 Corinthians 10:4)
our shield (Psalm 84:11)
Son of Man (Matthew 24:27)
Son of God, in whom is eternal life (1 John 5:11-12)
faithful and true (Revelation 21:5)
the one who will never leave or forsake His own (Hebrews 13:5)
the friend who welcomed sinners (Luke 15:2)
the performer of multitudes of true miracles (Matthew 4:24)
the Counselor (Isaiah 9:6)
the Prince of peace (Isaiah 9:6)
the author and finisher of our faith (Hebrews 12:2)
the Lamb of God, the perfect sacrifice for the sins of all humankind (John 1:29)
the righteous judge (2 Timothy 4:8)
the great I Am (John 8:58), the self-existent One, who said I am

> the good shepherd (He gave His life for the sheep; John 10:11-14)
> the door of the sheep (John 10:7-9)
> the bread of life (John 6:35, 41, 48, 51)
> the light of the world (John 8:12; 9:5)
> the resurrection and the life (John 11:25)
> the way, the truth, and the life (John 14:6)
> the true vine (John 15:1-5)

All of the "I am" statements were made by Jesus. If they were not true of Him, wouldn't He be a liar?

His character was

Holy
Righteous
Just
Guileless
Sinless
Spotless
Innocent
Gentle

Merciful
Humble
Gracious
Truthful
Forgiving
Compassionate
Loving

Jesus was Lord, Yahweh, the Jehovah of the Old Testament, manifested in a human body, as is recorded in the New Testament. This was prophesied by Isaiah: "The voice of one crying in the wilderness: 'Prepare the way of the LORD; make straight in the desert a highway for our God'" (Isaiah 40:3). The fulfillment was announced by John the Baptist: "For this is he who was spoken of by the prophet Isaiah, saying: 'The voice of one crying in the wilderness: Prepare the way of the LORD, make His paths straight'" (Matthew 3:3). Notice the confirmation in 1 Timothy 3:16:

> And without controversy great is the mystery of godliness:
> God was manifested in the flesh,
> Justified in the Spirit
> Seen by angels,
> Preached among the Gentiles,
> Believed on in the world,
> Received up in glory.

But let's not forget, He is coming again to establish His earthly kingdom. It will be governed righteously, not like the corrupt governments of the world today.

What has been presented are a few of the titles for and attributes of Jesus. They are really inexhaustible.

Jesus is different from the leaders of other religions. Jesus never carried a sword and never used a sword. Joseph Smith, founder of Mormonism, shot at those who were forcing their way into the jail where he and his brother were incarcerated. Joseph Smith's successor, Brigham Young, had people massacred because they were "unbelievers" who did not accept what he was teaching.

Charles Taze Russell perjured himself in a court of law.

Muhammad encouraged Jihad to force others to become Muslims or suffer the consequences.

But the Christian principle is to turn vengeance over to God. His Word says He will repay: "Beloved, do not avenge yourselves, but rather give place to wrath; for it is written, 'Vengeance is Mine, I will repay,' says the Lord. Therefore if your enemy is hungry, feed him; if he is thirsty, give him a drink; for in so doing you will heap coals of fire on his head. Do not be overcome by evil, but overcome evil with good" (Romans 12:19-21). Christians don't need to avenge themselves. God will take care of that. Christians don't have to force people to believe.

Jesus said to turn the other cheek. He said to love your enemies and pray for them. Jesus told Peter to put up his sword when he cut off the ear of one of those who was out to arrest Jesus. Jesus put the ear back on and fixed the damage that was done. He delighted in mercy, always giving opportunity for repentance.

Based on what the Scriptures reveal, we can conclude with this question: Is Jesus different from Muhammad, Joseph Smith, or Dr. Russell? Undoubtedly the answer is yes, and the Jesus they portray cannot be the same Jesus portrayed in the Bible, the Word of God.

The Jesus I know is the purest example of love, because God is love. His love was proven when He endured the cross for us. I truly love Him and know He loves me. The Jesus of the Bible, though tolerant of others, never backed away from relating the truth even in difficult circumstances, but He did so with grace and truth. The Scripture says Jesus was full of grace and truth. What will you do with Jesus? Will you fall at His feet and like Thomas declare, "My Lord and my God"? Or will you substitute a religion of works instead?

A works system never releases one from bondage and operates on the basis of fear to hold a person to the religious philosophies of people and their traditions, which encumber their followers. People refused to take Jesus at His Word, even in His day, and they still do. Jesus confirmed this when He said, "Which of you convicts Me of sin? And if I tell the truth, why do you not believe Me?" (John 8:46). Jesus emphasized the importance of His Words in John 6:63: "It is the Spirit who gives life; the flesh profits nothing. The words that I speak to you are spirit, and they are life."

What were some of the truths that Jesus told those He confronted? Here are a few from the Gospel of John:

> Philip found Nathanael and said to him, "We have found Him of whom Moses in the law, and also the prophets, wrote—Jesus of Nazareth, the son of Joseph."
>
> And Nathanael said to him, "Can anything good come out of Nazareth?"
>
> Philip said to him, "Come and see."

Jesus saw Nathanael coming toward Him, and said of him, "Behold, an Israelite indeed, in whom is no deceit!"

Nathanael said to Him, "How do You know me?"

Jesus answered and said to him, "Before Philip called you, when you were under the fig tree, I saw you."

Nathanael answered and said to Him, "Rabbi, You are the Son of God! You are the King of Israel!" (John 1:45-47)

"And as Moses lifted up the serpent in the wilderness, even so must the Son of Man be lifted up, that whoever believes in Him should not perish but have eternal life. For God so loved the world that He gave His only begotten Son, that whoever believes in Him should not perish but have everlasting life. For God did not send His Son into the world to condemn the world, but that the world through Him might be saved." (John 3:14-17)

"Most assuredly, I say to you, he who hears My word and believes in Him who sent Me has everlasting life, and shall not come into judgment, but has passed from death into life." (John 5:24)

"Do not think that I shall accuse you to the Father; there is one who accuses you—Moses, in whom you trust. For if you believed Moses, you would believe Me; for he wrote about Me. But if you do not believe his writings, how will you believe My words?" (John 5:45-47)

Martha said to Him, "I know that he will rise again in the resurrection at the last day." Jesus said to her, "I am the resurrection and the life. He who believes in Me, though he may die, he shall live. And whoever lives and believes in Me shall never die. Do you believe this?" She said to Him, "Yes, Lord, I believe that You are the Christ, the Son of God, who is to come into the world." (John 11:24-27)

"Little children, I shall be with you a little while longer. You will seek Me; and as I said to the Jews, 'Where I am going, you cannot come,' so now I say to you. A new commandment I

> give to you, that you love one another; as I have loved you, that you also love one another. By this all will know that you are My disciples, if you have love for one another." (John 13:33-35)

> Jesus said to him, "Have I been with you so long, and yet you have not known Me, Philip? He who has seen Me has seen the Father; so how can you say, 'Show us the Father'? Do you not believe that I am in the Father, and the Father in Me? The words that I speak to you I do not speak on My own authority; but the Father who dwells in Me does the works. Believe Me that I am in the Father and the Father in Me, or else believe Me for the sake of the works themselves." (John 14:9-11)

> "And now, O Father, glorify Me together with Yourself, with the glory which I had with You before the world was." (John 17:5)

In these words of this last portion of Scripture, isn't it significant that Jesus is sharing in the glory with the Father, that is, the same glory He had with the Father before the worlds ever came into existence? If these words spoken by Him are not true, then Jesus is a blasphemer and a delusional fake. Certainly the evidence is on the side of the apostles and the holy Word of God. Jesus referred to the Old Testament as the Word of God and said that He had fulfilled all of the law.

No wonder He is the Alpha and the Omega, the First and the Last. He is the Almighty God in human flesh. One must not shove to the background or deny the following Scriptures that clearly reveal who Jesus is:

> In the beginning was the Word, and the Word was with God, and the <u>Word was God</u>. He was in the beginning with God. All things were made through Him, and without Him nothing was made that was made. (John 1:1-3)

> And <u>the Word became flesh</u> and dwelt among us, and we beheld His glory, the glory as of the only begotten of the Father, full of grace and truth. (John 1:14)

The Word, who is God, became a sinless human being who dwelled here in a fleshly body like the one you and I have. This is what the Scriptures express to us. To say otherwise is to deny the Word of God.

The following portion from Philippians speaks to Jesus' complete humanness and His awesome deity:

> Let this mind be in you which was also in Christ Jesus, who, being in the form of God, did not consider it robbery to be equal with God, but made Himself of no reputation, taking the form of a bondservant, and coming in the likeness of men. And being found in appearance as a man, He humbled Himself and became obedient to the point of death, even the death of the cross. Therefore God also has highly exalted Him and given Him the name which is above every name, that at the name of Jesus every knee should bow, of those in heaven, and of those on earth, and of those under the earth, and that every tongue should confess that Jesus Christ is Lord, to the glory of God the Father. (Philippians 2:5-11)

Jesus is revealed as the visible expression of the invisible God, and it was through Him that everything was brought into existence and is kept in existence through the word of His power:

> He is the image of the invisible God, the firstborn over all creation. For by Him all things were created that are in heaven and that are on earth, visible and invisible, whether thrones or dominions or principalities or powers. All things were created through Him and for Him. And He is before all things, and in Him all things consist. And He is the head of the body, the church, who is the beginning, the firstborn from the dead, that in all things He may have the preeminence.
>
> For it pleased the Father that in Him all the fullness should dwell, and by Him to reconcile all things to Himself, by Him, whether things on earth or things in heaven, having made peace through the blood of His cross. (Colossians 1:15-20)

Because Christ Jesus is the Word, the Creator God, it was no problem for Him, during His earthly ministry, to say to the blind man, "Receive your sight," and immediately the man was able to see. Jesus commanded Lazarus, who had been in the grave for four days, to come forth from the grave, and he did. This wasn't an isolated case or two. Matthew 4:24 clearly states His miraculous power: "Then His fame went throughout all of Syria; and they brought to Him all the sick people who were afflicted with various diseases and torments, and those who were demon possessed, epileptics, and paralytics; and He healed them."

Possibly it was the fame of all these healings that captured the ear of Nicodemus and stirred him to seek out Jesus one night (John 3).

Also, because Jesus is a man, He is able to fulfill the high priestly office in heaven on behalf of the children of God. He offers and brings release to those who at one time were entangled in the bondage of religious ritual and feared death but were hopeful their religious actions would gain them favor in the hereafter thus avoiding eternal doom:

> Inasmuch then as the children have partaken of flesh and blood, He Himself likewise shared in the same, that through death He might destroy him who had the power of death, that is, the devil, and release those who through fear of death were all their lifetime subject to bondage. For indeed He does not give aid to angels, but He does give aid to the seed of Abraham. Therefore, in all things He had to be made like His brethren, that He might be a merciful and faithful High Priest in things pertaining to God, to make propitiation for the sins of the people. For in that He Himself has suffered, being tempted, He is able to aid those who are tempted. (Hebrews 2:14-18)

The one God, unique in His Tri-unity, requires a human mediator who is a perfect man and can therefore have the role of a righteous advocate between man and God, as 1 Timothy 2:5-6 says: "For there is one God and one Mediator between God and men, the Man Christ Jesus, who gave Himself a ransom for all, to be testified in due time."

Thomas comes to a full realization of who Jesus is: "And after eight days His disciples were again inside, and Thomas with them. Jesus came, the doors being shut, and stood in the midst, and said, 'Peace to you!' Then He said to Thomas, 'Reach your finger here, and look at My hands; and reach your hand here, and put it into My side. Do not be unbelieving, but believing.' And Thomas answered and said to Him, 'My Lord and my God!'" (John 20:26-28).

In the following portion from Revelation we read of the Son of Man, who is Jesus. Jesus will not come to earth and die again, as Islam teaches, because He is alive forevermore:

> Then I turned to see the voice that spoke with me. And having turned I saw seven golden lamp stands, and in the midst of the seven lamp stands One like the Son of Man, clothed with a garment down to the feet and about the chest with a golden band. His head and hair were white like wool, as white as snow, and His eyes like a flame of fire; His feet were like fine brass, as if refined in a furnace, and His voice as the sound of many waters; He had in His right hand seven stars, out of His mouth went a sharp two-edged sword, and His countenance was like the sun shining in its strength. And when I saw Him, I fell at His feet as dead. But He laid His right hand on me, saying to me, "Do not be afraid; I am the First and the Last. I am He who lives, and was dead, and behold, I am alive forevermore. Amen. And I have the keys of Hades and of Death."
> (Revelation 1:12-18)

According to all of these Scriptures, Jesus was both divine and human. His incarnation (human birth) and His resurrection from the dead are evidence of His continued humanness forever. In taking on humanity, He became one of us. He had a humble beginning. Although His human body did not fully show His divine glory, His deity was not diminished thereby. He was fully God. The Scriptures say God is Spirit, invisible, and though the Spirit could not be seen physically in Jesus, He was God. It was in His flesh that He died to defeat him through whom came the power and sting of death, the devil. Jesus the man is the only mediator (advocate, representative) between God and humankind. He was absolute God and perfect human, two distinct natures in one person.

In His humanness, would Jesus feel pain if He stubbed His toe? Of course He would. If He cut Himself while learning the carpenter's trade from His father Joseph, would He bleed? Of course He would. In His human nature, Jesus at His birth was not completely physically or intellectually developed. Luke 2:52 says, "And Jesus grew in wisdom and stature, and in favor with God and men." Wisdom and stature obviously refer to intellectual and physical development. Jesus had to go through the same developmental stages of life that you and I had to go through or He could not have experienced the same trials and temptations that you and I encountered. He would not have been fully human. As God, He was not limited. However, He laid aside some of His divine rights to fulfill His work on earth. As a human, He was tempted in all areas of life as we are, but because He was all of God in a human body, He did not sin. Colossians 1:15 says, "He is the visible image of the invisible God," and Colossians 2:9 adds, "For in Him dwells all the fullness of the Godhead bodily." That is, in Christ there is all of God in a human body. And in Hebrews 4:15 we read that Jesus, as fully man, was tempted as we are: "For we do not have a High Priest who cannot sympathize with our weaknesses, but was in all points tempted as we are, yet without sin." Being tempted is not sin, but yielding to it is.

There are times in Scripture when Jesus spoke from a human perspective and other times from a divine perspective. In His humanity He was limited to the human strength and wisdom He had, but through His divine nature He was unlimited in power and knowledge. Scripture is full of incidents when these two natures were demonstrated. Only as a man could He be tempted of Satan, but as God He would not yield to the temptation. If Jesus did not have the human limitations He would not be a human being like us, but He was fully human and fully divine.

Some day God's children will have immortal bodies like that of the resurrected Jesus, and the last enemy to be destroyed will be death. At that point Christians will be sinless, blameless, and faultless, able to stand in the presence of the holy and righteous God who will be all and in all, as Scripture promises in 1 Corinthians 15:20-28:

> But now Christ is risen from the dead, and has become the firstfruits of those who have fallen asleep. For since by man came death, by Man also came the resurrection of the dead. For as in Adam all die, even so in Christ all shall be made alive. But each one in his own order: Christ the firstfruits, afterward those who are Christ's at His coming. Then comes the end, when He delivers the kingdom to God the Father, when He puts an end to all rule and all authority and power. For He must reign till He has put all enemies under His feet. The last enemy that will be destroyed is death. For "He has put all things under His feet." But when He says "all things are put under Him," it is evident that He who put all things under Him is excepted. Now when all things are made subject to Him, then the Son Himself will also be subject to Him who put all things under Him, that God may be all in all."

The resurrection of Jesus from the dead is the focal point of Christianity. That's why false religions and humanists deny the resurrection. The resurrection brings about a dynamic to humans that changes so many things. It was the resurrection that changed the apostles. Can you imagine the fear and excitement when some of the apostles saw the empty tomb? What joyous excitement when some saw Him alive for the first time, and they told the others, "He is risen, He is alive!" I can imagine them questioning by echoing back, "He's alive?" "Yes, He's alive." Thomas said, "I won't believe it unless I see Him myself." When he did, he declared, "My Lord and my God." Did Jesus correct him when he made that statement? No, because that was who He was.

Why would all the disciples die at the hands of others for something that was a lie? Why would they continue the message of the risen Savior if it was all a hoax? No, it was the same resurrection power, the Spirit of holiness, that raised Jesus from the dead and indwelled the bodies of the disciples and all Christians since that time. It is the resurrection power that changes people. Things we used to crave are no longer so important. Things we liked before we dislike. Eternal values become more precious than earthly treasure.

Eternal life is more than living forever. It is the very life of Christ that invades our body, soul, and our spirit. First John 5:11-12 tells us that eternal life is in God's Son and if we have His Son we have eternal life. That life brings changes in all aspects of true Christians' life and future. They want to share that good news that Jesus is risen. He truly is alive. The apostle John declared that the Word who became flesh was full of grace and truth (John 1:14). And His grace is sufficient for you, regardless of the depth of your sin. You can be changed and live God's will for your life: "Therefore, if anyone is in Christ, he is a new creation; old things have passed away; behold, all things have become new" (2 Corinthians 5:17).

Just as you can be subject to your human will, Jesus the perfect man subjected His human will to the will of God, because in Him was all the fullness of God. He was, is, and always will be God. As God He is the rightful ruler over all humanity. As the Lord God Messiah He was rejected by His own people, and He is being rejected by the masses today. Even though God is gracious, merciful, and long-suffering, there will be a day of reckoning. God's justice must be served on those who refused His offer of justification through faith. It is a fearful thing to fall into the hands of the living God. Will Jesus be your Mediator and advocate today, or will He be your Judge at the judgment for unbelievers who will have no excuse?

The Holy Spirit

The Scriptures teach that the Holy Spirit has all the perfect attributes of God and therefore is God and one of the Tri-unity. Do I understand everything about the Tri-unity of God? Absolutely not. It is difficult for mere mortal humans to wrap their mental reasoning around this divine wonder. But does that make it impossible to believe? Again, absolutely not, for the Bible teaches this, and that is when faith must be exercised, if we believe the Bible to be the Word of God.

What does the Bible have to say about the Holy Spirit?

The Spirit of God was introduced in Genesis 1:1-2: "In the beginning God created the heavens and the earth. The earth was without form, and void; and darkness was on the face of the deep. And the Spirit of God was hovering over the face of the waters."

It is 2 Peter 1:16-21 that expresses how the sure Word of prophecy came about:

> For we did not follow cunningly devised fables when we made known to you the power and coming of our Lord Jesus Christ, but were eyewitnesses of His majesty. For He received from God the Father honor and glory when such a voice came to Him from the Excellent Glory: "This is My beloved Son, in whom I am well pleased." And we heard this voice which came from heaven when we were with Him on the holy mountain.
>
> And so we have the prophetic word confirmed, which you do well to heed as a light that shines in a dark place, until the day dawns and the morning star rises in your hearts; knowing this first, that no prophecy of Scripture is of any private interpretation, for prophecy never came by the will of man, but holy men of God spoke as they were moved by the Holy Spirit.

What is the ministry of the Holy Spirit?

The Holy Spirit is the Comforter of believers: "But when the Helper comes, whom I shall send to you from the Father, the Spirit of truth who proceeds from the Father, He will testify of Me" (John 15:26).

The Holy Spirit reproves the world: "And when He has come, He will convict the world of sin, and of righteousness, and of judgment" (John 16:8).

He is the Spirit of truth: "However, when He, the Spirit of truth, has come, He will guide you into all truth; for He will not speak on His own authority, but whatever He hears He will speak; and He will tell you things to come" (John 16:13).

He is a teacher: "But the Helper, the Holy Spirit, whom the Father will send in My name, He will teach you all things, and bring to your remembrance all things that I said to you" (John 14:26).

The Spirit energizes believers: "But if the Spirit of Him who raised Jesus from the dead dwells in you, He who raised Christ from the dead will also give life to your mortal bodies through His Spirit who dwells in you" (Romans 8:11).

He fills receptive believers: "And do not be drunk with wine, in which is dissipation; but be filled with the Spirit" (Ephesians 5:18).

He dwells in believers: "Do you not know that you are the temple of God and that the Spirit of God dwells in you?" (1 Corinthians 3:16).

He empowers believers to be strong in the things of God: "that He would grant you, according to the riches of His glory, to be strengthened with might through His Spirit in the inner man" (Ephesians 3:16).

The Holy Spirit must indwell believers, or they do not have the Spirit of Christ: "Now if anyone does not have the Spirit of Christ, he is not His" (Romans 8:9).

The Holy Spirit leads the children of God in their endeavors for God: "For as many as are led by the Spirit of God, these are sons of God" (Romans 8:14).

The Spirit of God brings to remembrance the assurance that comes from the holy Scriptures: "The Spirit Himself bears witness with our spirit that we are children of God" (Romans 8:16).

We learned earlier that Ananias lied to the Holy Spirit and therefore lied to God. The Scriptures proclaim that the Holy Spirit is God both in His nature and by His actions.

Because the Holy Spirit indwells Christians, they can be receptive to the Spirit's leading and accomplish God's work. "Preach the word! Be ready in season and out of season. Convince, rebuke, exhort, with all longsuffering and teaching" (2 Timothy 4:4). When opportunities are available, even though we had no specific plans, or in essence we are out of season, we are to step instantly into the situation and make it in season.

I am convinced that Christ's love led me in the following encounter as an out-of-season challenge that became an in-season experience.

An inmate, who was a trustee/worker, was in the lobby of the prison reading a magazine during noon hour. I was returning from an early lunch and noticed a stack of magazines alongside of him. Among the magazines was what I supposed to be a Bible. I asked him, "Is that a Bible?" He replied, "Yes it is." "Do you read it?" "Yes, I do." "Do you believe it?" "I sure do." "Do you have eternal life?" With a concerned look on his face, he replied, "No, I don't!" Using his Bible, I asked him to turn to 1 John 5:11-13, where he read, "And this is the testimony:

that God has given us eternal life, and this life is in His Son. He who has the Son has life; he who does not have the Son of God does not have life. These things I have written to you who believe in the name of the Son of God, that you may know_that you have eternal life, and that you may continue to believe in the name of the Son of God."

He looked at me with a radiant smile on his face and with great joy and certainty exclaimed, "I have eternal life." What assurance we can receive from the promises of the Word of God. Truly faith and assurance come from God's unfailing, unchangeable Word.

Sin

Its Effect

Human sin started in the Garden of Eden shortly after the creation. Satan said to Eve, "Has God indeed said, 'You shall not eat of every tree of the garden'?" (Genesis 3:1). Notice how deceitful Satan was by getting Eve to believe what God had said was not really what God meant. What was Eve's answer? She indicated that God had told them if they ate of or touched the tree in the midst of the garden, which was the tree of the knowledge of good and evil, they would die. Satan said, "You will not surely die." Eve was told she would become like God, knowing good and evil. Just think: she would become like their Creator!

Eve looked at the fruit of the tree and, according to Genesis, thought it would be good for food, pleasant to the eyes, and would make them wise. In those three evaluations she was motivated by the lust of the flesh, the lust of the eyes, and the pride of life. Yielding to those three temptations caused Adam and Eve's relationship with God to be broken. Through disobeying their Creator, the curse of sin and death came into the world.

Those three motivating factors still plague humankind today. We are reminded of this in the letter written by the apostle John: "For all that is in the world—the lust of the flesh, the lust of the eyes, and the pride of life—is not of the Father but is of the world" (1 John 2:16).

These three motivations are instilled in the values of many people in society today. Said another way, if it feels good, do it; if it is appealing, go for it; and if you are smart, then manipulate and walk over others to gratify yourself. The world system considers greed to be a good thing. Books have been written about the benefits of greed. However, many believe this to be the reason for the world's financial collapse of 2008 through 2010. Many "small people" have been hurt significantly by this giant named Greed. Man calls this wisdom. God calls it sin.

Satan is full of pride, a deceiver, and according to God's Word a liar and a murderer from the beginning. Satan gloats over evil and getting others to follow his ways. Look at what Isaiah 14:12-15 says: "How you are fallen from heaven, O Lucifer, son of the morning! How you are cut down to the ground, you who weakened the nations! For you have said in your heart: 'I will ascend into heaven, I will exalt my throne above the stars of God; I will also sit on the mount of the congregation On the farthest sides of the north; I will ascend above the heights of the clouds.' Yet you shall be brought down to Sheol, to the lowest depths of the Pit."

I believe that Satan was jealous of the authority God gave Adam in his dominion or rule over the earth and wanted Adam and Eve to obey and thus honor him instead of God. By getting Adam and Eve to obey him it would place them in his kingdom of darkness, and Satan would become the ruler rather than Adam. This sinful act of Adam and Eve brought the curse of mortality and death to humanity. It also brought a curse on the cosmos, so chaos and calamity interrupt the lives of humans in the course of everyday life. This curse will continue until the second coming of the Messiah.

Later, God gave the Ten Commandments to Moses for the people of Israel. God knew they could not and would not keep those rules. Why did He give them? Because they are the perfect law, which reflects the character of God and shows how far we humans fall short of God's standard and why God in His grace would have to make provision for humans to be redeemed. The intent of the Ten Commandments is for our good. If every human in the world could keep them, what a different world this would be. The Ten Commandments are found in Exodus 20:3-17:

> "You shall have no other gods before Me.
>
> "You shall not make for yourself a carved image—any likeness of anything that is in heaven above, or that is in the earth beneath, or that is in the water under the earth; you shall not bow down to them nor serve them. For I, the LORD your God, am a jealous God, visiting the iniquity of the fathers upon the children to the third and fourth generations of those who hate Me, but showing mercy to thousands, to those who love Me and keep My commandments. "You shall not take the name of the LORD your God in vain, for the LORD will not hold him guiltless who takes His name in vain.
>
> "Remember the Sabbath day, to keep it holy. Six days you shall labor and do all your work, but the seventh day is the Sabbath of the LORD your God. In it you shall do no work: you, nor your son, nor your daughter, nor your male servant,

> nor your female servant, nor your cattle, nor your stranger who is within your gates. For in six days the LORD made the heavens and the earth, the sea, and all that is in them, and rested the seventh day. Therefore the LORD blessed the Sabbath day and hallowed it.
>
> "Honor your father and your mother, that your days may be long upon the land which the LORD your God is giving you
>
> "You shall not murder.
>
> "You shall not commit adultery
>
> "You shall not steal.
>
> "You shall not bear false witness against your neighbor.
>
> "You shall not covet your neighbor's house; you shall not covet your neighbor's wife, nor his male servant, nor his female servant, nor his ox, nor his donkey, nor anything that is your neighbor's."

Anyone who reads through these Ten Commandments will see they are good for humankind. Disobeying them is sinning against God. The ultimate result of sin produces separation from God through death. Forgiveness is attainable, but it must be on God's terms. His Word says that without the shedding of blood there is no forgiveness. The sacrifice of a sinful person would fall short, so God would provide the perfect Lamb. The shed blood must be from a perfect human, the only sacrifice acceptable for imperfect people. And that's why John the Baptist, when he saw Jesus coming from a distance, declared, "Behold! the Lamb of God who takes away the sin of the world" (John 1:29).

When we do look at that law we see how far we fall short and our need to depend on God's grace and mercy. Only one human kept all of the law, and that was the blessed Messiah Jesus. "Do not think that I have come to abolish the Law or the Prophets; I have not come to abolish them but to fulfill them" (Matthew 5:17).

Sin will always take people further than they want to go, and once they arrive they wish they had taken a different road. They often live with remorse, regrets, and the guilt of having followed a path that often hurts others as well during their wayward journey. But there is a remedy. There is a path to forgiveness and peace for all who accept God's way. God specializes in recovering those who have strayed off the path and will repent and accept God's forgiveness.

Dr. Karl Menninger, who had a famous psychiatric clinic in Missouri, wrote a book giving evidence from clinical cases that is titled *Whatever Became of Sin?*

What he wrote was that people try to disguise their sin, only to find they can't eliminate their guilt. It was his opinion that guilt is the major cause for mental stress and depression.

The Word of God tells us that people can know release from their guilt if they are willing to acknowledge they are sinful and repent of their sin. They will find that freedom from guilt and forgiveness in the grace and truth of the One who was full of grace and truth, Jesus the Messiah.

Sin is devastating and can eternally separate people from what God intended for them. But God, because of His great love, put together a plan to recover man from that fateful destiny. That plan looked forward from the Garden of Eden to the future redemptive work of a coming Messiah, and for all those who came after the act of God's grace at the cross, that plan looks back to that completed redemptive work. God wanted Satan to know that he might win a few battles, but he was not going to win the war. An early prophecy in Genesis 3:15 says, "Because you [Satan] have done this, you are cursed more than all the cattle, and more than every beast of the field; on your belly shall you go, and you shall eat dust all the days of your life. And I will put enmity between you and the women, and between your seed and her Seed; He shall bruise your head, and you shall bruise His heel."

The Seed of the women is the coming Messiah. Jesus was born of the Seed of the woman that was fertilized by the power of the Holy Spirit. No seed of man was involved. This combination of the virgin Seed and the power of God the Holy Spirit birthed a sinless God-man, Jesus. "Behold, the virgin shall conceive and bear a Son, and shall call His name Immanuel" (Isaiah 7:14b). The word "Immanuel" means "God with us."

The Gospel of Luke (Luke 1:26-38) says about this miraculous birth:

> Now in the sixth month the angel Gabriel was sent by God to a city of Galilee named Nazareth, to a virgin betrothed to a man whose name was Joseph, of the house of David. The virgin's name was Mary. And having come in, the angel said to her, "Rejoice, highly favored one, the Lord is with you; blessed are you among women!"
>
> But when she saw him, she was troubled at his saying, and considered what manner of greeting this was. Then the angel said to her, "Do not be afraid, Mary, for you have found favor with God. And behold, you will conceive in your womb and bring forth a Son, and shall call His name JESUS. He will be great, and will be called the Son of the Highest; and the Lord

> God will give Him the throne of His father David. And He will reign over the house of Jacob forever, and of His kingdom there will be no end."
>
> Then Mary said to the angel, "How can this be, since I do not know a man?"
>
> And the angel answered and said to her, "The Holy Spirit will come upon you, and the power of the Highest will overshadow you; therefore, also, that Holy One who is to be born will be called the Son of God. Now indeed, Elizabeth your relative has also conceived a son in her old age; and this is now the sixth month for her who was called barren. For with God nothing will be impossible."
>
> Then Mary said, "Behold the maidservant of the Lord! Let it be to me according to your word." And the angel departed from her.

There was a specific time for the birth of the promised Messiah (Messiah means "Savior"). This birth was not an afterthought but was ordained by the eternal God before the foundations of the world were formed. "But when the fullness of the time had come, God sent forth His Son, born of a woman, born under the law" (Galatians 4:4).

Satan probably thought Jesus had been defeated when He died on the cross, but through His resurrection Jesus triumphed over Satan and death. Satan's final defeat will come when Christ, at the end of His thousand-year reign, destroys Satan's gathered armies that will be carrying out the evil one's orders in this final battle of the nations. Those congregated armies are enemies of the Lord and His people. They will be destroyed by fire that God sends down from heaven. Then Satan will be cast into the lake of fire and brimstone, never to be heard from again. The victory will be complete.

In the meantime, Satan continues to accuse God's redeemed people. God will not tolerate this forever and will finally cast Satan and his angels to the earth. Satan loses again, but today he is not through influencing the nations' leaders and the unredeemed people within his kingdom of darkness. He is a masterful deceiver vying for the souls of mankind. God's Word reveals the power and wiles of Satan against the believer, but also the Word tells us how to be an overcomer through faith in Jesus Christ: "You are of God, little children, and have overcome them, because He who is in you is greater than he who is in the world" (1 John 4:4). "He who is in the world" is Satan. God's people overcome the evil spirit of Antichrist through the Holy Spirit living within them.

In Revelation 12, we read of Satan being cast out of heaven during the tribulation period. Satan empowers the man of sin, the Antichrist, who goes to persecute Israel and the tribulation saints, those who refused to accept the mark of the beast:

> And war broke out in heaven: Michael and his angels fought with the dragon; and the dragon and his angels fought, but they did not prevail, nor was a place found for them in heaven any longer. So the great dragon was cast out, that serpent of old, called the Devil and Satan, who deceives the whole world; he was cast to the earth, and his angels were cast out with him. Then I heard a loud voice saying in heaven, "Now salvation, and strength, and the kingdom of our God, and the power of His Christ have come, for the accuser of our brethren, who accused them before our God day and night, has been cast down. And they overcame him by the blood of the Lamb and by the word of their testimony, and they did not love their lives to the death. Therefore rejoice, O heavens, and you who dwell in them! Woe to the inhabitants of the earth and the sea! For the devil has come down to you, having great wrath, because he knows that he has a short time."
>
> Now when the dragon saw that he had been cast to the earth, he persecuted the woman who gave birth to the male Child. But the woman was given two wings of a great eagle, that she might fly into the wilderness to her place, where she is nourished for a time and times and half a time, from the presence of the serpent. So the serpent spewed water out of his mouth like a flood after the woman, that he might cause her to be carried away by the flood. But the earth helped the woman, and the earth opened its mouth and swallowed up the flood which the dragon had spewed out of his mouth. And the dragon was enraged with the woman, and he went to make war with the rest of her offspring, who keep the commandments of God and have the testimony of Jesus Christ. (Revelation 12:7-17)

In this context we read of the dragon, who is Satan; the woman is the nation Israel from whom the male child, the Messiah, came through the tribe of Judah. Part of the nation Israel escapes the persecuting tactics of the Antichrist by finding refuge in the wilderness for three and a half years. In the Bible, a time and times and half a time is three and a half years, which represents half of the seven-year tribulation period.

These future events will unfold in their time as ordained by God. God has never failed to bring to pass His prophecies or His promises. It is one of the reasons why we can depend on the Bible as the infallible Word of the Creator God. Because we can trust the God of the Bible, we can fully depend on the promises He offers in His Word.

We have seen that the introduction of sin into the human race brought death as the consequence of that sin, and the continuing results of sin in the events related above, but also we can count on God's grace and mercy through His plan of redemption. The purchase price for salvation and forgiveness for sinful man was made possible through the shed blood of the Lamb of God. Who is that Lamb? None other than the sinless, spotless, sacrificial Lamb Jesus, the Son of the eternal God.

Here are some scriptural points on why the remission (forgiveness) of sins is possible:

> "For this is My blood of the new covenant, which is shed for many for the remission of sins" (Mark 1:4)
>
> "To give knowledge of salvation to His people by the remission of their sins" (Luke 1:77)
>
> "and that repentance and remission of sins should be preached in His name to all nations" (Luke 24:47).
>
> "To Him all the prophets witness that, through His name, whoever believes in Him will receive remission of sins" (Acts 10:43)

Those points from God's Word are plain and understandable. The blood of Jesus was shed to meet the righteous demands of the holy and just God, and this message of forgiveness is to be preached to all nations. And all who believe in Him will receive forgiveness. Jesus' death paid the price for our sins. His shed blood makes it possible to be forgiven, but only those who believe will receive forgiveness. Not to believe is to call God a liar. Jesus' bodily resurrection is the means of our being made right in God's sight: "Not by works of righteousness which we have done, but according to His mercy He saved us" (Titus 3:5). It is all of God. This doesn't happen through any of man's efforts to establish his own righteousness, which always falls short. "For He made Him who knew no sin to be sin for us, that we might become the righteousness of God in Him" (2 Corinthians 5:21).

Jesus took our sins in His own body and became sin for us that we might be made right with God. What an awesome act of love, grace, and mercy. Grace is giving us something we don't deserve, and mercy is keeping us from something we do deserve.

What is sin, and what does it do to self and others?

Sin is not a disease; it is the cause of disease.

Sin is wrong; it never makes things right.

Sin hurts others; it doesn't help others.

Sin corrupts; it doesn't bring health.

Sin deceives; it covers up.

Sin is envious; it wants what others have.

Sin is against God's will; it is self-serving.

Sin is greedy; it always wants more.

Sin hates; it doesn't embrace true love.

Satan loves sin because he is evil. Those who love and practice sin are carrying out Satan's will.

God hates sin, because His character is pure and perfect.

Isn't it interesting that sin opposes and is absent of love? It is difficult for humans to admit they are sinners. People say, "There are a lot of people who are far worse sinners than I am. I'm not so bad; deep down I've got a good heart." The problem is that you are comparing yourself with your own standards and the standards of others, and not God's. You are establishing the standard; therefore you have become your own god. It is God's standard that we are judged by, and not ours. Put another way, even our righteous acts fall short, because they are soiled by our sinful ways: "But we are all like an unclean thing, and all our righteousnesses are like filthy rags" (Isaiah 64:6). God is not talking about our sin here, but about human concepts of righteousness. God's righteousness is perfect, and ours falls short. God's standard is perfection, and that's the reason that God required a perfect sacrifice to take our place, so that we can enjoy being released from the curse and dominion of sin and to have victory over eternal death.

Sin is awful, isn't it? But it doesn't have to rule us. Aren't you glad God has a plan for you and me to experience His salvation and restoration?

Eternal Destiny

Do you think there is a heaven and a hell? Sometimes the answer I get to that question is, "I believe there is a heaven, but the only hell is here on earth." I believe people make that statement because they do not want to face the reality of an awful eternity. There are only two places of judgment mentioned in Scripture, and people's response to God's Word determines where people will spend eternity.

According to the Word of God, when the soul and spirit of man leave the human body, the body is dead, and one of two events happens at that time. The soul and spirit depart the body and either ascend into heaven to be with the Lord or descend into a place called Hades. Those who ascend into heaven will always be where the Lord is and will be rewarded for their godly acts done while they were alive on earth. Works they did that were not godly in nature will be burned up. There will be a loss of reward for those ungodly acts or works. What that loss of reward means I do not know, but I do know there will be a loss.

Rewards or loss of rewards will take place at the judgment seat of Christ (2 Corinthians 5:10), which is in Greek the bema seat of Christ. The bema seat was a place in the Greek market square where matters were brought before the elders of the community to determine their outcome. I saw the remains of one during a tour of Corinth in Greece. The church in Corinth could readily relate to Paul the apostle's writings to them regarding the bema seat. At the bema seat for believers, judgment will be made regarding whether the works done in the body will be rewarded or burned up. Believers will be rewarded for their works that are of eternal value. They are considered the works of gold, silver, and precious stones. Fire will not destroy those works. But the works represented by wood, hay, and straw are of no eternal value and will be burned up. This experience for the believer has no impact on his or her eternal salvation; in fact, this is made clear in 1 Corinthians 3:11-15:

> For no other foundation can anyone lay than that which is laid, which is Jesus Christ. Now if anyone builds on this foundation with gold, silver, precious stones, wood, hay, straw, each one's work will become clear; for the Day will declare it, because it will be revealed by fire; and the fire will test each one's work, of what sort it is. If anyone's work which he has built on it endures, he will receive a reward. If anyone's work is burned, he will suffer loss; but he himself will be saved, yet so as through fire.

The apostle Paul, speaking to the Christians of the church at Corinth, says, "For we must all appear before the judgment seat of Christ, that each one may receive the things done in the body, according to what he has done, whether good or bad" (2 Corinthians 5:10).

When will this judgment take place? According to God's Word, this will take place in heaven after the church, which is called the body of Christ, has been taken to heaven, while on earth the seven-year tribulation is taking place. That bema seat judgment is only for Christians.

There is another throne of judgment, the great white throne, and that is for unbelievers. This judgment will take place at the end of the thousand-year reign of Christ, after Satan's last attempt to dethrone Christ:

> Now when the thousand years have expired, Satan will be released from his prison and will go out to deceive the nations which are in the four corners of the earth, Gog and Magog, to gather them together to battle, whose number is as the sand of the sea. They went up on the breadth of the earth and surrounded the camp of the saints and the beloved city. And fire came down from God out of heaven and devoured them. The devil, who deceived them, was cast into the lake of fire and brimstone where the beast and the false prophet are. And they will be tormented day and night forever and ever.
>
> Then I saw a great white throne and Him who sat on it, from whose face the earth and the heaven fled away. And there was found no place for them. And I saw the dead, small and great, standing before God, and books were opened. And another book was opened, which is the Book of Life. And the dead were judged according to their works, by the things which were written in the books. The sea gave up the dead who were

> in it, and Death and Hades delivered up the dead who were in them. And they were judged, each one according to his works. Then Death and Hades were cast into the lake of fire. This is the second death. And anyone not found written in the Book of Life was cast into the lake of fire. (Revelation 20:7-15)

The Word of God teaches us that our eternal destiny is determined before we leave earth. After that, the judgment will take place either at the bema seat or at the great white throne. There is no evidence in the Word of God that indicates there is a place after death where a person can go to atone for his or her sins. There is no teaching in Scripture that says a person goes to a place, such as purgatory, to do penance for sinful works. The Bible, in fact, indicates otherwise. Hebrews 9:27 says, "And as it is appointed for men to die once, but after this the judgment." There will be no escaping this judgment, unless you are born again and become a member of the family of God. "But as many as received Him, to them He gave the right to become children of God, to those who believe in His name: who were born, not of blood, nor of the will of the flesh, nor of the will of man, but of God" (John 1:12-13).

People like to think there are other ways to pay for their sins and thus earn their salvation. But listen to God's Word: "How shall we escape if we neglect so great a salvation, which at the first began to be spoken by the Lord, and was confirmed to us by those who heard Him" (Hebrews 2:3). Notice that these words originated with the Lord Himself.

Those who are judged and receive their rewards at the bema seat will spend eternity with the Lord, and Scripture states that no one knows all that God has planned for those who have believed and accepted Jesus as their Lord and Savior. It will be exciting to participate in the things God has planned for those who are His people and love Him: "But as it is written: 'Eye has not seen, nor ear heard, nor have entered into the heart of man, the things which God has prepared for those who love Him'" (1 Corinthians 2:9). Heaven will be a wonderful place!

But where will those go who have refused God's great salvation? Revelation 20:14-15 says that the "lake of fire" is the place where each person goes who is judged for his or her works. They will be there forever in an existence of torment, remorse, and with all the other anxious emotions that the mind can envision. Our life here on earth is so brief in light of eternity. Doesn't it make sense to take the time to seriously think about our eternal destiny? Where will you be when your last breath is taken and your heart fails? Is that really the end, and nothing more?

You say, "How can God be so cruel as to send people to hell?"

Many people believe God will excuse their sinful deeds on judgment day, because God wouldn't send someone to an eternal destiny of separation from His presence for a few wrongdoings. After all, you may think, *I never killed anyone, I've always paid my taxes, I have been good to my family and friends, I am a moral person, I have a good heart.* This is justification from man's perspective.

God, because He is just, cannot excuse even a sin that men would consider insignificant. Will God be just if He excused the so-called least of our sins? Will God be unfair in these cases? I think not.

In the first book of the Bible, it says, "Shall not the Judge of all the earth do right?" (Genesis 18:25). This is a rhetorical question, and the answer is, of course, yes. God's judgment will not be done with revenge but is based on His righteous character.

Suppose a person was guilty of repeating the same crime, and each time he stood before the bench the judge would say, "That's all right, but try not to do that again." Each time the person appeared before the court, the judge would say, "You are forgiven." Would this be fair to the victims, and would the judge be a righteous judge? I think not!

But suppose the judge were to come down from the bench and decide to take the punishment the person deserves. The judge says, "I'll be your redeemer and pay the penalty so justice will be served." Suppose the guilty refuses the offer and says, "I don't think I am guilty." Think about that. Isn't this exactly what the righteous, sinless Jesus did for you and me? He paid the price for all the sins of our lives. His once-for-all sacrifice satisfied the righteous demands of the holy God. Sin required a death payment of a perfect human sacrifice, and the sinless Jesus, because of His love for us, gave Himself to endure that cruel and excruciating death on the cross. The price He paid is indescribable. We are purchased by His precious blood. There are those who refuse to admit their sin and accept God's payment for their sin and thus refuse His offer of salvation.

God loves the sinner but detests the sins. In line with this is the often-asked question, "If God loves people so much, why would God send innocent people to hell who have never heard God's message of salvation?"
This is assuming that there are some people who are innocent. The Bible is specific that there are none righteous, none good, but that all humans are guilty sinners falling short of God's standard, which is perfection.

God foreknew that even if they heard the message of God's offer of salvation, they would turn a deaf ear. If those people would receive the offer, God would have one of His servants reach them. For example it is recorded in Acts 8:26-40:

> Now an angel of the Lord spoke to Philip, saying, "Arise and go toward the south along the road which goes down from Jerusalem to Gaza." This is desert. So he arose and went. And behold, a man of Ethiopia, a eunuch of great authority under Candace the queen of the Ethiopians, who had charge of all her treasury, and had come to Jerusalem to worship, was returning. And sitting in his chariot, he was reading Isaiah the prophet. Then the Spirit said to Philip, "Go near and overtake this chariot." So Philip ran to him, and heard him reading the prophet Isaiah, and said, "Do you understand what you are reading?" And he said, "How can I, unless someone guides me?" And he asked Philip to come up and sit with him. The place in the Scripture which he read was this:
>
> > "He was led as a sheep to the slaughter;
> > And as a lamb before its shearer is silent,
> > So He opened not His mouth.
> > In His humiliation His justice was taken away,
> > And who will declare His generation?
> > For His life is taken from the earth."
>
> So the eunuch answered Philip and said, "I ask you, of whom does the prophet say this, of himself or of some other man?" Then Philip opened his mouth, and beginning at this Scripture, preached Jesus to him. Now as they went down the road, they came to some water. And the eunuch said, "See, here is water. What hinders me from being baptized?" Then Philip said, "If you believe with all your heart, you may." And he answered and said, "I believe that Jesus Christ is the Son of God." So he commanded the chariot to stand still. And both Philip and the eunuch went down into the water, and he baptized him. Now when they came up out of the water, the Spirit of the Lord caught Philip away, so that the eunuch saw him no more; and he went on his way rejoicing. But Philip was found at Azotus. And passing through, he preached in all the cities till he came to Caesarea.

The Bible has many examples where the Holy Spirit of God guides the servants of God to carry His message to those to be reached.

A little aside here that ties in with the above incident: Several years ago, before I ever was involved in prison ministry, I was sitting in the lobby of RBC Ministries reading a little pamphlet while waiting to see Richard DeHaan. Dr. M. R. DeHaan, founder of RBC, and Richard's father, happened to walk by and asked, "Do you understand what you are reading?" I answered, "Yes, Philip!" He smiled and walked on.

Another incident from the book of Acts involves a man named Cornelius and the apostle Peter. God had to work in the heart of Peter before Peter would go to Cornelius, who was a Gentile. Peter considered his calling was to proclaim the message of the crucifixion and the message of the risen Savior to his people, the Jews, but God knew that Cornelius, a centurion in the Italian Regiment, was a devout man who feared God and prayed continually to God. I believe Cornelius was truly seeking God, and God touched the heart of one of His apostles to go to him, because God knew Cornelius would respond to the message of salvation. To get the full story, read Acts 10.

This is another example of the Good Shepherd going after a lost sheep. He rewards those who seek Him: "But without faith it is impossible to please Him, for he who comes to God must believe that He is, and that He is a rewarder of those who diligently seek Him" (Hebrews 11:6). This pertains to those seeking the Creator God of the Bible. Whosoever will may come. The God of the Bible turns no one away who accepts Him and the promises of His Word.

God continues to reach out through His servants. Let me share with you a personal encounter. I had spent a week in Minneapolis calling on business accounts. It was Friday, and I was returning home on a commercial flight. It was about time for closing the door to the plane, and I noticed the seat next to me was vacant. I then sent a call up to the Lord and asked, if it was His will, to seat someone next to me who might be facing some burden for which I could offer some encouragement.

Just before the door was closed, a well-dressed young businessman came rushing in and walked the aisle to the empty seat next to me. He took off his coat and tossed it, along with his briefcase, into the overhead rack. With a big smile on his face he plunked down in the seat next to me. I thought to myself, *Lord, this fellow seems to have it all put together*, but as he sat down he heaved a great sigh. I said, "Rough day." He said, "It's a hassle out there trying to make it." I said, "A man's life consists not in the abundance of the things he possesses." He said, "D___, that's good. Where did that come from?" I said, "The Bible." "Oh," he said. I said, "Things will never satisfy or bring us the peace that deep down people are seeking."

I then offered him a little pamphlet, "Steps to Peace with God," written by Billy Graham. He read it through and replied, "I've been looking for the answer to that for thirteen years." I said, "You can have that peace by receiving God's offer of salvation and reconciliation [peace] by acknowledging Jesus the Christ as your Lord and Savior." After further discussion he bowed his head and prayed a prayer of faith.

We were arriving at Milwaukee, where he was getting off, and I was continuing on to Grand Rapids to my family. When I arrived I was able to share with them how God answered prayer and showed the power of His Word to change hearts and lives.

I did obtain the man's name, address, and phone number, asking him if it was okay to forward them to a contact in Milwaukee who would follow up with him and help him in his newfound faith. He was receptive to that and was thankful that our paths had crossed and that he had found what he had been seeking for so long. I never cease to be amazed at God the Holy Spirit's ways of working through sinful but redeemed people to reach those who are seeking.

In summary, according to God's Word, there are only two places to spend eternity: heaven or hell. Do you have the full assurance of heaven if you leave this earthly scene? If not, why not?

Salvation

There may have been times when you may have heard someone say he or she is saved or born again. The words "born again" come from a spiritual experience that is spoken about in Scripture, but those words are used sometimes in worldly conversation to describe a turnaround of direction for a person or a business venture. However, from a Christian perspective, what is meant by the term "born again" or "saved"?

The meaning is found in the Word of God. The two words are intertwined. You can't have one without the other. The Bible teaches you must be born again in order to be saved and to have the assurance of salvation. To be forgiven is dependent on salvation. So much is at stake concerning our eternal destiny.

Jesus had an encounter with a devout Jew, who was one of a group of seventy religious leaders called the Sanhedrin. This group not only had political influence but also was the last word when it came to ruling over the Jewish religious community. The work of similar groups of rabbis down through the years led to the development of all the traditions and religious practices that were a burden to the Jewish people. Those same traditions caused much confrontation between Jesus and the Jewish religious leaders. We read about this encounter:

> There was a man of the Pharisees named Nicodemus, a ruler of the Jews. This man came to Jesus by night and said to Him, "Rabbi, we know that You are a teacher come from God; for no one can do these signs that You do unless God is with him."
>
> Jesus answered and said to him, "Most assuredly, I say to you, unless one is born again, he cannot see the kingdom of God."
>
> Nicodemus said to Him, "How can a man be born when he is old? Can he enter a second time into his mother's womb and be born?"
>
> Jesus answered, "Most assuredly, I say to you, unless one is born of water and the Spirit, he cannot enter the kingdom of God. That which is born of the flesh is flesh, and that which is born of the Spirit is spirit. Do not marvel that I said to you, 'You must be born again.' The wind blows where it wishes, and you hear the sound of it, but cannot tell where it comes from and where it goes. So is everyone who is born of the Spirit."
>
> Nicodemus answered and said to Him, "How can these things be?"
>
> Jesus answered and said to him, "Are you the teacher of Israel, and do not know these things? Most assuredly, I say to you, We speak what We know and testify what We have seen, and you do not receive Our witness. If I have told you earthly things and you do not believe, how will you believe if I tell you heavenly things? No one has ascended to heaven but He who came down from heaven, that is, the Son of Man who is in heaven. And as Moses lifted up the serpent in the wilderness, even so must the Son of Man be lifted up, that whoever believes in Him should not perish but have eternal life. For God so loved the world that He gave His only begotten Son, that whoever believes in Him should not perish but have everlasting life. For God did not send His Son into the world to condemn the world, but that the world through Him might be saved." (John 3:1-17)

Nicodemus was also a member of the Pharisees, a sect of Judaism that was very legalistic. They observed all kinds of sacrifices and washings for cleansing before going into the temple; they were particular about getting too close to unclean people, especially those with leprosy. (The Pharisees thought they would become unclean if even the shadow of a leper would be cast on them.) It is true to say they were some of the most religious people on earth, all with sincerity and good intentions, believing they were carrying out God's will. And they certainly displayed a form of outward self-righteousness that on various occasions Jesus referred to: "For I say to you, that unless your righteousness exceeds the righteousness of the scribes and Pharisees, you will by no means enter the kingdom of heaven" (Matthew 5:20).

Why would Nicodemus need to be born again? Nicodemus believed in God. Wasn't he trying to follow the religious rituals of the Jewish religion? Wasn't he a good neighbor? Didn't he care for his family? Nicodemus probably rated "A" in all these areas. Then why did he have to be born again? Simply put, the righteousness of man always falls short, because God's standard for righteousness is perfection. Read carefully what God's Word says about the spiritual condition of man's nature: "for all have sinned and fall short of the glory of God" (Romans 3:23), and there is a terrible consequence for sin. We read about this in Romans 6:23: "For the wages of sin is death, but the gift of God is eternal life in Christ Jesus our Lord."

There is a payment to be made for sin, and that is death. That death means to be separated from God's love and presence for all eternity. That would be awful in itself, but that separation will be accompanied by eternal torment. Because we are all sinners, we all deserve this dreadful eternal destiny. But what we need to see is the brighter side, in that God offers everyone a gift. That gift is eternal life, a future to be lived in a joyful atmosphere created by God where everything will be right. But there is only one way to be included in that marvelous future, and that is by obtaining the salvation that God makes available. We must possess this salvation before we exit this worldly scene. This gift can be obtained only while we are engaged on our earthly journey. The Scripture says, "It is appointed for men to die once, but after this the judgment" (Hebrews 9:27). The decision one makes before dying determines where he or she will be in the eternal status and is the basis on which the person will be judged.

Man, with all of his good intentions, still has a sinful nature, and God cannot forgive one sin without the payment that satisfies the righteous requirements of a holy and just God. God's Word tells us that without the shedding of blood, there is no possibility of forgiveness. Furthermore, forgiveness is obtained as part of our relationship with Christ, not through fulfilling the requirements of religious rules, traditions, and practices.

The last part of Romans 6:23 speaks of a gift of eternal life that requires acknowledging that Christ Jesus the Lord is the one through and in whom that gift is obtained. Eternal life is possessed through a relationship with Jesus Christ and excludes the works required by the rituals of religion. If one could work for salvation and eternal life, then it wouldn't be a gift. True Christianity is not a religion but a relationship with Jesus Christ. It is the way to the Father, whose throne room is in heaven.

How is this relationship established? Jesus gives us the answer that He gave to the apostle Thomas: "I am the way, the truth, and the life. No one comes to the Father except through Me" (John 14:6). Jesus is not saying He is one of the ways to the Father who is in heaven; He is the only way. He is not part of the truth; He is the truth. He is the only means of life, because He is the giver and sustainer of all life. Jesus either means what He is saying here or He is being delusional and a deceiver. It can only be one or the other.

How can we know that we have that gift of eternal life? Again we must go to God's Word for the answer:

> If you confess with your mouth the Lord Jesus and believe in your heart that God has raised Him from the dead, you will be saved. For with the heart one believes unto righteousness, and with the mouth confession is made unto salvation. For the Scripture says, "Whoever believes on Him will not be put to shame." For there is no distinction between Jew and Greek, for the same Lord over all is rich to all who call upon Him. For "whoever calls on the name of the LORD shall be saved." (Romans 10:9-13)

Humans look at their life and want to believe that they are not bad people. They hope that their life in comparison with that of others will be acceptable to God and He will be lenient with them. In addition, they try to follow the religious requirements of their faith. But this is considering salvation only from a human perspective. What about God's perspective? God's holiness and justice require a sacrifice to redeem people from the bondage of sin. That sacrifice must be without any blemishes.

Consider the sacrifices that were made as part of the tabernacle ceremonies during the wilderness wanderings of the Israelites. These sacrifices were to be the firstborn lambs, and all the other types of sacrifices had to be the best possible, without blemishes or flaws. These sacrifices were acceptable only as a covering for sin until the perfect Lamb of God would come and make a once-for-all sacrifice for all the sins of humans.

A sinful human sacrifice with all of its blemishes would not be acceptable from God's perspective, and that's why all the efforts of man to redeem himself by good works always fall short. It would be a sacrifice that is blemished. Instead, God provided the perfect sacrifice so that salvation could be offered to humans with justice having been served. If salvation is all of God, then how do we approach God? What are the steps to salvation?

The **first step** is repentance, turning from self to God and realizing you do not have the power to save yourself because of your sin and guilt. "The Lord is not slack concerning His promise, as some count slackness, but is longsuffering toward us, not willing that any should perish but that all should come to repentance" (2 Peter 3:9). In the context of 2 Peter 3, some people are asking, "Where is the promise of Jesus' coming again from heaven?" Peter tells them God is holding out for those who will repent and be saved. Maybe you are one of them? Please don't miss out. The day of grace will come to an end.

The **second step** is to confess vocally that Jesus is the Lord and that you want Him to be your Lord.

The **third step** is to believe in your heart that God has raised Jesus from the dead. Believing with your mind is just information, but believing with your heart requires faith in God's Word and accepting that God means what He says. Where does that faith come from? It is a gift that comes from hearing God's Word. Romans 10:17 says, "So then faith comes by hearing, and hearing by the word of God," and Ephesians 2:8-9 tells us, "For by grace you have been saved through faith, and that not of yourselves; it is the gift of God, not of works, lest anyone should boast."

The Word of God rules out man's works as a requirement for salvation. That Scripture in Ephesians is clear that salvation is not accomplished through works. Is it not based on what the Scripture says, and not in what I want it to say? It is dependent on what I believe and not based on my feelings. Feelings are part of our emotional being and can change in a moment of time. I can feel saved today and lost tomorrow. Feelings must be brought under control. I need to depend on the written Word of God, and that takes faith, and faith pleases God.

So we see then that faith truly is obtained from the Word of God. This faith results in salvation. We are saved when that faith turns to belief, and that belief into complete trust in what God's Word promises, for we know that God will perform. None of this is possible without the Holy Spirit's conviction and enlightenment, because when we turn to God's Word truly seeking God, the Holy Spirit rewards us for that diligence. Hebrews 11:6 says, "But without faith it is impossible to please Him, for he who comes to God must believe that He is, and that He is a rewarder of those who diligently seek Him." And with what does God reward us? Salvation and being declared righteous in His sight. At that moment in time when we truly believe, we experience God's salvation. We receive the righteousness of God in Christ that is so necessary, since we have no righteousness of our own. "For He made Him who knew no sin to be sin for us, that we might become the righteousness of God in Him" (2 Corinthians 5:21).

When was Jesus made sin for us? Let's start in the Garden of Gethsemane. Jesus was there with all of His disciples, with the exception of Judas the betrayer, who was busy selling Jesus for the prophesied thirty pieces of silver. In this garden, Jesus prayed to His Father, asking the Father to take away the cup: the coming trial, false accusations, beatings, the crown of thorns, the scoffing and derision, the brutal manhandling by the soldiers, the whipped bloody back, the agony of the cross, all for the purpose to be made sin for us. Jesus had to endure all that this represented in the process of redemption; otherwise we could not be reconciled to God. Jesus came to be the sacrificial Lamb of God. He shed His blood to make it possible for us to be forgiven. "John saw Jesus coming toward him, and said, 'Behold! The Lamb of God who takes away the sin of the world!'" (John 1:29).

This entire scene reveals that Jesus was fully human. He was crying out to God the Father expressing all of the human emotions that He experienced, except they were more intense than we would have experienced, because He was perfect. Jesus had no divine immunity to escape the horror that He, the one who never committed sin, faced to accomplish salvation for us, when He would become sin for us. Love for we humans was at the center of that sacrifice, because all the sacrifices of lambs could never remove our sin. Even if we were to sacrifice our own lives, that would not be enough. They or we would not be a spotless, perfect sacrifice.

"You were not redeemed with corruptible things, like silver or gold, from your aimless conduct received by tradition from your fathers, but with the precious blood of Christ, as of a lamb without blemish and without spot. He indeed was foreordained before the foundation of the world, but was manifest in these last times for you" (1 Peter 1:18-20).

From all that Jesus went through in payment for our salvation, it could only be offered as a gift, for anything we did would be an insult to His grace. Why would He leave the glory He had with the Father to come to earth and to go through all He went through if man could achieve salvation on his own? Salvation is obtained when a person begins the new life through faith in Christ that is confirmed by the indwelling Holy Spirit.

It is the Holy Spirit who ministers, through the Word of God, Christ to seekers and those who believe. The natural man does not understand the things of God apart from the Spirit of God. The Word says salvation, eternal life, forgiveness of sins, and heaven are all gifts received when we exercise faith in the promised Messiah and all that He went through.

It was on the cross that Jesus, with sorrowful eyes and a heart full of compassion, pleaded with the Father to forgive people, for they knew not what they were doing. He also cried out, "My God, My God, why have You forsaken Me?" (Mark 15:34). It is my opinion that at that moment in time on the cross, Jesus was forsaken of God, and the man Jesus took in His own body the horrible sins of all mankind. It was in His body full of our sins that Jesus paid the price of death to satisfy God's requirement that without the shedding of blood there would be no remission or forgiveness of our sins. Both He and the prophecies of Scripture said all of this would happen. And if Jesus had not been resurrected from the dead and if the tomb was not empty, our faith would be useless:

> And if Christ is not risen, your faith is futile; you are still in your sins! Then also those who have fallen asleep in Christ have perished. If in this life only we have hope in Christ, we are of all men the most pitiable. But now Christ is risen from the dead, and has become the firstfruits of those who have fallen asleep. For since by man came death, by Man also came the resurrection of the dead. For as in Adam all die, even so in Christ all shall be made alive. (1 Corinthians 15:17-22)

The possession of all the promises of God's Word, including the gift of salvation, is possible only by taking God at His word. That's what faith is all about.

Even our faith, we learned, is a gift that is obtained from the Word. Thus, salvation is a gift obtained when a person begins the new life through faith in Christ that is confirmed by the indwelling Holy Spirit, who ministers Christ to us through the Word of God. The natural man does not understand the things of God apart from the Spirit of God. The Holy Spirit or an angel of God will never ever reveal anything that is inconsistent with the written Word of God, such as the requirement of works for salvation.

"Oh," you say, "that's too easy." Not when you consider all that Jesus went through to make the gift of salvation available, a great display of God's love and amazing grace. What is God's grace? Grace is unmerited favor, that is, giving us something we don't deserve and cannot earn. Mercy is keeping us from something we do deserve. When you study the Scriptures, you will find that all that we have comes from God: faith, salvation, forgiveness, eternal life, the indwelling Holy Spirit all are gifts paid for through the sacrifice on the cross by the perfect, sinless Lamb of God. He died so that we might have life, eternal life that is a gift.

But when we get right down to basics, gifts come from the Father in heaven. Listen to what Scripture says in James 1:17: "Every good gift and every perfect gift is from above, and comes down from the Father of lights, with whom there is no variation or shadow of turning."

I hope you see the consistency of God's Word and its power. You and I can experience the new birth of God's salvation based on the authority and promises of His Word. We can depend on God's Word because it is life-giving and endures forever. How powerful is that!

Scripture teaches that Christ fulfilled all of the law, and in doing so He removed the curse of the law so that it no longer has dominion over those who have been set free through faith in Christ and His death on the cross:

> Not by works of righteousness which we have done, but according to His mercy He has saved us, by the washing of regeneration and renewing of the Holy Spirit. (Titus 3:5)

> Knowing that a man is not justified by the works of the law but by faith in Jesus Christ, even we have believed in Christ Jesus, that we might be justified by faith in Christ and not by the works of the law; for by the works of the law no flesh shall be justified. (Galatians 2:16)

> I do not set aside the grace of God; for if righteousness comes through the law, then Christ died in vain. (Galatians 2:21)

> O foolish Galatians! Who has bewitched you that you should not obey the truth, before whose eyes Jesus Christ was clearly portrayed among you as crucified? This only I want to learn from you: Did you receive the Spirit by the works of the law, or by the hearing of faith? Are you so foolish? Having begun in the Spirit, are you now being made perfect by the flesh? (Galatians 3:1-3)

According to God's Word, we were dead in trespasses and sin until we were quickened, or made alive, because of God's love, grace, and mercy:

> And you He made alive, who were dead in trespasses and sins, in which you once walked according to the course of this world, according to the prince of the power of the air, the spirit who now works in the sons of disobedience, among whom also we all once conducted ourselves in the lusts of our flesh, fulfilling the desires of the flesh and of the mind, and were by nature children of wrath, just as the others. But God, who is rich in mercy, because of His great love with which He loved us, even when we were dead in trespasses, made us alive together with Christ (by grace you have been saved). (Ephesians 2:1-5)

Regarding that third step to salvation, some say this proves that Jesus was not God because God had to raise Him up. But listen to what Jesus told His apostles: "Therefore My Father loves Me, because I lay down My life that I may take it again. No one takes it from Me, but I lay it down of Myself. I have power to lay it down, and I have power to take it again. This command I have received from My Father" (John 10:17-18). This gives evidence and consistency to the fact that Jesus had this power because He was fully God. When a person places complete trust in Jesus Christ alone for salvation, that person is born again on the authority of God's Word and receives the righteousness of God in Christ. That person's sins are forgiven, to be remembered no more by God. That person becomes a new person in Christ.

Look at what the apostle Peter says in his first letter: "having been born again, not of corruptible seed but incorruptible, through the word of God which lives and abides forever" (1 Peter 1:23). This tells us that this new birth comes through the Word of God. Jesus said in John 6:63 that His words are Spirit and life. The power of God's Word is overwhelming. We can depend on it.

God tells us in His Word that we can know we have eternal life: "And this is the testimony: that God has given us eternal life, and this life is in His Son. He who has the Son has life; he who does not have the Son of God does not have life. These things I have written to you who believe in the name of the Son of God, that you may know that you have eternal life, and that you may continue to believe in the name of the Son of God" (1 John 5:11-13).

If I were to offer you a gift, what would you have to pay for it? Nothing! But if, after you took possession of the gift, I said to you, "Now that you accepted this gift, I expect you to pay for it," it never was a gift. That's in essence what some religions teach, and that's what keeps people in bondage. They are afraid to leave the rituals of religion for the freedom and release that come through God's free gift of eternal life. That eternal life is in God's Son. Some religions do not believe there is a God who has a gift of salvation for them, and they rely on a works-based religion. How tragic to disregard God's offer.

Please remember that God's Word tells you and me that by the works of the law no one will be justified. We cannot be made right in the sight of God by keeping the law. That would mean that Jesus, the Son of God, died in vain if our righteousness could be established by our works. Does that mean we do not need to do good works? Not at all. It's just that our good works cannot save us. I depend on God the Father's grace through faith in the sacrifice of His perfect Son, who on the cross made the full payment for my redemption and pardon. I am set free from the bondage and curse of the law. I become overwhelmed with the joy His salvation brings. You too can enter into this joy.

A couple of hundred years ago, at a slave auction in the South, an old, worn-out slave was put up for bid. His former owner had treated him spitefully and had burdened him with difficult tasks that had caused him to age rapidly. Now he was no longer useful to the slave owner and was put up for auction. No one seemed to be bidding, when finally a man offered an unusually high bid for the slave that was readily accepted. The slave thought, *Why would this man pay such a high price for someone who is worn out by years of degrading labor?* The transaction was completed. The old slave said, "Master, why did you purchase me? I'm old, abused, and worn out." The new master said, "I bought you so I could free you." The slave couldn't believe what he was hearing and in reply said, "You mean I am free and I can do whatever I want?" "That's right." The slave replied, "If that's why you bought me, I will serve you the rest of my life."

That's a beautiful story of grace and gratitude. Are you still a slave to sin, and your cruel slave master is Satan? You were bought at a great price—the precious blood of Jesus the Christ—to be set free from the bondage of sin and the evil slave master Satan. Do you want to stay with your old master or the new one? Why wouldn't you want to serve a kind and gracious Master?

It might be that as you read the Scriptures presented that you heard God speaking to your heart through His Word. That's the way God the Holy Spirit convicts us of sin, righteousness, and judgment. Don't try to quench that thirst for the truth by drinking from the wells of manmade religion. Jesus said that that those who hunger and thirst after righteousness (to be made right) will be filled. The thirst and hunger of your inner being can be satisfied only by the living water and the bread of life that Jesus brings when you open the door of your spiritual heart and life to him. "Behold, I [Jesus] stand at the door and knock. If anyone hears My voice and opens the door, I will come in to him and dine with him and he with Me" (Revelation 3:20).

Fellowship with God was destroyed in the Garden of Eden due to disobedience, as related in Genesis, the first book of the Bible. Fellowship can be restored only by obeying the voice of Jesus, as stated in the last book of the Bible, when you open the door of your heart and let Him in. He promises to come in if invited and will bring spiritual food to the table. You can dine and fellowship with royalty, the King of kings and the Lord of lords.

God, however, did not make you a robot. Jesus will not force His way into your heart and life. You can either open the door or ignore Him and keep the door shut. The decision is yours. Consider carefully the following questions:

> Realizing you are a sinner, are you willing to turn from sinful self to God?
>
> Do you desire God's forgiveness of all of your sin?
>
> Will you acknowledge Jesus as the Lord and believe He died for your sins, was buried, and rose from the dead?
>
> Are you willing to open the door to your heart and life and invite Christ to come in?
>
> Are you ready to do this now?

If you answered yes to all of those questions, then by accepting Jesus Christ as your Lord and Savior by faith you are transferred from the kingdom of darkness into the kingdom of God's dear Son. You are born again. Your sins are forgiven. You have eternal life and citizenship in heaven. You have made peace with God and have the peace of God. You are a new person. "Therefore, if anyone is in Christ, he is a new creation; old things have passed away; behold, all things have become new" (2 Corinthians 5:17).

You say that is too simple. It is simple, because God wants little children to understand it. You say it's too easy. Yes, but look at what Jesus went through to make it possible for you. That's why salvation is all of God and is provided as a gift by His grace. People have nothing they can do for salvation, because it's all been done. Salvation is free and made possible only by God's marvelous grace and His profound love for you and me who are sinners. Don't stay turned away from God's great salvation. It is free and will fill you with the deepest joy when you turn from self to Jesus, who is the only way to God the Father in heaven, both for this life and the life to come. May His love, joy, and peace flood your soul.

Prophecies

Throughout this book there have been references to prophecies that were fulfilled or must still be fulfilled. Let's look at what is still to come. These future events involve the nations of the world. Israel will see some remarkable but also troublous times, because Israel will be a thorn in the flesh to the nations. The true church will be taken out of this scene, and then will come the seven-year period of tribulation. During those seven years, God's people, the tribulation saints, will see increasing persecution. Millions will be beheaded because the tribulation saints refuse to take the mark of the beast. Also, just prior to or at that period of time, Israel will be threatened by a gathering of nations that involves present-day Iran, Libya, Turkey, Sudan, and Russia. You can see this developing currently, as was prophesied.

God's Word tells us that a leader is coming who will appear on the world scene and will seem to have all the answers for all the world's ills and problems. The Scriptures state that this leader will bring about a world government, a world religion, and a world economy. People will buy into his program thinking he is the real Messiah, only to be deceived later. This charismatic leader is none other than the prophesied Antichrist. This Antichrist, who rules all the nations of the world through ten kingdoms, will have set up an alliance and a seven-year peace treaty with Israel. Israel will look to the Antichrist as if he were the promised Messiah, but halfway through the peace treaty, the Antichrist will establish himself as God in the temple in Jerusalem, and Israel will realize that the Antichrist is a false Messiah.

It is during this tribulation period that the 144,000 Jewish evangelists, 12,000 each from the twelve tribes of Israel, circle the globe with the kingdom message. Those evangelists anger the Antichrist, who is the embodiment of Satan, and he attempts to annihilate all of Israel, but Israel will be rescued. When all the nations of the world, under the leadership of the Antichrist, gather at the plains of Meggido in the north of Israel, it looks like doomsday for Israel, but it is then that the Lord Jesus, accompanied by His saints from heaven, returns to the Mount of Olives in all His glory.

Jesus as the Lord of lords destroys the enemies of Israel with the brightness of His coming and establishes His rightful kingdom on the throne of David in Jerusalem. It is then the thousand-year reign of Christ begins after Satan is chained and thrown into the bottomless abyss. The Antichrist and the false prophet are cast into the lake of fire, and those who had received the mark of the beast are sent to Hades awaiting the judgment at the great white throne at the end of the millennial reign of Christ. At the end of the thousand years, Satan is released from the bottomless pit for a short time to go out to gather the discontented rogue nations, including Gog and Magog, to destroy the kingdom of Jesus the true Messiah, who is the Lord of lords and the King of kings. Fire comes down from heaven and defeats Satan and the rebellious nations. Satan is cast into the lake of fire, where the Antichrist and the false prophet are, to be tormented day and night forever and ever.

After the judgment, a renovated new earth, new Jerusalem, and new heaven appear, wherein dwells righteousness. Those who are God's redeemed will enjoy God's kingdom as God shares His glory with His people throughout the endless ages of eternity.

I hope, dear reader, you will be there, for it will be glorious! If you're not there, you will share in Satan's torment forever in his ultimate kingdom, which is hell and the lake of fire. Choose eternal life, not eternal death. The source of these future events comes from the Scriptures: Ezekiel 36–39; Daniel 7–9; the book of Zechariah; the book of Revelation, particularly chapters 5–19; 1 Thessalonians 4:13-18; and Jesus' prophecy in Matthew 24.

You have probably said to yourself, "Where is the proof that all this is really going to happen?" It says so in the Word of God. Every prophecy in the holy Bible that has been fulfilled came to pass exactly the way predicted, so why wouldn't prophecies yet to be fulfilled also come to pass?

Even with all these prophetic evidences that the Bible is true and had to be inspired by other than human wisdom, the Bible itself, in 2 Peter 2:1-3, says that in the last days scoffers of the Word will live according to their own lusts. Their eternal existence will be graphically horrible.

Jesus was who He said He was: the Son of Man and the Son of God. His apostles, the disciples of Jesus' day, and millions on millions of people since that time have found Him to be all that the Bible says He is. He is our Lord and Savior who will come again. It may be sooner than you think! Dear friend, be ready for His coming. To not do so is to not believe the offer and the warning of God's Word, and continued unbelief is the unpardonable sin.

Are you a scoffer, or are you accepting God's Word and His offer?

You decide!

Appendix A

The Divine Name in the New World Translation

Chapter 12: A Conclusion

"From the study we just finished, we see that there is no manuscript evidence of any kind showing that the Tetragrammaton was used in the original Christian Scripture (N.T.) manuscripts. Secondly, we understand the futility of using Hebrew versions to prove that the Christian Scripture writers used the Tetragrammaton because these versions are merely translations from a Greek text that does *not* use the Tetragrammaton. Finally, we realize that there is no evidence from history to support the theory that a heresy in the early Christian congregations resulted in the removal of the Tetragrammaton from the Christian Scriptures.

In this concluding chapter we must consider the implications of this information.

An irreconcilable conflict

The Watch Tower Society introduces an irreconcilable conflict in its *Kingdom Interlinear Translation* footnote material. If the Greek text published by the Watch Tower Society is truly inspired by Jehovah and therefore absolutely reliable, then the correct word in these 237 Christian Scripture "Jehovah" passages in the *New World Translation* is ***Kyrios***.[1] Generally, ***Kyrios*** is translated as *Lord,* and would be a reference to Jesus. (This is the preferred choice of the *New World Translation* in 406 cases.[2]) On the other hand, the *New World Translation* uses the divine name

1 This statement does not overlook the many copying errors made during the transmission of the Christian Scriptures. However, it recognizes that today, through the careful work of textual critics such as Westcott and Hort, we have an almost exact reproduction of the original Christian Scriptures.

2 Refer to Appendix C, page 235 of The Tetragrammaton and the Christian Greek Scriptures. This and other downloadable books are available through the web site **www.tetragrammaton.org**.

Jehovah in these same 237 instances. If *Jehovah* is indeed the word used by the inspired Christian writers, then the Greek text is in error.

This irreconcilable conflict is evident in three viewpoints that cannot coexist without compromise. Yet, the Watch Tower Society independently defends each of these viewpoints:

1. **We possess faithful copies of the Christian Scriptures.** We agree with the authors of *"All Scripture Is Inspired of God and Beneficial"* that the Greek Scriptures we have today are substantially the same as they were when originally written. Sir Frederic Kenyon says, "The interval then between the dates of original composition and the earliest extant evidence becomes so small as to be in fact negligible, and the last foundation for any doubt that the Scriptures have come down to us substantially as they were written has now been removed."[3]

2. **The text of the *Kingdom Interlinear Translation* is trustworthy.** This Greek text demonstrates that ***Kyrios*** (*Lord*) was the word used by the inspired Christian writers. Manuscripts from the third and fourth centuries C.E. substantiate its presence. The *Kingdom Interlinear Translation* clearly demonstrates that ***Kyrios*** (*Lord*) was accepted as the proper word from as early as 105 years—and no later than 301 years—from the time of its writing. (John wrote Revelation about 96 C.E. The third century began in 201 C.E., or 105 years after John wrote Revelation.)

3. **The "J" reference sources are from a much later period of time.** The Hebrew versions used to substantiate the inspired Christian writers' use of the Tetragrammaton were translated no earlier than 1385 C.E.

If the Greek text is reliable, then its words must be reliable. But if the Greek text is reliable, how can the Tetragrammaton in a 14th century C.E. Hebrew translation have precedence over a fourth century C.E. Greek text that uses ***Kyrios*** (*Lord*)? We could not argue that all of the words in the Greek text are reliable except for 237 instances that have no manuscript or historic evidence of change. Inasmuch as the evidence for the use of the Tetragrammaton is far less verifiable than that for any other word in the original Christian Scriptures, if these

3 "All Scripture Is Inspired of God and Beneficial," Watch Tower Bible and Tract Society, 1990, page 319.

237 instances of the use of ***Kyrios*** are doubtful, then no part of the Christian Scriptures can be regarded as reliable.

Yet, this is not a mere issue of scholarly research or distant debates about ancient manuscripts. It has a very practical application to each of us. If the written word of Jehovah was so fragile and tenuous that the divine name could be lost without any trace in less than 200 years, can we continue to trust it today? Followers of Jehovah's word, the Bible, are unique. Unlike other religions, true Christianity is not a mere philosophy of good acts and kindnesses. Rather, true Christianity is based upon specific truths that are precisely recorded in Jehovah's word. If our Bible is not a trustworthy translation of reliable Greek (and Hebrew) manuscripts that can be traced directly back to the inspired writers, we cannot be certain as to the trustworthiness of our faith.

Jehovah does not intend that we have an uncertain faith. He did not "lose" his written word only to have it reappear 1300 years later in Hebrew versions translated from Greek manuscripts in which the lost words had not yet been "found."

Hebrew Scripture quotations

In some instances, the Christian Scripture writers used ***Kyrios*** in such a way as to convey the thought that they were referring to the Jehovah of the Hebrew Scriptures. There is no doubt but that this is the case in such verses as:

In the course of one of the days [Jesus] was teaching, and Pharisees and teachers of the law who had come out of every village of Galilee and Judea and Jerusalem were sitting there; and (**Jehovah's** power—*NWT* or, the power of **Lord** [***Kyrios***]—*KIT*) was there for him to do healing. (Luke 5:17)

Clearly, this verse does not say that *Jesus' own power was there in order that he could heal.* That would be an unlikely statement inasmuch as Jesus' power was *always* present. Luke is drawing our attention to Jehovah's power. Luke used ***Kyrios*** in a way that conveyed the thought as expressed in the *New World Translation*: "... and Jehovah's power was there for him [Jesus] to do healing." Nonetheless, Luke did not use the word his reader Theophilus (Luke 1:3) would know as the Hebrew name of God. Instead, Luke used ***Kyrios***. The reader today must be able to grasp that same meaning by reading the word *Lord* rather than *Jehovah*.

There are *many* passages throughout the Christian Scriptures that identify Jehovah as the subject.[4] We will quote just two such verses. Matthew 1:22-23a (with an identifiable quotation from Isaiah 7:14 that is attributable to Jehovah) says:

> All this actually came about for that to be fulfilled which was spoken (by **Jehovah**—*NWT* or, by **Lord** [***Kyrios***]—*KIT*) through his prophet, saying: "Look! The virgin will become pregnant and will give birth to a son…. "

Even though Matthew used the Greek word ***Kyrios***, he certainly must have intended the reader to understand it to mean, "which was spoken by Jehovah…" (*New World Translation*).

The third illustration of a ***Kyrios*** passage clearly referring to *Jehovah* also comes from Luke. When the angel Gabriel was sent to Mary with the announcement of the birth of Jesus, she responded according to Luke 1:38:

> Then Mary said; "Look! (**Jehovah's** slave girl!—*NWT* or, The slave girl of **Lord** [***Kyrios***]—*KIT*) May it take place with me according to your declaration."

Certainly Luke indicated that Mary was addressing *Jehovah* when she offered herself in humble obedience. It would be most unusual to explain this passage by saying that Mary was addressing her yet unborn son.

These verses show us that in certain instances, Christian Scripture writers used the word ***Kyrios*** when referring to *Jehovah*. That is, *since there is no historical or biblical record to indicate that they used the Tetragrammaton in the inspired writings,*

---

4 The reader should understand that we are not excluding the person of Jesus from this statement. For more information, see Chapter 14 "The Indistinct Meaning of **Kyrios**" in the book The Tetragrammaton and the Christian Greek Scriptures, available as a downloadable book at **www.tetragrammaton.com**.

*we know from the best ancient manuscript evidence that they used the Greek word **Kyrios**[5] when referring to Jehovah.*

In conclusion, we must briefly consider two issues resulting from the inspired authors' use of the word ***Kyrios.***

We must let the inspired writers speak

On the surface, it seems as though the inspired writers made a mistake when they used the single word ***Kyrios*** to refer to both *Jehovah* and *Lord.*

Yet, all the evidence shows us that that is exactly what they intended to do.

At this point we must be honest with ourselves. Often, we want the inspired writers to say that which will support our own group's theological beliefs. Listen to any group explaining what they think an inspired writer meant and you will realize how much they want to show that the Scripture writer used words that validate their doctrinal position.

It is understandable that the Watch Tower Society would prefer to have the inspired writers separate the identity of *Jehovah* and the *Lord Jesus* in the Christian Scriptures. If these writers had used the Tetragrammaton 237 times, we would be able to see a clear distinction between *Lord* and *Jehovah.*

But they did not. They used the single word ***Kyrios*** for both. In some instances it is clear that they were speaking of *Jehovah.* In others, it is clear that they were speaking of the *Lord Jesus.* There are, however, a large number of verses in which they appear to have purposely allowed the identities of *Jehovah* and *Jesus* to overlap. Notice the sharp contrast between the sense of the following verses in the *New World Translation* and the *Kingdom Interlinear Translation.* The translators of the *New World Translation* have made it appear as though the verse is identifying *Jehovah.* On the other hand, the inspired writer used the word

5 Again, at this point we must make a strong statement affirming the inspiration of Scripture. As we have seen, there is no evidence that the original manuscripts contained the Tetragrammaton. Therefore, unless we deny the inerrancy and inspiration of the Christian Scriptures, we can only conclude that God directed the inspired writers to use the Greek word **Kyrios** rather than the Hebrew word יהוה. If—in our desire to protect a theological position—we still must insist that the Tetragrammaton from Hebrew versions has precedence, then we must be willing to relinquish our claim that the Scriptures we have today are "inspired of God."

Kyrios, thereby conveying an entirely different meaning. (The quotation from the *Kingdom Interlinear Translation* comes directly from the interlinear portion. Consequently, the word order is that of the Greek sentence itself.)

New World Translation	Kingdom Interlinear Translation
I am the Alpha and the Omega," says **Jehovah** God, "the One who is and who was and who is coming, the Almighty." Revelation 1:8	I am the Alpha and the Omega, is saying **Lord**, the God, The (one) being and the (one) was and the (one) coming, the Almighty. Revelation 1:8
"We thank you, **Jehovah** God, the Almighty, the One who is and who was, because you have taken your great power and begun ruling as king." Revelation 11:17	We are giving thanks to you, **Lord**, the God, the Almighty, the (one) being and the (one) was, because you have taken the power of you the great and you reigned. Revelation 11:17
And I heard the altar say: "Yes, **Jehovah** God, the Almighty, true and righteous are your judicial decisions." Revelation 16:7	And I heard of the altar saying Yes, **Lord**, the God, the Almighty, true and righteous the judgment of you. Revelation 16:7
"Praise **Jah**, you people, because **Jehovah** our God, the Almighty, has begun to rule as king." Revelation 19:6	Hallelu**jah**, because reigned **Lord** the God of us, the Almighty. Revelation 19:6

The book of Revelation alone has many similar examples. (See Revelation 4:8 and 11, 15:3, 18:8, 19:6, 21:22, and 22:5-6.) There are many other examples throughout the Christian Scriptures as well. In fact, all of the 237 Jehovah references should be examined.

In all of these instances, we must allow the inspired writer to say to us exactly what he said to the readers of his day. In turn, that is what Jehovah wants us to understand today.

The translator must communicate the writers' thoughts

In the first chapter we stated a principle that all Bible translators must follow. We said, "The translator must choose words that communicate the same idea to the reading audience today that the inspired writer communicated to the reader of his day." We then made the application that a present-day Bible translator must allow the "Old Testament" writers' words to communicate the revered name of God to the reader. An English Bible translator today must therefore identify God by name to his English reading audience just as the Hebrew Scripture author had.

Applying this same principle to the Christian Scripture translator is no different. Irrespective of the word used by the original Christian Scripture writers, the translator of an English Bible today must convey the same meaning to his readers that the authors did. This is true even if a word they used has a less sharply defined meaning than the word (or words) we would prefer today.

Inasmuch as the Tetragrammaton is *not* used in the Greek Scriptures, all passages translated as *Jehovah* in the *New World Translation Christian Scriptures* must rightfully be translated as *Lord* where ***Kyrios*** is found in the *Kingdom Interlinear Translation.*[6]

The translator must communicate the exact thoughts of the original writers to his reading audience. The translator cannot become a commentator, explaining what he (the commentator) believes the Scripture writer intended to say.[7] A commentator may do that later, using properly translated Scripture passages.

---

6 It is important that we not be misunderstood. The Tetragrammaton was used almost 7,000 times in the Hebrew Scriptures. The author holds in high regard those translators who have made the effort to use a proper translation of הוהי rather than Lord. However, inasmuch as the Tetragrammaton is not found in any existing manuscripts of the Greek Scriptures, it is a violation of inspiration to insert the name where there is no evidence that the original Christian writers used it.

7 This does not ignore the fact that a translator must often make subjective choices when translating a word or a phrase from Greek into English. In many instances, that decision will involve the personal opinion of the translator regarding word meanings according to the context. **Kyrios** was a common secular word in the Greek language of Jesus' day. It is appropriately translated in the New World Translation as Sir [Mark 7:28], owner [Matthew 21:40], master [Matthew 25:26], a protocol form of address for an emperor [Acts 25:26], and slave master [Ephesians 6:5]. However, this does not give the translator the privilege of substituting one known word for another with an entirely different meaning as would be the case in substituting the divine name for Lord.

Even the translator may do that later. But the translator is not free to use his translation as a statement of personal opinion."

Appendix B

Specific Topics from the Qur'an

At the dinner in Bombay, when the sheikh invited me to visit him in Bahrain, I mentioned I would like the privilege to share what I believe with him, and he could share what he believes.

During our first visit, on his desk was a copy of the Arabic Bible that a friend at Thomas Nelson Publishing was able to obtain and send to the sheikh on my behalf. He showed it to me and thanked me. He also showed me the little booklet I had given him in India, "Steps to Peace with God."

I began to share some material with him, but he asked if I could come back the next day, when he would have his interpreter there. The next day I shared through the interpreter, which took twice as much time, but the sheikh was interested and gracious as we went through the suras one by one.

Each sura (the name of the sura is given) and verse (*ayah*) from the Qur'an is followed with my explanation. The following is what I shared, and I left copies for him.

What the Qur'an Says about the Bible

We gave the people of Abraham (the Jews) the Book and the Wisdom and We gave them a mighty Kingdom. (Woman 4:54)

Explanation: *The Almighty gave the Jews His book (Torah), the Old Testament.*

And We sent, following, Jesus son of Mary, and gave unto him the Gospel. And We set in the hearts of those who followed him tenderness and mercy. (Iron 57:27)

Explanation: *God gave the Injeel (New Testament) to Jesus. True followers of Christ have a changed heart of tenderness and mercy.*

Yet how will they (the Jews) make you (O Muhammad) their judge, seeing they have the Torah wherein is God's judgment? . . . Surely We sent down the Torah,_wherein is guidance and light; thereby the Prophets who had surrendered themselves gave judgment for those of Jewry, as did the Masters and rabbis, following such portion of God's book as they were given to keep and witness to.

So fear not men but fear you Me; and sell not My signs for a little price. Whoso judges not according to what God has sent down, they are the unbelievers. (Table 5:43-44)

Explanation: *The Jews have the Torah, containing everything from which to be judged. What the Torah prophets said will judge Israel and guide them. Muhammad believed God had a book in heaven. He gave a portion of it to the Jews, a portion to the Christians, and a portion to him. Muhammad said if the Jews follow the book that's all that is needed.*

So let the People of the Gospel (the Christians) judge according to what was sent down therein. Whoever judges not according to what God has sent down, they are the ungodly. (Table 5:47)

Explanation: *God sent down the Injeel (Gospel). If Christians do not follow what God has sent down, they are the ungodly. Muhammad does not say Christians are to follow the Qur'an.*

Surely they that believe, and those of Jewry, and Sabeans, and those Christians, whoever believes in God and the Last Day, and works righteousness, no fear shall be upon them, neither shall they sorrow. (Table 5:69)

Explanation: *If Jews and Christians follow their own books, they have nothing to fear, according to Muhammad.*

Say, "People of the Book (Muslims), you do not stand on anything, until you perform the Torah and the Gospel, and what was sent down to you from the Lord." (Table 5:68)

Explanation: *A true Muslim must obey the Torah and the Injeel, that is, the Old Testament and the New Testament.*

There is no changing the Words of God; that is the mighty triumph. (Jonah 10:64)
No man can change the Words of God. (Cattle 6:34)
You shall never find any changing the wont of God, and you shall never find any altering the wont of God. (Angels 35:43)

Explanation: *Sometimes people say the Bible has been tampered with and changed. Muhammad says people can never change the Word of God.*

Considering the above it is evident from the Qur'an that Muhammad said that Jews and Christians are to follow the Word of God that was given to them. Also, good Muslims are to read and obey the Torah and the Injeel.

What the Qur'an Says about Jesus

When the angels said, "Mary, God gives you good tidings of a Word from Him whose name is Messiah, Jesus, son of Mary; highly honored shall He be in this world and the next, near stationed to God." (House of Imran 3:45)

Explanation: *Jesus is referred to as the Word of God and given a position at the right hand of God. Thus He is in a position to intercede for us.*

We gave Jesus son of Mary the clear signs, and confirmed him with the Holy Spirit. (Cow 2:87)

Explanation: *"We" refers to the majesty of God. "Signs" refer to the miracles. "Confirmed" means God gave Jesus the Holy Spirit to help sustain and defend Him. Muhammad speaks of no other prophet other than Jesus having the Holy Spirit. Others were inspired by the Holy Spirit but did not have the Holy Spirit.*

The Messiah, Jesus son of Mary, was indeed the messenger of God, and His Word that He committed to Mary, and a Spirit from Him. (Woman 4:171)

Explanation: *God committed His Word to Mary, which became Jesus the Christ. Only Christ of all the persons in the Qur'an is called the Word of God. This is confirmed to a greater degree in John 1:1-14.*

He said I am but a messenger come from thy Lord, to give thee (O Mary) a boy most pure'_(without sin). (Mary 19:19)

Explanation: *Muhammad here states Christ Jesus is sinless. Muhammad does not claim this for himself. He asked God for forgiveness.*

But she Mary who guarded_her virginity, so We breathed into her of Our Spirit and appointed her and her son to be a sign unto all beings. (Prophets 21:91)

Explanation: *Jesus is born of a virgin and conceived by the power of the Holy Spirit.*

When I (God) confirmed you (Jesus) with the Holy Spirit, to speak to men in the cradle and of age. (Table 5:110)

Explanation: *God gave Jesus the Holy Spirit so as a child He could speak as a grown man to the people. (This story is in one of the Gnostic gospels). However, the Bible records Jesus speaking with great wisdom at the age of twelve in the temple in Jerusalem. See Luke 2:41-47.*

Those messengers, some We have preferred above others . . . some He raised in rank. And we gave Jesus son of Mary the clear signs, and confirmed him with the Holy Spirit. (Cow 2:253)

Explanation: *Messengers are prophets. Some are preferred above others. Christ is the highest messenger (prophet) because He has the signs (miracles) and the Holy Spirit.*

So when he (Moses) came to it, he was called, "Blessed is He Who is in the fire and he who is about it. Glory be to God, the Lord of all being. Moses behold, it is I, God, the All-Mighty, the All-Wise." (Ant 27:8-9)

Explanation: *If God can speak to Moses from a burning bush, why can't God prepare a human body to indwell and reveal Himself? Why not the body of Jesus?*

What the Qur'an Says about Jesus' Death, Resurrection, and Ascension

We gave Moses the book . . . and We gave Jesus Son of Mary the clear signs, and confirmed him with the Holy Spirit and whenever there came to you a Messenger with that your souls had not desired for, did you become arrogant, and cry lies to (Moses and Old Testament prophets),and some slay (Jesus and New Testament prophets). (Cow 2:87)

Explanation: *In this sura Muhammad explains the difference between the prophets of the Torah (Old Testament) and the Injeel (New Testament). Moses and his party were accused of being liars by the unbelievers, Christ and his apostles were persecuted and slain by unbelievers.*

Christ said to God, "I was a witness over them (the people) while I remained among them; but when you made me die, You Yourself were the watcher over them." (Table 5:117)

Explanation: *The Qur'an says God made Jesus to die.*

"Peace be upon me the day I was born, and the day I am raised up alive." That is Jesus , son of Mary, the Word of Truth, concerning which they are doubting. (Mary 19:33-34)

Explanation: *Jesus the Christ, the Word of Truth, died (previous sura 5:117)_ and according to this sura rose again.*

When God said, "Jesus, I will make you die and will raise you up to me, and I will purify you of those who believe not. I will set your followers above the unbelievers till the resurrection day." (House of Imran 3:55)

> **Explanation:** *This sura states that Jesus died and ascended to God before the resurrection day. Christ's followers will be God's choice people before the judgment or the resurrection day.*

They (the Jews) did not slay him . . . not of a certainty, no indeed. (Woman 4:157)

> **Explanation:** *This sura is used to say that Jesus was not crucified by the Jews. True, Jesus was crucified by the Roman authorities. The Romans were incited by the Jews. Crucifixion was a Roman method of execution.*

And We [God] ransomed him (the son of Abraham, God's friend) with a mighty sacrifice. (Rangers 37:107)

> **Explanation:** *Abraham, according to the Bible, killed a ram in Isaac's place (the Qur'an says in Ishmael's place). But a "mighty sacrifice" cannot mean a mere ram. It can only mean God; thus, this is a type of Christ that looks toward the ultimate sacrifice, when Jesus, the Lamb of God, would be sacrificed for the sins of all humankind.*

The All-mighty, All-wise God has raised him up. (Woman 4:158)

> **Explanation:** *Christ Jesus was raised by the all-powerful and all-knowing God. Jesus told His disciples before His crucifixion that He would lay down His life and would have the power to take it back up again. Was Jesus telling a lie?*
>
> *Was the apostle John lying when he recorded this in John 10:15-18:*
>
> > "As the Father knows Me, even so I know the Father; and I lay down My life for the sheep. And other sheep I have which are not of this fold; them also I must bring, and they will hear My voice; and there will be one flock and one shepherd. Therefore My Father loves Me, because I lay down My life that I may take it again. No one takes it from Me, but I lay it down of Myself. I have power to lay it down, and I have power to take it again. This command I have received from My Father."

In addition to this material from the Qur'an, I had the privilege to share the essentials of my Christian faith. That visit and subsequent visits with the sheikh were learning experiences for me. I trust they were for him as well. There are elements of truth in the Qur'an, but it also contradicts the Bible in areas that are extremely important.

On my way back to the hotel, the driver, Zakir, one of the sheikh's servants, gave me an authorized copy of the Qur'an that was translated by Yusuf Ali. It had both Arabic and English side by side, along with footnotes in English. I thanked him for this considerate act. I have read the English portions along with many of the footnotes.

After that first visit the sheikh said that he wanted his sons to meet my son, and on one of our visits my son David and a friend of mine, Bill, and his son spent time with the sheikh and his sons. This resulted in a fishing trip on the Gulf waters in one of his yachts. Also on that visit the sheikh gave my friend's son a purebred Arabian horse. Knowing the sheikh had a great admiration for horses, especially Arabians, on one of my visits I presented him with a Lalique figurine of a horse. He displayed it in a prominent place in his office.

On one of the trips we were treated to dinner at a beautiful home on his personal island a short distance from Bahrain. At that dinner he invited some staff from the American Missions Hospital, which is located in the capitol city, Manama. That hospital was established in Bahrain more than a hundred years ago by the Reformed Church of America. In its early years, the staff had administered a vaccination that saved the lives of the royal family of Bahrain, and others, from an outbreak of yellow fever. Sheikh Mohammad and his brothers Isa and Khalifa were educated and taught English by a British lady associated with the hospital. It is because of those kind acts that the royal family still shows kindness to the AMH staff.

Appendix C

The Qur'an, History, and Jihad

The history of the early days of Islam, centuries of warring, especially the Crusades, and the message of the Qur'an have given radical Muslim their position for Jihad. They point to this position to justify their actions and believe they are carrying out the will of Allah.

The Qur'an, the Hadiths, and Jihad

It has been related in a biography of Muhammad that the first person he wanted to be rid of was a Jewish man. He asked, "Who will rid me of Ibnu'l Ashraf?" One of his men said, "I will deal with him for you. O apostle of God. I will kill him." Muhammad gave his blessing, but later the man returned to Muhammad and said that in order to kill this man he would have to lie. Again, Muhammad gave his blessing. So this man and a few other followers tricked the man into leaving his house so they could kill him. The account relates that "our attack upon God's enemy cast terror among the Jews, and there was no Jew in Medina who did not fear for his life" (64a).

Numerous other incidents of killings and exiling of tribes from Medina are described in that biography. It seems that the warner with a message was becoming a warrior with a sword destroying those who opposed submission to Allah and allegiance to Allah's Prophet.

Some Muslim theologians are quick to say that the sword is used for defensive purposes, but the history of Muhammad's day, the glorification in the Muslim world today of wars and terrorist devastation, and the monetary rewards to families of suicide bombers belie their assertion. There is a deeper underlying reason for these brutal killings. For those Muslims who want to take the Qur'an literally, as many devoted Muslims do not, they will find the language of the Qur'an and the Hadith sanctions and promotes these actions against unbelievers and infidels. Note some of Muhammad's quotes from the revered Hadith:

> Allah's apostle said, "Know that paradise is under the shade of swords" (Hadith 4:55)

> Allah's apostle said, "I have been ordered to fight with the people until they say, 'None has the right to be worshipped but Allah,' and whoever says, 'None has the right to be worshipped but Allah,' his life and property will be saved by men" (Hadith 4:125)
>
> It is not fitting for a prophet that he should have prisoners of war [and free them with ransom] until he has made a great slaughter [among his enemies] in the land (Hadith 4:161)
>
> Whoever changed his Islamic religion, then kill him (Hadith 9:45)

In some Muslim homes today, Hadith 9:45 is used to justify threatening or killing a family member who converts to Christ.

The Qur'an speaks about the rewards for dying while using the sword (sura 47:4-6):

> Therefore, when ye meet the Unbelievers (in fight), smite at their necks; At length, when ye have thoroughly subdued them, bind a bond firmly (on them): thereafter (is the time for) either generosity or ransom: Until the war lays down its burdens. Thus (are ye commanded): but if it had been Allah's Will, He could certainly have exacted retribution from them (Himself); but (He lets you fight) in order to test you, some with others, But those who are slain in the Way of Allah, He will never let their deeds be lost. Soon will He guide them and improve their condition, And admit them to the Garden which He has announced for them.

Radical Muslims find that the written words of the Qur'an foster using the sword and Jihad. To say only a few places in the suras and Hadiths approve this behavior is not being intellectually honest. Throughout the Qur'an, more than one hundred *ayahs* (verses) sanction and promote the need for Jihad.

Sura 9:14, which calls for Jihad, has been used by Osama bin Laden and his followers: "Fight them, and Allah will punish them by your hands, cover them with shame, help you (to victory) over them, heal the breasts of Believers" (8a).

Sura 9 is the last of the suras to be recited by Muhammad, and therefore any revelation therein must necessarily wipe out any contradictory teaching in all of the previous suras.

It is apparent that the Jihad Muhammad advocated is still embraced by many radical Muslim leaders and thousands of their followers. There is no question the Qur'an encourages Jihad. You can go to the web and search for "The Koran's 111 Jihad Verses by Yoel Natan." In addition, Appendix D of this book reproduces "History of Islam *Jihad*," which is a chronological listing of Jihad since the days of Muhammad.

Radical Muslim Leaders' Intentions

Iran's President Mahmoud Ahmadinejad (re-elected in 2009 in what many citizens of Iran call a rigged election) and Iran's Islamic religious leader, Ayatollah Ali Khameini, believe they are called by Allah to accomplish a change before their messiah, the Mahdi, returns to establish the one-world Islamic theocracy:

> God willing, with the force of God behind it, we shall soon experience a world without the United States and Zionism. (Mahmoud Ahmadinejad)
>
> Today, the time for the fall of the satanic power of the United States has come, and the countdown to the annihilation of the emperor of power and wealth has started. (Mahmoud Ahmadinejad)
>
> Get ready for a world minus the U.S. (Mahmoud Ahmadinejad)
>
> It is the mission of the Islamic Republic of Iran to erase Israel from the map of the region. (Ayatollah Ali Khameini)
>
> The end of the U.S. will begin in Iraq. As the Imam [Khomeini] said, "One day the U.S., too, would be history." (Ayatollah Ali Khameini)

> The American regime can expect a resounding slap and devastating fist-blow from the Muslim nation for its support of the Zionist crimes and criminals. (Ayatollah Ali Khameini) (25a)

It is not just the militant leaders of the Islam nations but also millions of indoctrinated young Muslims who believe the above statements are their destiny. Their influence is felt worldwide. These threats come continuously from the leaders of a nation that wants to develop nuclear weapons and advocates use of biological weapons:

> Al-Jazeera recently aired footage of Kuwaiti professor Abdallah al-Nafisi. In the video, translated by the Middle East Media Research Institute (MEMRI), Nafisi expresses ardent support for terrorism and suggests that terrorists use biological warfare against the United States in order to kill hundreds of thousands of civilians.
>
> Nafisi also suggests that Muslims pray for success of white supremacists groups that seek to carry out attacks within the U.S.
>
> In addition, Nafisi attacks those in the Arab world whom he perceives as traitors, to laughter and applause from his audience.
>
> Among those in the Arab world who should be silenced using "any means possible" are journalists who oppose terrorism, any one who supports dialogue with Jews, and senior Palestinian Authority Officials Saeb Erekat and Mahmoud Dahlan, Nafisi says. (78)

Muslims are quick to say their actions are justified because the horrible history of the Crusades was conducted under the banner of Christianity. That may be their claim, but the Crusades could never be justified based on a biblical mandate. Instead, the Crusades were motivated by corrupt and misguided religious leaders who did not want to lose their political power.

The New Testament, or the New Covenant, issued in a new dispensation of God's grace, says we are to love our enemies and to pray for them. The Qur'an, as far as I can see, doesn't indicate a change in its later writings that does away with Jihad but rather calls for a holy Jihad and says that Allah hates unbelievers. This hatred has been taught in Islamic elementary and high schools, and based on Professor Nafsi's comments, it is apparently encouraged and taught in universities.

Their textbook for fighting is the Qur'an (sura 9:5, 14), which is quoted in three different English translations (Yusuf Ali, Pickthal, and Shakir) as follows:

> But when the forbidden months are past, then fight and slay the Pagans wherever ye find them, an seize them, beleaguer them, and lie in wait for them in every stratagem (of war); but if they repent, and establish regular prayers and practise regular charity, then open the way for them: for Allah is Oft-forgiving, Most Merciful. (Yusuf Ali)

> Then, when the sacred months have passed, slay the idolaters wherever ye find them, and take them (captive), and besiege them, and prepare for them each ambush. But if they repent and establish worship and pay the poor-due, then leave their way free. Lo! Allah is Forgiving, Merciful. (Pickthal)

> So when the sacred months have passed away, then slay the idolaters wherever you find them, and take them captives and besiege them and lie in wait for them in every ambush, then if they repent and keep up prayer and pay the poor-rate, leave their way free to them; surely Allah is Forgiving, Merciful. (Shakir)

> Fight them, and Allah will punish them by your hands, cover them with shame, help you (to victory) over them, heal the breasts of Believers. (Yusuf Ali)

> Fight them! Allah will chastise them at your hands, and He will lay them low and give you victory over them, and He will heal the breasts of folk who are believers. (Pickthal)

> Fight them, Allah will punish them by your hands and bring them to disgrace, and assist you against them and heal the hearts of a believing people. (Shakir)

This gives militants a foundation for carrying out actions against those they identify and judge as unbelievers and infidels, as well as other Muslims whom they consider to be apostates.

Hatred of the Jews

In one of my visits to Bahrain, my friends and I were at a modern, all-white-marble shopping mall, and as an American tourist one draws attention. I was approached by an Arab man who spoke very good English. We exchanged pleasantries, and he wondered why we were in Bahrain. I told him I was visiting my friend Sheikh Mohamed. This aroused some curiosity, which led him to promote Islam, and as he expressed his views there filtered through a strong dislike for the Jews. This has been going on for centuries but has intensified as oil money is used to foster terrorist actions against unbelievers. Targeted are Jews and people from Western cultures.

In fact, I received a follow-up letter from that mall acquaintance that had a paragraph ending with this sentence: "Remember it was the Jews who killed your Jesus" (the Jews to whom Jesus came as the Messiah and was rejected). I guess he thought this statement would influence me to hate Jews and Israel and embrace Islam. However, statements like these indicate complete misunderstanding and unbelief regarding the purpose for the death, burial, and resurrection of the Messiah Jesus.

If anyone had reason to detest the Jews it would have been Jesus, but Jesus knew why He was going to be nailed to the cross. On it He, through His eternal Spirit, cried out with compassion, "Father, forgive them for they know not what they do." This wasn't a thoughtless statement but an amazing act of God's grace and love. The Christian position is that without the crucifixion there is no forgiveness of sins!

It is my opinion that humankind's misunderstanding of the purpose of the crucifixion is central to the ongoing violence and hatred in the world. Jesus, the Prince of peace, was rejected, and now people are working hard to prove they don't need Him while carrying out their frustrating attempts to bring about permanent peace. It is still "away with Him, we will not have Him to rule over us." God gave His chosen people Israel the first opportunity to accept the Messiah, but they would not. Nonetheless, God's desire is for humankind, which includes Jews and non-Jews (and that includes Muslims), to be reconciled to Himself. The crucifixion was necessary to obliterate the curse of sin that separated people from God. God always gives opportunity for repentance, but He will not always strive with people. There will be a day of judgment.

Jesus' rejection as the Messiah by the majority of Jews and the leaders of the nation of Israel continues. The Prince of peace was rejected, but it will not always be so. Biblical prophecy says there is coming a day, just before the Messiah Jesus' return, when Jewish evangelists will carry the message of the kingdom of God that Jesus was and is the true Messiah to the people of Israel and to the nations of the world.

Under a future seven-year peace treaty put together by a charismatic world leader, the Antichrist, Israel will still be a thorn in the flesh to that leader and to all the nations. These nations, with all their evil forces, will prepare for the battle at Armageddon, only to be instantaneously defeated by the coming of Jesus. How soon will this happen? Only God knows, but in the meantime militant Muslim leaders and their followers continue their great hatred toward Israel, and because the United States has been a solid friend of Israel, the United States is included on their hate list.

Should we believe that the Israeli government does everything right? The answer is no! Should we believe that all Muslim governments do everything wrong? The answer is no! We should hate the evil purposes and practices of all earthly governments, but we are to pray for and love all the people of all nations, including their leaders.

In relations between the United States and Israel there is continued pressure by the United States and the United Nations for Israel to give up more land for peace, but this has proven to be an endless demand from Palestinians, who fail to fulfill the promised ensuing peace. What radical Islamic world leaders want is all of the land and the annihilation of Israel, as the following report suggests:

> Israeli leaders and citizens are feeling very much alone these days. They see the Radical Islamic world led by Iran preparing to annihilate the Jewish State. And they see very few, if any, around the world willing to stand with them against the forces of barbarism.
>
> Historically, an Israeli Prime Minister and his people could always count on the strong friendship and strategic support of the United States. But that is no longer the U.S. and Israel position over the Iran issue. The White House and State Department do not seem to understand the radical Shia eschatology [beliefs about the last days] that is driving Tehran, and thus do not understand how high the stakes are. Worse, they are getting dangerously close to becoming appeasers of the Ahmadinejad regime.
>
> An editorial this week in a major Israeli newspaper, *Yediot Aharonot*, notes the applause with which many delegates at the Durban II conference in Geneva greeted Iranian President Mahmoud Ahmadinejad's speech and asserts that, "The harsh

> conclusion is that more than one country in the world, more than ten, and not all of them Islamic, are ready to support wiping the State of Israel off the map." The author declares that, "Prime Minister Benjamin Netanyahu was absolutely right when he said and says that we are alone," and believes that, "The Americans will not lift a finger unless it becomes clear that the main target is America." The paper says Israel should "prepare for war in an arena and at a time not to our liking." (79)

The majority of Muslims do not like the actions of the radical militants and the terrorism that is being carried on. If, however, the militants, who are the heavily armed, were to gain political and military control of the brotherhood of Islam, they would enforce an atmosphere of Jihad that would have to be carried out by that brotherhood. We cannot ignore the potential threat to all peoples of the world. We must listen to what is being said by the militants and look at the last sixty years of persecution of non-Muslims in Muslim-controlled nations.

In my research, I found an August 1997 issue of *Readers Digest* that included an article titled "The Global War on Christians." The article detailed the kidnapping and abuse of a Coptic Christian girl by Muslim extremists in Cairo and the use of *Shari'a* laws "to invoke discrimination and outright persecution against Christians" (80a), according to Paul Marshall (the author of *Their Blood Cries Out* and the senior fellow at the Institute for Christian Studies in Toronto, Canada). "No nation illustrates this more brutally than the Sudan." The article continued:

> Since 1989 the Sudanese government has been engaged in a wholesale war against Christians, who constitute roughly one-fifth of the population. Marshall reports that the goal of the ruling National Islamic Front led by Hassan Al-Turabi who some consider the country's de facto leader is to "eradicate non-Islamic religion."
>
> In the North, Al-Turabi's forces control the necessities of life. "Non-Muslims are given the choice of converting to Islam or being denied food, clothing and shelter," Marshall says. "Thousands of women and children have been sold into slavery to Muslim masters who force them to convert to Islam."
>
> Sudan's Nuba Mountains, where Christians have lived since the sixth century, are now a wasteland of mass graves, destroyed

> villages and camps filled with starving women and children. Half a million Nuba Christians, virtually all men, have been killed in the past decade. "The word *genocide* is thrown around too frequently," says Marshall. "In the case of Sudan, however, it is a factual description."
>
> American ally Saudi Arabia is another country where, Shea says, freedom of religion simply does not exist. [Nina Shea is the author of *In the Lion's Den.*] All citizens must be Muslims. Expressions of Christianity wearing a cross, reading a Bible or uttering a non-Muslim prayer are prohibited.
>
> The *Matawwa'in,* the Saudi religious police, search out hidden church services among the millions of Filipinos, Koreans, Indians and other foreign workers. In December 1992 two Filipino Christians, allegedly arrested for preaching Christianity, were sentenced to death on Christmas Day. After an international outcry, the sentence was commuted to deportation. (80b)

An interesting fact about the intolerant religious atmosphere in Saudi Arabia is that its government sponsors the promotional booklet "Understanding Islam and the Muslims" (Washington, DC: The Embassy of Saudi Arabia, 1989 [three years before the above incident]). In this booklet is the article "Does Islam Tolerate Other Beliefs?" According to the article, "It is one function of Islamic law to protect the privileged status of minorities, and that is why non-Muslim places of worship have flourished all over the Islamic world."

Yet, years after the publication of these articles, things are not better, and reports about suppression and persecution continue. Actions do speak louder than words!

Sudan's Al-Turabi declared in a *fatwa* (religious ruling), "Muslims who . . . try to question or doubt the Islamic justifiability of *jihad* are hereby classified as 'hypocrites' who are no longer Muslims, and also 'apostates' from the religion of Islam; and they will be condemned permanently to the fire of Hell" (25b).

Since its early days, and even for many Muslims today, Islam is the religion with a sword taking vengeance on those who oppose their religious beliefs and world goals. Many Muslims try to explain away those portions of the Qur'an by saying what is meant is the spiritual internal war of the individual, or they ignore these suras and insist that Islam means "peace." However, Islam means "submission," and Muslim means one who "submits," obviously to Allah and

His Prophet. Today's mantra among the Jihadists is, "*Islam* is the answer, and *Jihad* is the way." We can't deny these attitudes and actions.

In all of these portions from the Qur'an it is interesting to see the influence on the prophet Muhammad from his exposure to the Jewish and Christian people, their religious teachings, and their culture. To say that Muhammad had no contact with the teaching from followers of Judaism or Christianity contradicts the Qur'an.

What's also interesting is the change in the hostility toward Jews and Christians in the earlier suras compared with the later. With some exceptions, one would have to read the Qur'an from sura 114 backwards to follow the order in which they were revealed and recited by Muhammad. Reading the Qur'an in that order you can see that over a period of twenty-three years Muhammad turned from a warner to a warrior. What brought about this change?

The early history of Islam would indicate that the refusal of Jewish and Christian communities to accept Muhammad as a prophet and his message, refusal of people to convert to Islam, and threats to his life caused Muhammad to become militant and declare war on unbelievers and infidels.

Although those militant actions were not warranted then and should not be warranted today, they are undoubtedly the reasons radical Muslims carry on the way they do. The sheer numbers of militants and the amount of oil money available to finance their activities has made radical Muslims determined to pursue the centuries-old goal of an Islamic world theocratic government. Islamic rule as mandated by Allah and governed by Shari'a law will be the basis for meting out justice. To reach this goal, militant leaders say Israel and the satanic western cultures must be wiped from the face of the earth all in the name of Allah (14a).

Appendix D
Islam and Persecution

Muhammad created one of the largest . . . and longest lasting empires to ever exist on this planet. Unfortunately, unlike the empires of Rome, Byzantine or even the French and English, Islam refuses to go away. These are people who are still fighting the last Crusade, as they seek to retake land they took from others . . . and add new land to it. Their recent military conquests in places like the Sudan, Indonesia and the Philippines have seen Christians and Jews slaughtered to make room for Sharia. What many people refuse to acknowledge, is that this Jihad has been going on for the last 1400 years, since 622 A.D.

In these last 1400 years Moslems have invaded:
Mecca in 622 (Beginning of the Moslem Hegira Era)
Autas (Arabia) in 624
Tayef (Arabia) in 626
Assyria (portions of Iraq, Iran, Syria, Turkey) in 630
This happened during the lifetime of the prophet Mohammed. Unlike Jesus who spread the Glory of God through the WORD, Mohammed spread HIS word through the SWORD. He himself led these attacks, where all Arabs who refused to submit to Islam were mercilessly killed. All Jews were killed, all Christians were killed. After that most Arabs decided that prudence was the better part of valor and became Moslems. After Mohammed died, Moslems invaded the following countries under Abu Bakr:
Palestine/Ertez Israel in 636
Syria and Jerusalem in 637
Zoroastrian Persia (Iran) in 637
Egypt in 638-659
The other Khalifas (Caliphs) continued the Jihad by attacking and forcibly converting the people of the following countries to Islam:
North Africa in 650
Spain in 680
Sindh (India) in 715
France in 732 (Battle of Tours when we defeated the Moslem and stopped their advance into Western Europe)

Khotan (Eastern China) in 1050
Punjab (India) in 1191, (destruction of Buddhism in India by 1192)
Kosovo in 1369
Indonesia and Malaysia in 1450
Constantinople (Istanbul) in 1453
Ottomans annex Serbia in 1456
Ottomans annex Bosnia/Herzogovina in 1461
Ottomans annex Albania in 1462
Vienna in 1689
This marked the end of the first phase of the Jihad, when European navigators took charge of the seas in the 15th century all over the world. This, however, still didn't stop Muslim atrocities from occurring as the Ottoman Empire continued through WWI:
Asia Minor/Smyrna in 1877-1923. Over 1.5 million Armenian Christians slaughtered; 750,000 Assyrians murdered (3/4 their population); over 400,000 Greeks killed in WWI.
While the Cold War and Soviet expansion focused attention elsewhere, Islam's aggression still continued:
Israel in 1948-2003
Lebanon in 1973
Cyprus in 1975
Indonesia/East Timor 1975-2000
Mindanao (Southern Philippines) 1980
Bosnia in 1996
Chechenya in 1997
Kosovo in 1998-99
Macedonia in 1998-99
Southern Sudan 1997
Ethiopia in 1999
Kashmir in 1999
Just about everywhere there is conflict in the world, today, you will find Islam at war with its neighbors . . . be they Christians, Jews, Buddhists, Hindus or whatever . . .
Whether it's the continuing violence in Chechnya, Sudan, Indonesia, Nigeria, Philippines or Israel, Islam seeks to depose all existing cultures.
Here is a brief list of the surviving Christian communities of the Middle East, courtesy of ArabicBible.com.
Egypt: The Copts of Egypt Orthodox, Catholics, and Protestants are estimated to be between 10 and 12 million, dispersed across the country. They are the

descendants of the ancient Egyptian people living under the Pharaohs. Their numbers shrank after the Arab-Moslem invasion in 740 A.D. and flourished under the British in the 19th century. One million Copts live in the diaspora, particularly in the United States and Canada.
Sudan: Seven million black Africans live in the south. Most of these tribes are Christians Anglicans, other Protestants, and Catholics. After the Islamic conquest, the Africans of Nubia were displaced to the south. Since the Islam takeover in the north in 1989, they have been submitted to ethnic cleansing and forced to abandon their faith in order to protect their lives. One million south Sudanese are living in exile.
Lebanon: The Christians Maronites, Orthodox, Melkites, and others, including Protestants number about 1.5 million. Since 1975, hundreds of thousands have been massacred, displaced, and exiled. Since 1990, the Christian areas of Lebanon have been under Syrian occupation. There are more than 7 million Lebanese Christians in the diaspora. More than 1.5 million Americans are of Lebanese descent.
Iraq: About 1 million Christian Assyrians, Nestorians, Chaldeans, and others live in Iraq. Most are concentrated in the north. The Assyrians are submitted to cultural and political repression. Approximately 1 million Christian Mesopotamians live in North America, Europe, and Australia.
Syria: One million Christians are Syrian citizens. Deprived of cultural and educational rights, Syria's Aramaeans, Armenians, Orthodox, and Melkites are present in the northeast and in the major cities.
Iran: Five hundred thousand Persian, Armenian, and Assyrian Christians from all denominations live in constant fear under the Islamic Republic of Iran. Christian spiritual leaders are executed by the government. There is slightly greater tolerance for varieties of Christianity that pre-date Islam in Persia. (65)

Chapter References

Parenthetical references within chapters include the number of the source as listed in the reference materials. The letter references the first and subsequent uses of that source in a chapter. The letter is followed by the page number(s) in the source.

Chapter 2: Jehovah's Witnesses

40a, 56
45a, 13
46a, 214
46b, 410
46c, 380, 381
46d, 407
49a, 426
49b, 456-58
50a, 34
50b, 32
50c, 35
50d, 40
50e, 108
50f, 114
50g, 298
50h, 231
50i, 270, 190
51a, 30
51b, 88-89
67a, 99-101
68a, July 15, 1894, 1677
69a, March 1, 1979, 16
69b, May10, 1972, 272
70a, 41

Chapter 3: Mormonism

53a, 93:21, 23.
53b, 84:4-5

54a, Joseph Smith, *History*, chapter 1, 18-19
71a, 214
72a, 345

Chapter 4: Islam

8a, 28
8b, 17
8c, 15-16, 75-76
15a, 46
15b, 31
18a, 65
18b, 46-47
24a, 71
24b, 90-91
24c, 192
65a, from the web
66a, 42
73a, 299-300
74a, 428
76a, 187-193
77a, 172
80a, 6
80b, 7
81a, 21-23

Chapter 5: Christianity

14b, 261

Appendix C: The Qur'an, History, and Jihad

64a, 367-68
25a, 26-27, 155-56
25b, 36
14a, 106
80a, 6
80b, 7

Reference Material

1. *The Holy Qur'an, Text, Translation and Commentary* by A. Yusuf Ali 1934 edition provided by info@harunyahya.com.
2. Ed Hinson and Ergun Caner, *The Popular Encyclopedia of Apologetics* (Harvest House Publishers).
3. Randall Price, *Fast Facts on the Middle East Conflict* (Harvest House Publishers).
4. M. R. DeHaan II, *The Message of the Prophets* (Radio Bible Class).
5. John Ankerberg and John Weldon, *The Facts on Islam* (Harvest House Publishers).
6. John Gilchrist, *The Uniqueness of Jesus in the Qur'an and the Bible* (Jesus to the Muslims, Republic of South Africa).
7. *Understanding Islam and the Muslims* (The Islamic Affairs Department, The Embassy of Saudi Arabia, Washington, DC; Consultants, The Islamic Texts Society, Cambridge, UK).
8. Kerby Anderson, *A Biblical Point of View on Islam* (Harvest House Publishers).
9. *Why Islam?* (Al-Shirkatul Islamiyyah, The London Mosque 16, Gressenhall Road, London SW18 5QL).
10. Harold A. Sevener, *Israel's Glorious Future* (Chosen People Ministries).
11. *Readers' Digest* (August 1997).
12. Raouf Ghattas and Carol B. Ghattas, *A Christian Guide to the Qur'an* (Kregel).
13. John Ankerberg and Dillon Burroughs, *What's the Big Deal About Other Religions?* (Harvest House Publishers).
14. Dean C Halverson, general ed., *The Compact Guide to World Religions* (Bethany House).
15. Harold J. Berry, *Islam: What They Believe* (Back to the Bible).
16. Kenneth Boa, *Cults, World Religions, and the Occult* (Victor Books, a division of Scripture Press Publications).
17. Ron Rhodes, *Islam, What You Need to Know: A Quick Reference Guide* (Harvest House Publishers).
18. Abdiyah Akbar Abdul-Haqq, *Sharing Your Faith with a Muslim* (Bethany House).
19. John Ankerberg and Ergun Caner, *The Truth About Islam and Jihad* (Harvest House Publishers).
20. Ernest Hahn, *How to Respond Muslims* (Concordia Publishing House).

21. E. M. Hicham, *Your Questions Answered: A Reply to Muslim Friends* (MPG Books Group, UK)
22. Timothy Demy and Gary P. Stewart, *In the Name of God* (Harvest House Publishers).
23. Ken Ham, general ed., *The New Answers Book 2* (Master Books, a division of New Leaf Publishing Group).
24. Norman Geisler and Abdul Saleeb, *Answering Islam* (Baker).
25. Joel C. Rosenberg, *Inside the Revolution* (Tyndale House).
26. Walter Martin, *The Kingdom of the Cults*, Ravi Zacharias, general ed. (Bethany House).
27. Watchtower Society, *New World Translation of the Holy Scriptures* (1984 ed.)
28. The Divine Name in the New World Translation (www.tetragrammaton.org).
29. Jehovah in the New Testament (www.tetragrammaton.org).
30. Robert M. Bowman Jr., *The Jehovah's Witnesses* (Zondervan).
31. Ron J. Bigalke Jr., *The Genesis Factor* (Master Books).
32. Harold J. Berry, *Jehovah's Witnesses* (Back to the Bible).
33. Scott Bixby, published lecture notes, August 2003, at Calvary Baptist Church
    Christianity vs. Jehovah's Witnesses
    Christianity vs. Mormonism
    Christianity vs. Islam
34. Is the *New World Translation* a Better Bible? (www.tetragrammaton.org).
35. Institute for Religious Research, *Ministering Truth to Jehovah's Witnesses.*
36. Ron Rhodes, *Jehovah's Witnesses, a Quick Reference Guide* (Harvest House Publishers).
37. Steven Cory, *The Spirit of Truth and the Spirit of Error: Two World Religions* (Moody Press).
38. Joel Groat, *Facts About the Jehovah's Witnesses* (Institute for Religious Research).
39. Institute for Religious Research, *Four Dangers of the Jehovah's Witness Organization.*
40. John Ankerberg, John Weldon, and Dillon Burroughs, *The Facts on Jehovah's Witnesses* (Harvest House Publishers).
41. Ralph O. Muncaster, *The Bible—General Analysis* (Strong Basis to Believe).
42. ———, *The Bible—Manuscript Reliability* (Strong Basis to Believe).
43. ———, *The Bible—Scientific Insights* (Strong Basis to Believe).
44. ———, *The Bible—Archaeological Facts* (Strong Basis to Believe).
45. *Israel My Glory* (July/August 2003).
46. Jehovah's Witnesses, *Reasoning from the Scriptures.*
47. ———, *You Can Live on Earth Forever.*
48. ———, *The Truth Shall Make You Free.*

49. ———, *Make Sure of All Things.*
50. ———, *Let God Be True.*
51. ———, *New Heavens and New Earth.*
52. *The Book of Mormon: Another Testament of Jesus Christ* (The Church of Jesus Christ of Latter-day Saints, Salt Lake City, Utah; 1989 ed.).
53. *The Doctrine and Covenants of the Church of Jesus Christ of Latter-day Saints* (The Church of Jesus Christ of Latter-day Saints, Salt Lake City, Utah, 1989 ed.).
54. *The Pearl of Great Price, including The Book of Abraham written by his own hand, Translated from the Papyrus by Joseph Smith* (The Church of Jesus Christ of Latter-day Saints, Salt Lake City, Utah, 1989 ed.); also includes Joseph Smith, *Matthew*, Joseph Smith, *History*, *The Articles of Faith* (The Church of Jesus Christ of Latter-day Saints, Salt Lake City, Utah, 1989 ed.).
55. Institute for Religious Research (1340 Monroe Avenue NE, Grand Rapids, MI, 49505), pamphlets:
    New Light on Joseph Smith's First Vision
    Is Mormonism Christian?
    Facts About the Jehovah's Witnesses
    Four Dangers of the Jehovah's Witness Organization
    The Book of Mormon Today
    Are Mormon Temples Christian?
56. Harold J. Berry, *Mormons* (Back to the Bible).
57. Institute for Religious Research, *Where Does It Say That? Photo Reprints of Hard-to-Get Mormon Documents.*
58. Josh McDowell, *More Than a Carpenter* (Living Books, Tyndale House).
59. *The Lost Books of the Bible* (Alpha House).
60. F. F. Bruce, *The New Testament Documents: Are They Reliable?* (Inter-Varsity Press).
61. Lee Strobel, *The Case for Faith* (Zondervan).
62. Joel C. Rosenberg, *The Last Jihad* (Tyndale House).
63. ———, *The Last Days* (Tyndale House).
64. *The Life of Muhammad: A Translation of Ishaq's Sirat Rasul Allah.*
65. On web go to "The Koran's 111 Jihad Verses,"compiled by Yoel Natan. At site scroll down to dennisw with opening comment, "Thanks, here's a little more on the Religion of Peace"
66. Kerby Anderson, *Islam* (Harvest House Publishers).
67. *The Time Is at Hand* (1906 ed.).
68. Watch Tower Society, *Zion's Watch Tower.*
69. ———, *Watch Tower Magazine.*

70. Edmond Gruss, *Jehovah's Witnesses* (Presbyterian and Reformed Publishers).
71. *History of the Pioneer Settlement of Phelps and Gorham's Purchase,* 1851.
72. Joseph Smith, *Teachings of the Prophet.* (LDS publication by church staff).
73. Dave Jackson and Neta Jackson, *The Complete Book of Christian Heroes* (Tyndale).
74. Bukhäri al-Sahih, volume 6, book LXVI: *Kitäb Fad'il l-Qur'än*, chapter 5, Hadith 4992.
75. Joel Rosenberg, "Flash Traffic" web newsletter report, April 10, 2009.
76. *The History of al-Tabari*, volume 1, *General Introduction and from the Creation to the Flood*, translated by Franz Rosenthal (Albany: State University of New York Press, 1989).
77. Josh McDowell and John Gilchrist, *The Islam Debate* (Here's Life, Publishers).
78. "Call for Biological Attack," broadcast aired on Al-Jazeera television and reported in the July/August 2009 issue of *Israel My Glory*.
79. Joel Rosenberg, "Flash Traffic" web newsletter, Washington update, April 24, 2009.
80. "The Global War on Christians," *Readers Digest* 1997.
81. Dr. Thomas Key, *Midnight Call* magazine, October 2002, items 1-3 in the article.
82. Joel Rosenberg, "Flash Traffic" web newsletter report, May 20, 2009.
83. Joel Rosenberg, "Flash Traffic" web newsletter report, January 7, 2011